THE COMPLETE GUIDE TO

DECORATIVE WOODWORKING

Detail of a particularly fine fifteenth-century misericord. These seats are usually found in church choirs and, traditionally, are decorated with every-day scenes and grotesque figures.

THE COMPLETE GUIDE TO

DECORATIVE WOODWORKING

ALAN AND GILL BRIDGEWATER

A QUARTO BOOK
Published by Phaidon Press Limited
Littlegate House
St Ebbe's Street
Oxford
OX1 1SQ

First published 1986

Library Cataloguing in Publication Data
Bridgewater, Alan
The complete guide to decorative woodworking:
techniques and materials.
1. Woodwork
I. Title II. Bridgewater, Gill
684'.08 TT180

ISBN 0-7148-2431-3

This book was designed and produced by
Quarto Publishing Ltd
The Old Brewery
6 Blundell Street
London N7 9BH

SENIOR EDITOR Polly Powell
PROJECT EDITOR Paul Stephen
ART EDITOR Nick Clark
EDITOR Keith Parrish
DESIGNER Peter Bridgewater
PHOTOGRAPHERS Paul Forrester and Kim Sayer
PICTURE RESEARCH Sheila Corr
ART DIRECTOR Pete Laws
EDITORIAL DIRECTOR Jim Miles

Typeset in Great Britain by
Central Southern Typesetters Limited, Eastbourne
Manufactured in Hong Kong by
Regent Publishing Services Limited
Printed in Hong Kong by
Leefung Asco Printers Limited

The authors would like to take this opportunity to thank Peter Bridgewater for his help, patience and expertise.

CONTENTS

INTRODUCTION 6
TYPES OF WOOD 14

1 DECORATIVE CONSTRUCTION 16
Making a dovetail joint in the arts and crafts tradition 18
Making a Shaker box 24
Making a turned bowl in the Scottish quaich tradition 30
Making a wedged mortise-and-tenon joint 36
Making a Windsor chair 42

2 VENEER, MARQUETRY AND TUNBRIDGE WARE 48
Making a marquetry design 50
Making a marquetry design in the Boulle tradition 56
Making a parquetry games board 62
Making a Nonesuch inlay 68
Making a Tunbridge ware design 74

3 RELIEF WOODCARVING 80
Working a medieval chip-carved roundel 82
Whittling a piece of treen: Ball-in-a-cage 88
Working a sunflower panel 94
Whittling and carving a love spoon 100
Carving an Art Nouveau appliqué relief 106

4 WOODCARVING IN THE ROUND 112
Carving an oak misericord in the English medieval tradition 114
Carving a naïve fairground horse's head 120
Carving a posy in the Grinling Gibbons tradition 126
Making a decoy duck in the American tradition 132
Carving an interlaced chair-back in the Chippendale style 138

5 FINISHING 144
French polishing 146
Stencilling and painting in the American folk tradition 152
Water gilding 158
Painting an American dower chest design 164
Stencilling in the American Hitchcock tradition 170

6 PATTERNS AND MOTIFS 176
BIBLIOGRAPHY
GLOSSARY
INDEX

INTRODUCTION

THE intention of this book is to explore and demonstrate the use of all the craft skills and techniques involved in producing decorative woodwork. The initial brief was broad and ambitious, but after much painstaking research and talking to interested parties that ranged from woodcarvers, artists, furniture-makers and museum and gallery keepers, to craft enthusiasts and students, we developed a much more focused idea of what was wanted. It certainly was not a wordy tome that groaned on about the Italianate intricacies of woodwork design — you know the sort of thing, half a million words and not an illustration in sight. What was needed was a book that described not only the When, Where and Why, but also, in highly visual terms, the How!

But where to start? Should we survey decorative techniques world-wide? Should we include designs, crafts and techniques from tribal and ethnic sources? Should the emphasis be on traditional Western furniture and interiors? The vast amount of exciting material on offer presented a challenge.

Not the least of our problems was the fact that although the natural beauty and easy working of wood has for centuries made it the primary decorative material, many of the techniques have become lost. The various crafts were either based on skills passed on by word-of-mouth tradition from father to son — in which case descriptions of the techniques were never written down — or if they have been described in books, these are ancient, out of print, in a foreign language or obscure. Our objectives have involved us searching out these lost skills and presenting them to you in a fresh way that is easy to understand and follow.

Detail of an English thirteenth-century chest. These simple chip-carved geometric shapes were popular motifs on furniture of this period.

Detail of a chest dated 1637. The sunflower motif has been worked in shallow relief, with naïvely worked modelling and a tool-textured ground.

Once we realized that there were thousands of crafters who wanted to become involved in the exciting and stimulating craft of decorative woodworking, we had to make firm decisions as to which crafts should be included and how they should be presented. Knowing that the majority of decorative woodworking crafts have their roots in ethnic, folk and country art and craft traditions, we decided that the techniques should relate to the use of traditional tools and materials. Our projects would use gouges, chisels, knives and saws rather than, say, power routers, heat presses and high-tech air-brushes. Each project, therefore, has been designed so that it can be worked with simple, easily obtained tools and materials.

As the various crafts and projects were researched, it became more and more apparent that decorative woodworking was not so much a story of highly trained specialists — although this is the case with some of the more sophisticated aspects — as that of many generations of simple and naïve country craftsmen. Using very basic, often village-made tools, these humble artisans shaped our homes, our churches and most of our everyday domestic objects — indeed, they shaped and decorated our whole lives. Where possible we have looked back beyond our recent industrial past, during which factory technicians seem to have applied decoration to everything and anything without due consideration to the appropriate use of wood. We look to a time when there was direct and honest contact between the craftsman, his material and its form and decoration.

This book is not concerned with the intellectual analysis of taste, fashion and style, those three impostors that have tried to talk us out of our decorative woodcraft traditions. It is a practical challenge, an invitation to roll up your sleeves and start working with wood, tools, glue and paint. We have tried to relate all the decorative techniques used in this book to periods when craftsmen were in touch with the close personal needs of their neighbours and consequently making and decorating objects in wood that reflected these needs. This is not to say that we want to make a slavish copyist of you. You should be moving forward in a state of continuous exploration and experimentation. Nevertheless, you will at the same time be looking over your shoulder and drawing inspiration from the craftsmen of the past.

The Complete Guide To Decorative Woodworking has been carefully shaped into six chapters which cover specific woodworking skills and distinct areas of interest, and there are 25 projects to make utmost use of the techniques described. On the understanding that the beginner can learn only by doing, each project has been designed so that there are working drawings and photographs, inspirational photographs, a series of detailed step-by-step, hands-on-tool illustrations and an easy-to-read text. A short introduction sets the particular craft in its context of time and place and then, by means of step-by-step illustrations and text, you are taken through all the project stages. Of course, we appreciate that our way is not the only way, so to balance our chosen techniques, methods and crafts, additional ideas and inspirational leads are presented alongside our projects to help you.

It is worth noting that the projects are not placed in chronological order or in a sequence relating to how difficult the techniques might be — in the contexts of complete projects and dealing with a variety of crafts such a classification is meaningless. Instead, we have divided the book into areas of similar interest. So, for example, if you want to achieve a painterly effect you would look at the projects in chapter five; if your big pleasure is relief carving you would go to chapter three. The projects and source material have been organized for easy access.

Whatever your decorative woodworking needs, we reckon that this book will go a long way to answering them. As to the choice of projects covered, it must be noted that a number of them are, as far as we know, described here for the first time. Certainly you would find reference to Nonesuch inlay, Shaker boxes and Dower chests in other books, but we do much more than place these decorative crafts in a historical and cultural context

Detail of seventeenth-century Dutch marquetry. It was during the seventeenth century that marquetry became fashionable, particularly in Holland, Germany and England.

— we show you how these uniquely beautiful works can be achieved. We take you through all the stages, from the initial museum research, the design sketches and workout drawings, through to the creative pleasure of cutting, gluing, painting and finishing. If you have ever wandered around a craft centre or folk museum and wondered how a particular piece of woodwork was decorated; or if you have run your fingertips over a piece of woodcarving, marvelled at the undulations and the grain and wondered how the craftsman felt as the keen-edged tools slipped through the sweet-smelling wood — then this book is definitely for you.

Relief carving, woodturning, whittling love tokens, gilding, painting and stencilling — these are all decorative woodworking pleasures that should not be missed. Every project in this book will present you with a new and exciting challenge. We tell you about the tools; we describe the wood; we describe the paints and we tell you how the tools should be held. In fact, we help you every step of the way. By working on such inspirational projects as Making a Turned Bowl, Making a Windsor Chair, Carving an Oak Misericord, Whittling and Carving a Love Spoon, and Painting an American Dower Chest Design, a keen beginner will be able to create uniquely decorative and beautiful woodworked articles. Decorative woodworking does not require a workshop full of complex and expensive tools; it requires only that you become involved in the close, physically satisfying and therapeutic experience of working wood — our most beautiful natural material — with silent, keen-edged hand tools.

We have included at the end of the book a series of inspirational designs, patterns and motifs. The beginner can work through the projects and then, having achieved a fair degree of expertise and craft experience, will be able to refer to the directory and perhaps advance to greater things. It may sound a little trite to talk about discovering your roots and getting away from the pressures of our pre-packed plastic age, but we believe that by working through the projects in this book you will discover

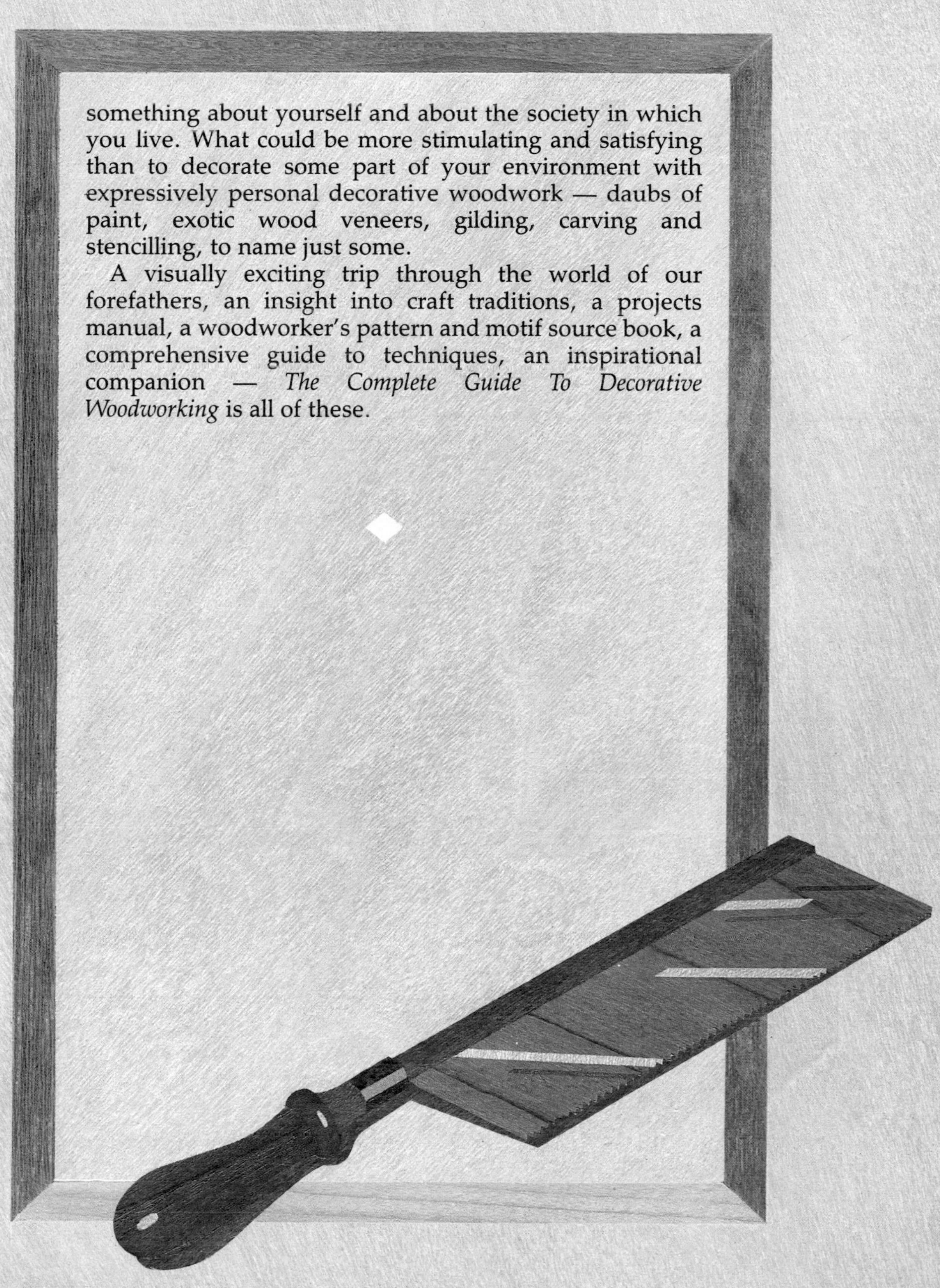

something about yourself and about the society in which you live. What could be more stimulating and satisfying than to decorate some part of your environment with expressively personal decorative woodwork — daubs of paint, exotic wood veneers, gilding, carving and stencilling, to name just some.

A visually exciting trip through the world of our forefathers, an insight into craft traditions, a projects manual, a woodworker's pattern and motif source book, a comprehensive guide to techniques, an inspirational companion — *The Complete Guide To Decorative Woodworking* is all of these.

TYPES OF WOOD

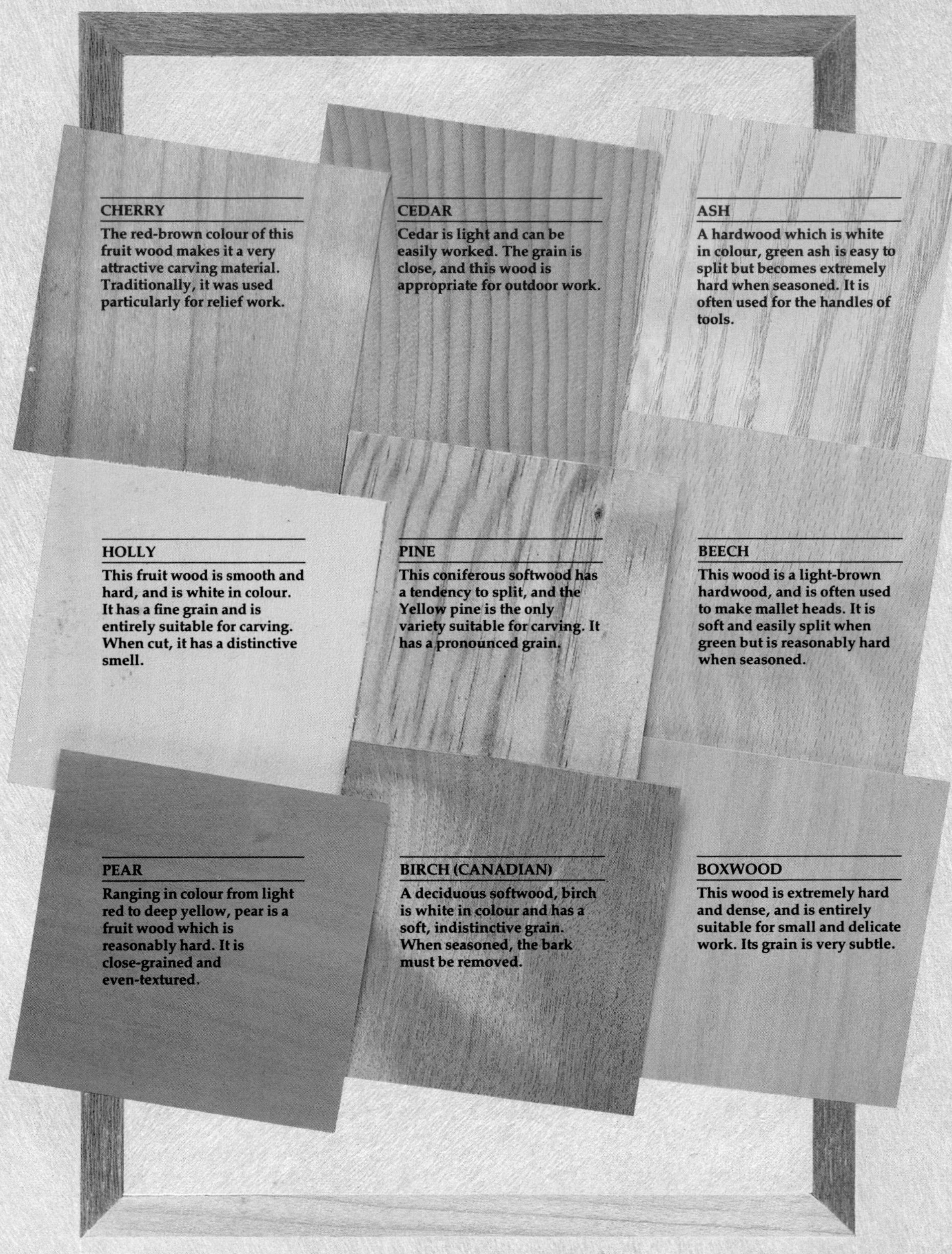

CHERRY

The red-brown colour of this fruit wood makes it a very attractive carving material. Traditionally, it was used particularly for relief work.

CEDAR

Cedar is light and can be easily worked. The grain is close, and this wood is appropriate for outdoor work.

ASH

A hardwood which is white in colour, green ash is easy to split but becomes extremely hard when seasoned. It is often used for the handles of tools.

HOLLY

This fruit wood is smooth and hard, and is white in colour. It has a fine grain and is entirely suitable for carving. When cut, it has a distinctive smell.

PINE

This coniferous softwood has a tendency to split, and the Yellow pine is the only variety suitable for carving. It has a pronounced grain.

BEECH

This wood is a light-brown hardwood, and is often used to make mallet heads. It is soft and easily split when green but is reasonably hard when seasoned.

PEAR

Ranging in colour from light red to deep yellow, pear is a fruit wood which is reasonably hard. It is close-grained and even-textured.

BIRCH (CANADIAN)

A deciduous softwood, birch is white in colour and has a soft, indistinctive grain. When seasoned, the bark must be removed.

BOXWOOD

This wood is extremely hard and dense, and is entirely suitable for small and delicate work. Its grain is very subtle.

CHESTNUT
A mid-brown coloured hardwood, chestnut is a durable wood but has a tendency to split. It has a very distinctive grain that responds well to finishes.
MAHOGANY
Rich reddish-brown in colour, this hardwood is now rare. It is suitable for carving although it tends to split if carved across the grain. When seasoned, it has a low moisture content.
SYCAMORE (PLANE)
Sycamore is a hardwood that resists splitting but is unsuitable for outdoor work. It has a whitish colour and is moderately hard, but can be quite difficult to work.
LIME
Lime is a hardwood which is light yellowish in colour. Although unsuitable for outdoor work, this wood is a good relief-carving material because it seasons well and has an indistinctive grain.
MAPLE (BIRD'S EYE)
Varieties of this hardwood have different textures but all are close-grained. Colours vary from light brown to red-brown, and all varieties respond well to finishing.
WALNUT
This dark-brown hardwood is excellent for carving but is expensive and hard to find. Its extremely decorative grain makes it suitable for veneering.
ELM
Dark red-brown in colour, Elm is a hardwood that tends to warp during seasoning, and is suitable for outdoor work. It resists splitting and has a distinctive grain.
OAK
This is a hardwood. The heart wood is suitable for carving and, after seasoning, continues to harden. The sap wood, which is yellowish in colour, should be removed before carving. The heart wood is durable in all conditions.
YEW
Hard and extremely durable, this hardwood has a distinctive grain. It varies in colour from a deep red-brown to a light yellow.

CHAPTER 1

DECORATIVE CONSTRUCTION

IN THE context of this book, decorative construction is defined as being methods, techniques or forms of woodwork that are in themselves structurally visible but at the same time visually dynamic. So not only is, say, a plain and simple dovetail joint an efficient means of jointing two bits of wood, it is also, by its very nature, attractive, grain-enhancing and pattern-making. This being so, when a woodworker chooses to make a table, box or similar piece using such a joint rather than a secret or mitred dovetail, he is aware that the joint will be an important feature in its own right.

So it is with all the projects in this chapter. Not only are they efficient in terms of construction and visually exciting woodworked forms, they also represent a conscious striving on the part of the craftsman to build items that express his craft. For example, the Shaker box could easily have been designed with straight-cut hoop ends or, in fact, have been knocked together from slats of wood — but, of course, there was more to it than that. Shaker craftsmen did not merely make functional utility items out of wood; through their work they made statements about their whole way of life. It was vital to them that the design and construction of all their woodwork displayed an open, honest integrity. The same could be said of Scottish quaich-makers. These naïve country craftsmen did not set out to dazzle our eyes with the stunning beauty of their quaich bowls; they intended no more than to use all available materials to create domestic items that were structurally sound and functionally fit for their purpose.

Windsor chairs, too, are much more than just bits of furniture; they are, so to speak, the culmination of hundreds of years of wood crafting. No single chairmaker could have designed such beautifully efficient and decorative forms. In many ways the whole history of woodworking is written in the Windsor chair — these wonderfully simple, open structures say it all: the ingenious saddle seats giving an illusion of thinness produced by skilful adzing and gouging; the way the sticks and legs are shaved, turned and plugged into the seats; the sculptural beauty of the steam-curved arms as they gently encircle and cradle the sitter — these are all classic examples of open, decorative construction. The joints are not covered up; indeed, the whole structure is a witness to the woodworker's craft. Each and every element is sound and has about it an inherent truthfulness.

The same could be said for most hand-built chairs, naïve country-made furniture and craftsmen-worked items. They all fulfil their function in ways that are boldly direct. It is almost as if there is a conscious striving between craftsman and nature to achieve a perfect balance of form, function and structure. Decorative construction should never shout but always quietly beckon. Next time you get the chance to visit a country museum, take a look at some of the rural woodcrafts, the farm gates, the country chairs, the hay wagons, the barrels and cartwheels. See how they are made up of simple, honest, open, self-decorated structures.

MAKING A DOVETAIL JOINT IN THE ARTS AND CRAFTS TRADITION

THE Arts and Crafts movement of the late nineteenth century was, in many ways, a nebulous movement that came to mean all things to all people. To the followers of William Morris, for example, it was a revival of traditional standards — standards that were concerned with romantic socialism and a rustic way of life. For Walter Crane, the movement gave inspiration to an idealistic crafts and life philosophy — 'the true root and basis of all art lies in the handicrafts; it is our mission to turn artists into craftsmen and craftsmen into artists'. A great many artist craftsmen of the period saw the movement as the key to some sort of return to unreal rural living.

Between 1889 and 1910, there was a group of English furniture-makers who were genuinely trying to break away from Victorian traditions and get back to designs and techniques that had their roots in rustic furniture and rural simplicity. They produced furniture that was natural, unstained and structurally decorative. One such inspired artist craftsman was William Richard Lethaby (1857–1931). Lethaby, who was later to be the first principal at the Central School of Arts and Crafts in London, concentrated on making furniture that used technique and structure as its primary design features. He was not interested in thick veneers or heavy over-embellished applied carving. Lethaby declared that the wood, techniques, joints and the grain must speak for themselves. When, later, he became Professor of Design at the Royal College of Art, he summed up the whole Arts and Crafts philosophy in his now famous saying: 'Design is right doing — design is simply arranging how work should be done.'

TOOLS & EQUIPMENT

- Workbench
- Marking gauge
- Square
- Measure
- Pencils
- Bevel
- Vice
- Dovetail saw
- Small tenon saw
- Coping saw
- Bench clamp
- Small straight chisel
- Mallet
- Small bevel-edged chisel
- Oilstone and strop

MATERIALS

- 2 pieces of straight-grained knot-free pine measuring 6 × ⅝in (length to suit)
- Workout paper
- PVA glue

The scale is four squares to 1in. Note the direction of the grain. With a project of this character it is essential that you choose the wood with great care: reject material that has grain splits and dead knots, and make sure that the wood at the joint is as near perfect as possible.

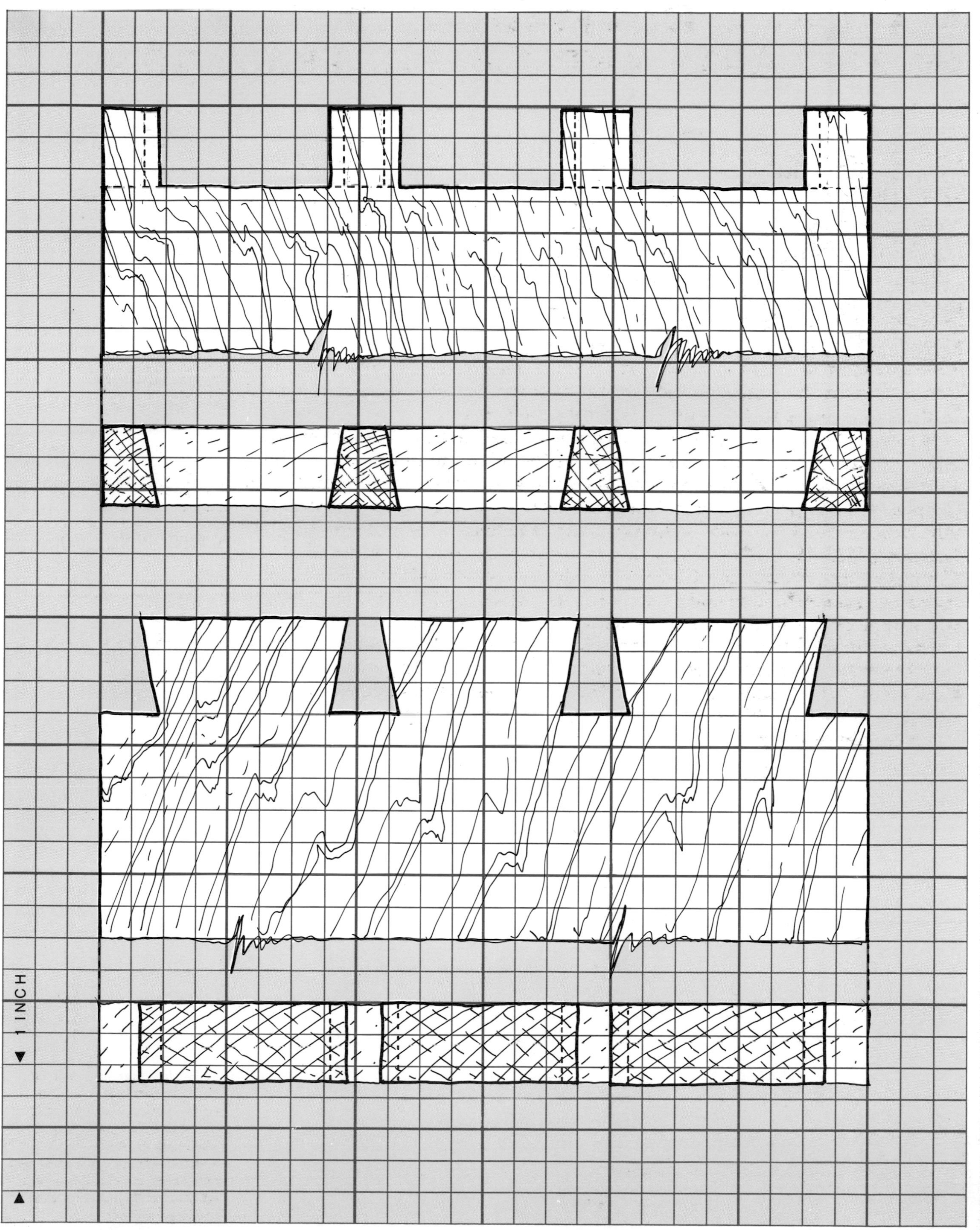
1 INCH

BELOW LEFT *Cabinet made by a student at the London College of Furniture. Worked in ash, this piece has been influenced by the Post-Modernists, and structural details are considered as decorative features. Note the delicacy of the wood sections.*

ABOVE LEFT *Roll-top bedside chest made by a student at the London College of Furniture. This delicate piece of furniture that draws its inspiration from the Arts and Crafts tradition uses carved 'through dowels' as a decorative feature.*

BELOW RIGHT *Veneered cabinet made by a student at the London College of Furniture. Sycamore and teak were used for this cabinet deeply influenced by the Arts and Crafts tradition. The mitred corners are held together with decorative dovetails patterned with veneer inserts.*

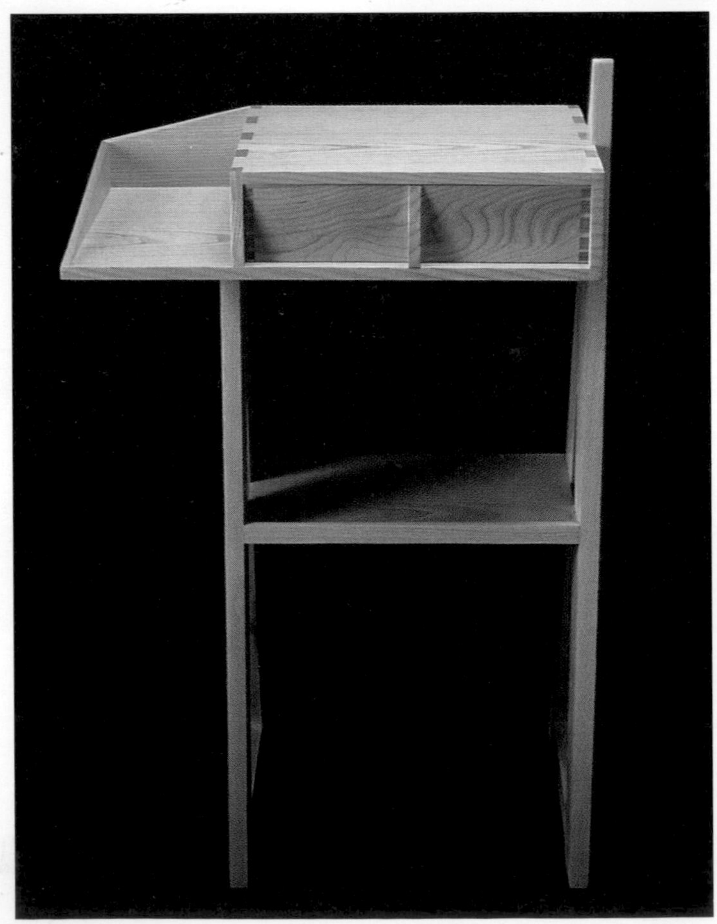

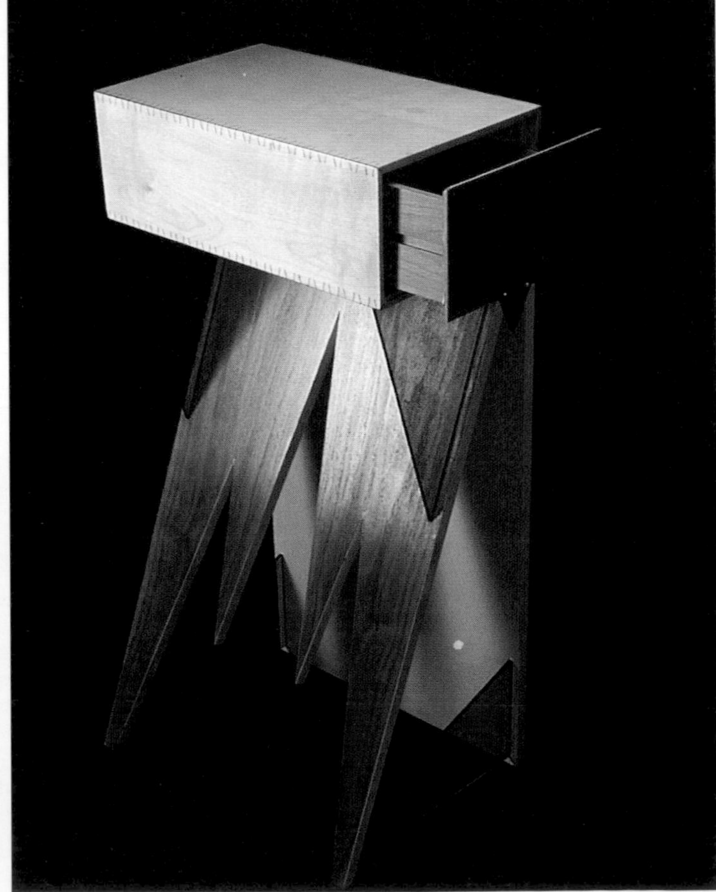

PROJECT PHOTOGRAPH *Arts and Crafts cabinet made by Ernest Gimson between 1889 and 1910. Furniture of this type and style has come to symbolize the Arts and Crafts period. It has a straightforward, sound construction, and the use of inlay decoration is restrained.*

Considering the joint and drawing the gauge lines

Take a magnifying glass to the project photograph of the Arts and Crafts cabinet (see page 21), and focus on the very delicate and beautifully worked dovetails. Look at the working drawing and details, and see how this project concentrates on the making of a classic dovetail joint with small pins.

If possible, visit a museum and search out Arts and Crafts furniture made between 1890 and 1900, particularly pieces by the Barnsley brothers, Gimson and Lethaby. If you get to see the pieces close-up, note how the joints are nearly always bold, honest and of the dovetail type. See how the beautifully worked dovetails are hardly ever secret or mitred, but rather are visible and part of the total design.

When you are familiar with the handmade furniture of the period, consider how you might use such a dovetail joint. If you are a beginner, it is advisable to use this project to build a simple exercise or exhibition joint. Noticing the thickness of the wood, set the gauge to ⅝in and run it around both pieces of prepared wood (as illustrated). Check the gauge lines with a square and label the two pieces of wood A and B.

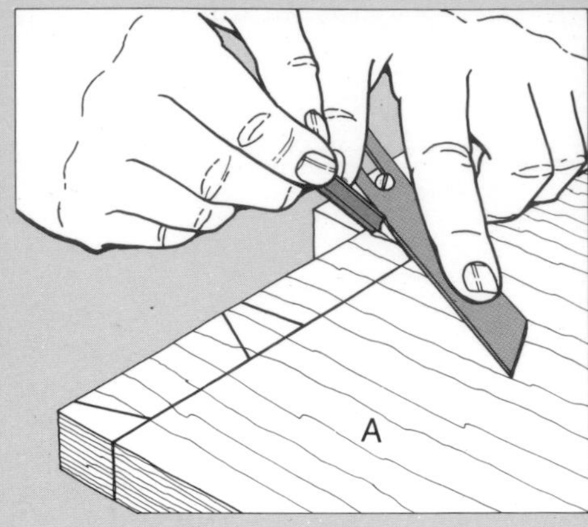

Setting out the wood

Lay out the marking tools, measure, pencil and bevel. Look at the working drawing, compare it with your chosen boards, and then consider how many divisions — or dovetails — are needed. There are no hard-and-fast rules as to the number of dovetails needed over a given length, but the nearer the dovetails are, the stronger the joint is.

Another point to note is the actual size and proportion of the dovetail pins and sockets. Certainly, large dovetails are easy to cut but using a wide tail tends to result in a weak joint. Beginners should compromise by having three dovetails to every 6in width of board, and working them so that they are ½in at the wide end and ¼in at the narrow end. In the working drawing the wood is set out in three equal parts in order to make two whole dovetails and two halved dovetails.

Now, take your workout paper, measure and pencil, and make a full-size working drawing. Set the angle of the bevel directly from the drawing. When all is as described, take the A piece of wood and begin to set out the lines of the dovetails — use the bevel to mark the socket angles (see illustration). Do this on both sides of the wood and run the angled lines down as far as the gauge lines. Finally, take a soft pencil and cross-hatch the waste wood between the dovetails.

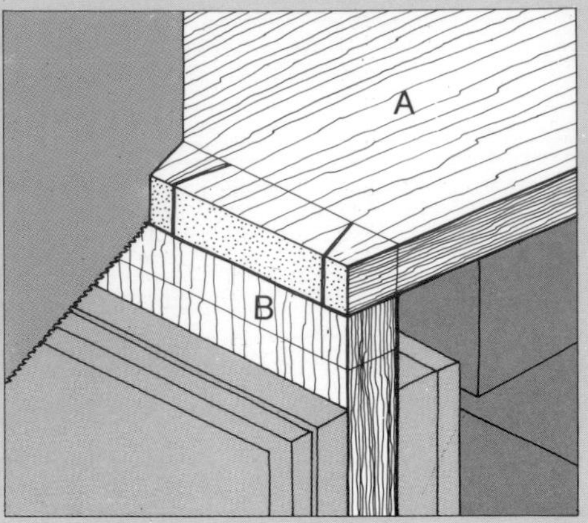

Cutting the bevel lines and transferring the cuts

Place the A piece of wood end up in the vice and arrange all the saws so that they are to hand. Making sure that you cut on the waste side of all drawn lines, take the dovetail or small tenon saw and cut down the drawn lines until the teeth of the saw just meet the gauged shoulder line. You will need to make six cuts in all.

Take the A piece of wood out of the vice and replace it with the B piece of wood. Now, with the aid of a block of scrap wood (as illustrated), arrange both pieces of wood so that they are supported and come together at right-angles. When you have done this, hold the wood secure with the left hand, and place the point of the saw in one of the saw cuts. Being very careful to avoid throwing the wood off true, draw the point of the saw gently outwards. Do this with all six cuts. If you now remove the A piece of wood, you will see that you have marked out the position of the four dovetail pins on the end-grain of the B piece of wood.

Using the square and pencil, run the saw-marked lines down the face of the B piece of wood until they strike the gauge line. Do this with both sides of the wood. Identify the areas of waste wood that are between the four pins, and cross-hatch them with a pencil. Finally, set both pieces of wood on the workbench, and check that they relate to the various working drawings and details.

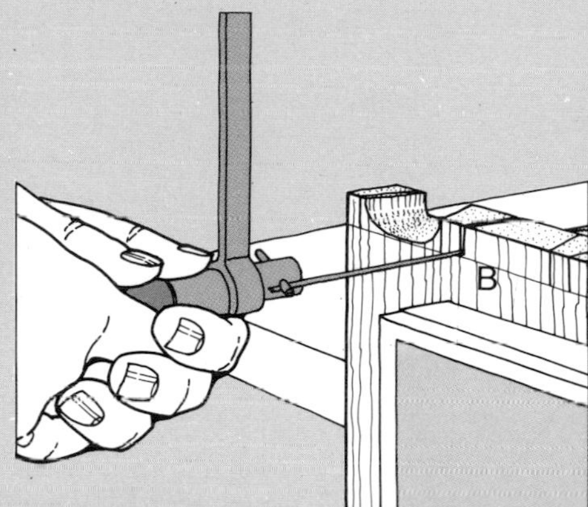

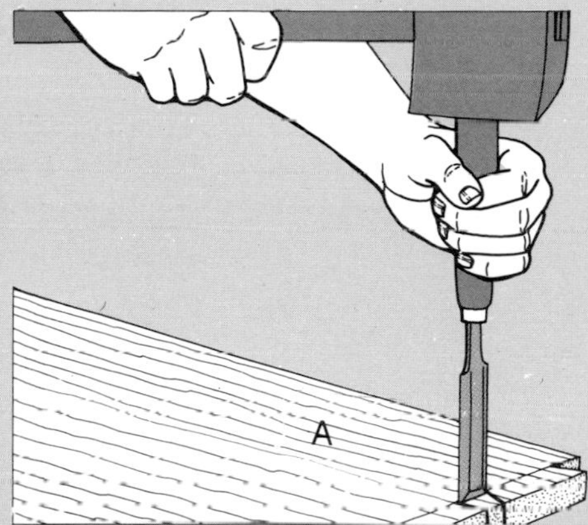

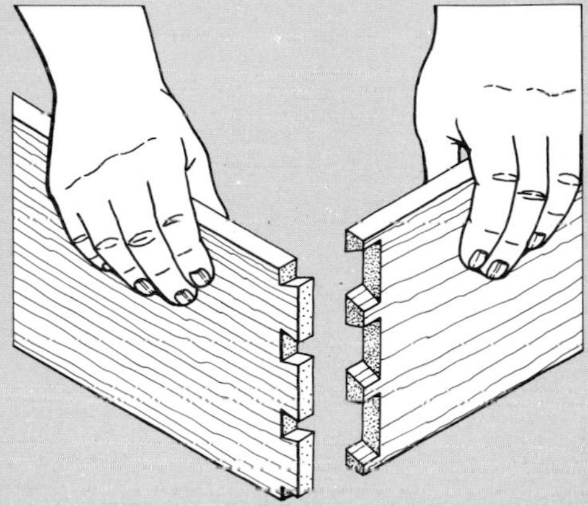

Cutting the dovetail pins

Once all the wood has been marked out as described, place the B piece of wood end up in the vice and place the dovetail and the coping saws so that they are to hand. First, take the dovetail saw and, making sure that the blade is held vertical and on the waste side, cut down the drawn lines and stop short, just a little before the gauge-marked shoulder lines.

Having cut all six lines, take the coping saw and swiftly remove the waste between each of the pins. Do not try to saw close to the gauge line, but rather aim to cut out most of the waste.

Put both saws to one side, take the wood out of the vice and clamp it side-down to the bench. Have a fresh look at the inspirational material and your working drawings, and take a small, sharp chisel and a mallet. Pare the waste wood back to the shoulder lines in all three areas. Turn the wood over and work the other side in the same way. Note: if the dovetail is small, it can be chopped out with a chisel and there is no need to use the saw.

Continue gradually paring at the wood between the pins until you reach the various pencil and gauge lines. Of course, as you approach the lines, you will have to work with increasing caution, so check that your chisel is really sharp.

Cutting the sockets

When you have cut out the areas of waste between the pins, put the B piece of wood to one side and place the A piece of wood end up in the vice. First, cut out the two half-sockets with the dovetail saw — saw down to the shoulder lines, re-position the wood side-up and saw along the gauge line.

Clamp the wood to the bench, clear away the bench waste and then be ready with the bevel-edged chisel and the mallet. Hold the flat side of the chisel towards the gauge line, make sure that the cutting edge is a little on the waste side, and then give the chisel a well-placed chop with the mallet. If you now move the blade a little further away from the gauge line and give it another tap with the mallet, a little chip of wood should fall away.

Continue cutting down into the wood, moving the chisel forward and chopping with the mallet. Repeat this action several times until the base of the V-cut is about halfway through the wood thickness.

Flip the wood over and work it from the other side. You can now either chop straight through the wood with a series of V-cuts (as already described) or you can make a clean cut with the chisel exactly on the shoulder line, flip the wood over and then cut right through it. Finally, when the waste has been removed, sharpen the chisel and clean up with a dozen or so paring cuts.

Putting together and finishing

Before you go any further, consider how this project works the dovetail by using the initial cuts on one piece of wood as the guide for the sockets on the other. This is, of course, just one way of working; you can use a template, and you could have made a more sophisticated joint with the workings concealed.

When you have cut the joint, clear the bench and set out the work and the PVA glue. Start by having a trial fitting: bring the two halves of the joint together and adjust them for an easy fit. Note: do not be tempted to force the wood because this will almost certainly result in the pins at the side splitting off along the grain. Finally, when you have a good fit, brush the joint with PVA glue, bring the wood together and clamp the joint. Wipe away the excess glue and put the whole work to one side to dry out.

Note: when you come to remove the waste, always double check with the working drawings because it is the easiest thing in the world to make a mistake and cut off the joint rather than the waste. When you are cutting out the waste at the shoulder, it is most important that the chisel is held upright. If you fail to do this, the shoulders will be slightly undercut and this, in turn, will result in a poor match.

Making a Shaker Box

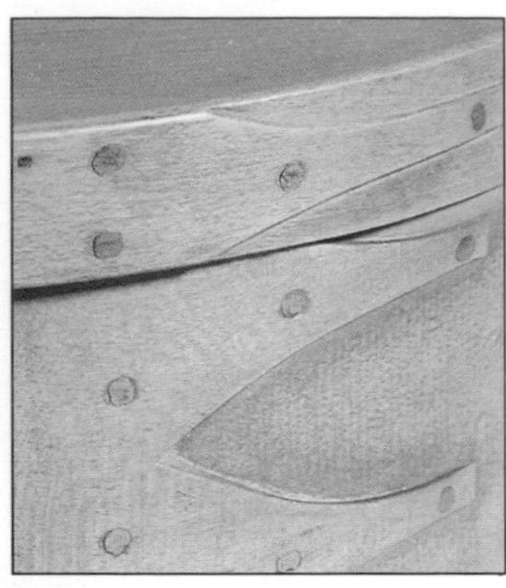

In 1774, the Shaker sect, led by their prophetess Mother Ann Lee, established a commune at Niskeyuna in America. Fundamentally, the Shakers believed that the Second Coming of Christ was close at hand and prepared themselves by withdrawing from the 'sinful' world and dedicating their hearts to God and their hands to work. This diligent, self-sufficient way of life prospered so much so that by about 1790 there were Shaker communes at Enfield, New Hampshire, Massachusetts and later in Ohio and Kentucky. From an early period the Shakers came to be known for their functional furniture – furniture that 'works, serves and avoids all pretence and superfluity'. Right up until the 1950s the Shaker craftsmen produced all manner of characteristic items: spindle-back rocking chairs, delicate taper-leg desks, trundle beds, etc. But perhaps the most interesting of all the Shaker pieces are the oval carriers. These beautiful boxes, some with lids and handles, were made in their thousands. Construction involved soaking, steaming and bending thin slats of maple, oak, birch or cherry around moulds, and the resultant hoops were then glued and nailed to lids and bottoms of thicker wood. These carriers were painted or stained, and sold in graduated nests. Although these boxes were originally made for utility purposes – groceries, tools, sewing cottons – their form, detailing and simplicity symbolizes the Shaker way of life.

TOOLS & EQUIPMENT

- Workbench
- Pencils
- Metal rule
- Scalpel
- Vice
- Coping saw
- Rasp
- Graded sandpapers
- Heavy craft knife
- Steamer (as illustrated)
- 2 template moulds (as illustrated in the working drawing)
- A pair of heat-proof gloves
- 6 dolly pegs
- Peen hammer
- Cotton cloth

MATERIALS

- 2 pieces of prepared pine measuring $7 \times 5 \times \frac{1}{4}$in
- 2 strips of maple, cherry or birch veneer measuring $21 \times \frac{5}{8} \times \frac{1}{16}$in and $20\frac{11}{16} \times 2\frac{3}{8} \times \frac{1}{16}$in
- Stiff card
- Tracing paper
- 12 copper rivet nails ($\frac{3}{16}$in)
- PVA glue
- Beeswax

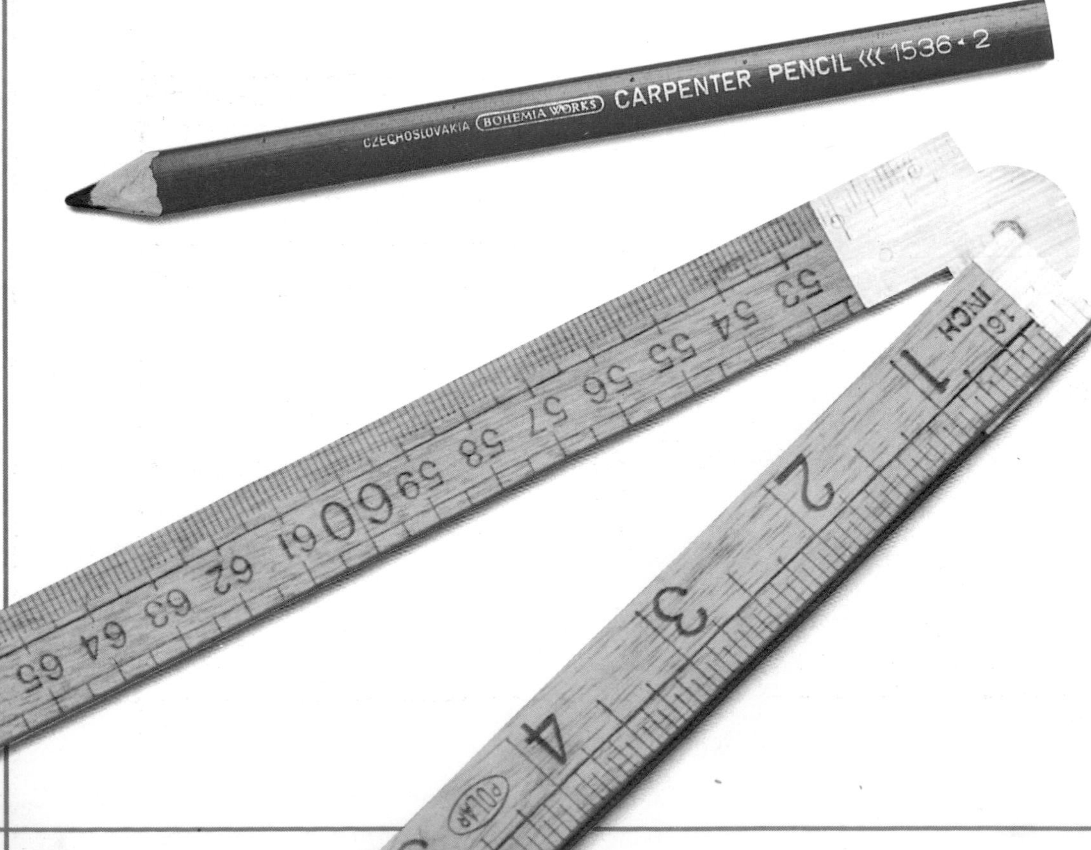

There are two scales for this working drawing: the upper drawing is two squares to 1in, and the lower detail is four squares to 1in. Note how the wooden mould has been worked so that there are two peg slots and three metal rivet-plates.

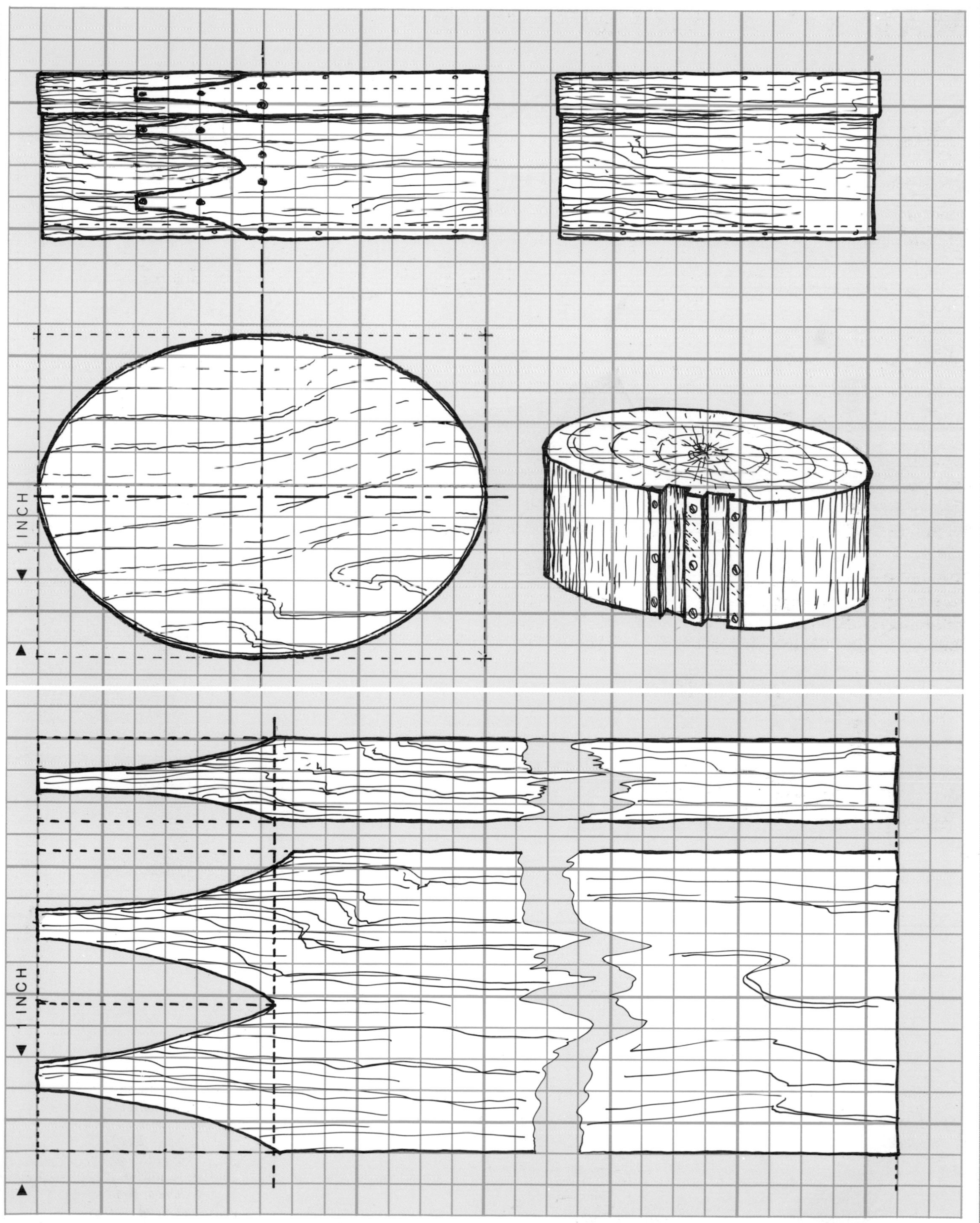
1 INCH
1 INCH

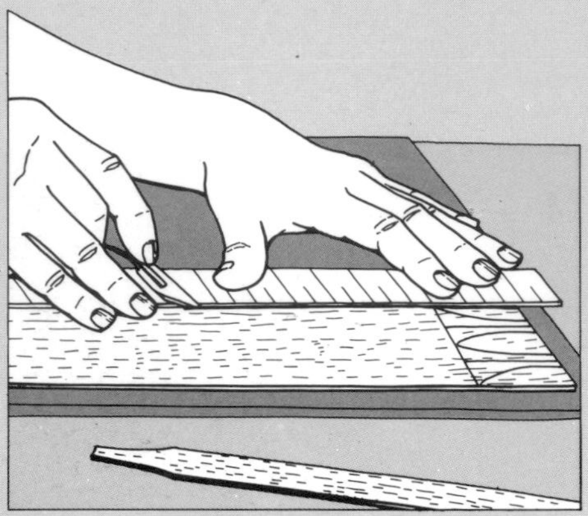

Considering the materials and making the templates

Set out the two pieces of pine and the two strips of veneer on the workbench and give them a thorough checking. Make sure that the wood is free from grain twists, end splits, stains and dead knots.

Have a long look at the working drawing and the photographs and see how Shaker boxes are designed and constructed. Note how the delicate 'fingers' or 'lappers' of the sides and rim have been tapered and bevelled, and see how the overlapped scarf joints have been fixed with flat-head copper rivet nails.

Consider how the alignment and placing of the various parts and the fine detailing makes these boxes both functional and beautiful. For example, there is nothing casual or haphazard about the proportions of the decorative lappers or the placing of the rivet nails – everything has been thought about and positively designed.

When you feel that you have a good understanding of how the box has been conceived, designed and constructed, draw up the templates to scale on stiff card using a pencil, tracing paper and a ruler. There are four templates in all; one for the lid rim, one for the box sides, one for the oval lid and one for the oval base (see working drawing). Finally, take a scalpel and a metal rule, and, with great care and caution, cut out the four template formers.

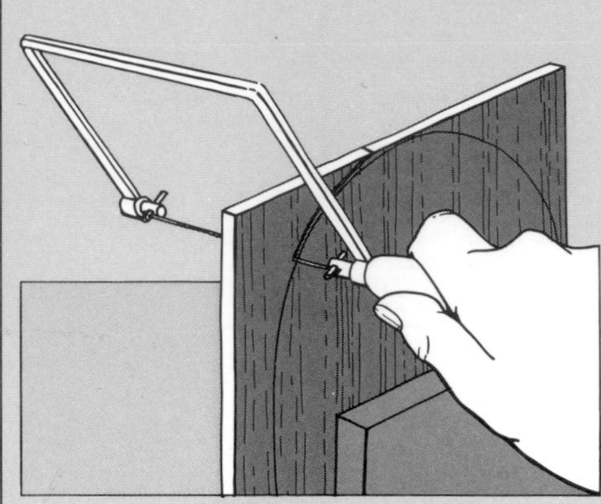

Cutting the base and lid boards

Take the two oval cardboard templates and transfer their forms to the working faces of the two pieces or pine. Use a soft pencil and label the two formers top and bottom. Note: have a look at the working drawing and see how the wood grain runs the length of the oval.

When you are sure that all is correct and as described, place the wood one piece at a time in the vice or clamp it to the bench if you prefer. With the wood well secured, cut out the oval profiles with the coping saw using steady, even strokes. Work the wood on the waste side of the pencil line and try to keep the angle of cut at 90° to the working face of the wood.

As you are cutting and manoeuvring the fine coping-saw blade around the various curves, you will have to take the wood out of the clamp from time to time, and re-position it so that the line of the next cut is uppermost.

Continue sawing until you have achieved two nicely worked blanks. Having done this, take the rasp and a medium-fine sandpaper, and smooth all the sawn edges to a swift, crisp finish.

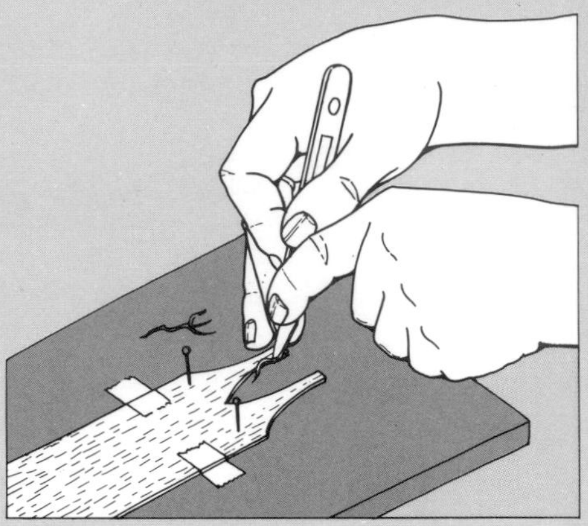

Cutting and bevelling the lappers

Take the side and rim templates, and transfer the forms to the working faces of the two strips of veneer. Now, with a sharp knife and a metal rule, cut and work the two slats until they are to size and you have a neat edge. Remembering that on no account must the knife blade slip and run into the grain, work the decorative lappers that go to make up the scarf joint. Draw the blade around the profiles so that the fingers taper in single, smoothly worked curves.

Place the two long strips on the workbench so that their outside faces are uppermost and pare away the thickness of wood at the tail or square end with a rasp, knife and sandpaper.

Aim to work a feathered taper over about 5–6in and try to grade the wood thickness so that it is smooth.

With the outside face still uppermost and the lappers nearest you, take the razor-sharp scalpel and cut the bevels. Work with a well-controlled and rather stiff wrist. Hold the knife at an angle and run the blade around the curves so as to achieve the swiftest and most delicate of bevels. If you feel less than confident at this stage, do not try to hack the bevel wood off in one great slice, but work it little by little.

Finally, take a sheet of fine sandpaper and, with a light stroking touch, rub off all burrs, splinters and rough edges.

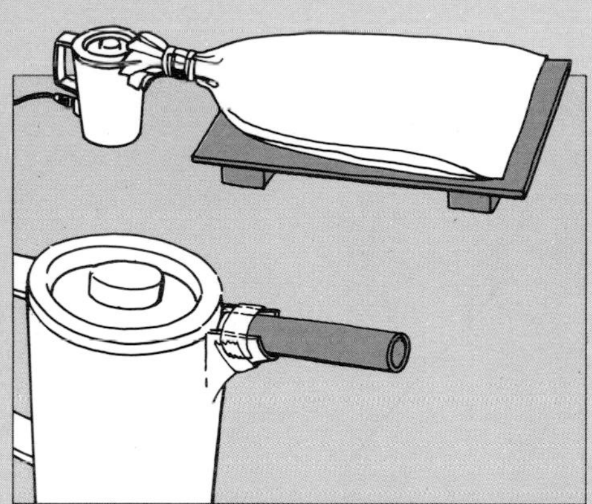

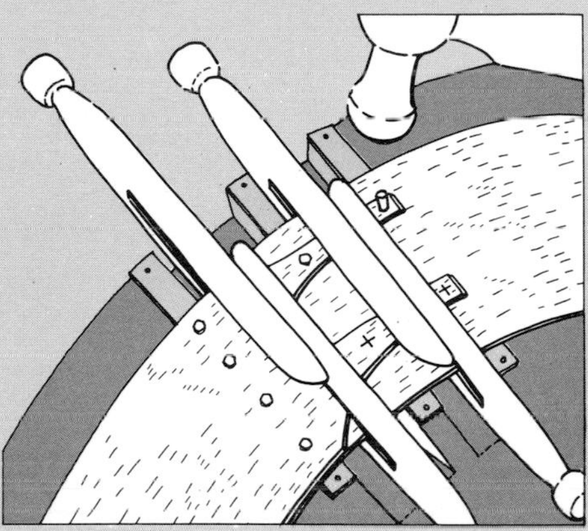

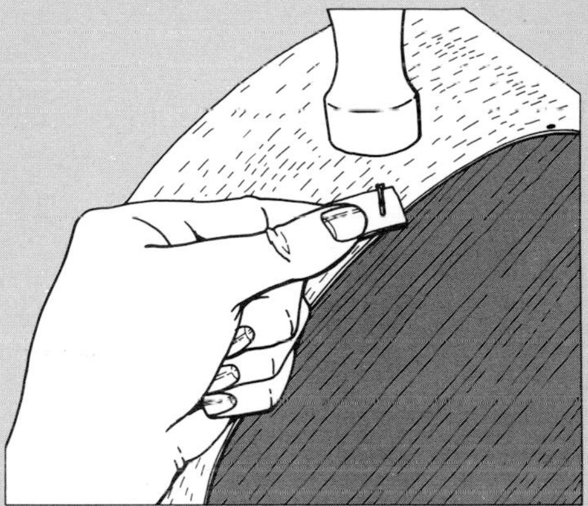

Steaming and bending

When the side and rim pieces have been nicely edged, tapered and bevelled, soak them overnight in hot water. Meanwhile, consider how the wood is to be steamed. You may build a sophisticated steamer of a long plywood box and a purpose-built gas or electric boiler, or, alternatively, you can use an electric kettle and a plastic bag apparatus as illustrated.

Place the soaked wood in the steamer for about 30–45 minutes, or until it can be easily flexed and bent. Note: wood varies in quality and structure from piece to piece and type to type, so it is important that you monitor the steaming and remove the wood as soon as it curls or sags.

While the wood is being steamed, it is necessary to organize the working area. Place the two oval template moulds (as described in the working drawing) on the workbench and place the gloves, six dolly pegs, 12 copper rivet nails and the peen hammer so that they are all comfortably to hand.

Moulding, clamping and rivet-nailing

As soon as the veneer slats are pliable take them out of the steamer, one piece at a time. With controlled haste, bend them around the template moulds. When the slats are in place and the decorative lappers are precisely aligned, take the dolly pegs and clamp them over the scarf overlap (as illustrated).

Pencil mark the position of the 12 rivet nails. Wait until the wood has cooled off and remove the pegs, smear a little PVA glue under the overlapping fingers of the joint and replace the pegs.

Take the nails and the peen hammer, and, with great care, drive the nails through the fingers of the overlap. (It may be advisable to have a trial run with a scrap of wood and some rivet nails.) Strike each nail with a few well-placed blows so that the point is driven and peened against the metal mould-plates.

Ideally, the riveting should be worked while the wood is still damp and warm so that there is less risk of the wood splitting. However, if in doubt, drill a pilot hole. Aim to work joints that are tightly clenched but, at the same time, try to keep the wood free from hammer damage. Finally, wipe off the excess glue with a damp cloth and put the rim and box hoops to one side to dry out.

Putting the box together

When all 12 rivet nails have been clenched and the points have been peened over, the box can be put together. Take the side and rim hoops and, being careful not to force or split the wood, ease them onto the base and lid ovals. Place the lid on the box and adjust the decorative finger lappers of the lid so that they are perfectly aligned with those on the base. Fix the hoops to the base and top with half a dozen copper nails set at regular intervals.

Now, with a piece of fine-grade sandpaper supported against your open palm, rub the whole box down – inside and out – until the wood is free from burrs, hard glue dribbles and rough edges. When the box is completely smooth to the touch, take a soft cotton cloth and bees-wax, and bring the wood to a good finish.

Note: traditionally these boxes were also finished with varnish and red, yellow, blue and green milk paints. To create a similar finish, paint the box with a flat watercolour and let the paint dry. Break the colour with sandpaper, and then wax and polish.

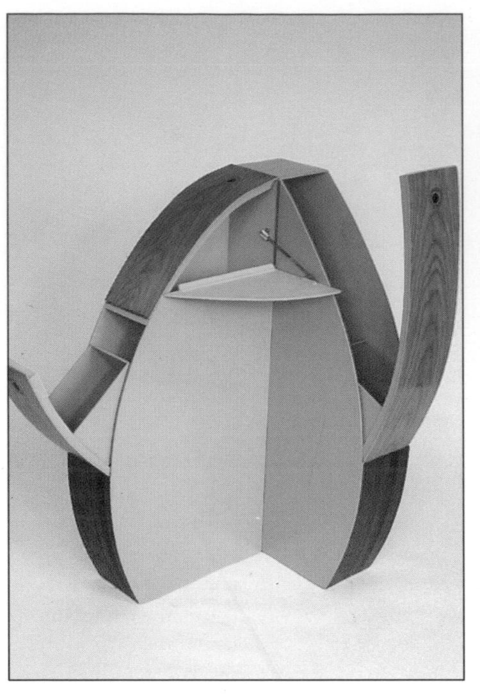

ABOVE LEFT *and* RIGHT *Small decorative container made for a project at the London College of Furniture. The container has been worked with laminated veneers, and although novel, has obviously been inspired by traditional woodworking. Note the rather ingenius way in which the form of the container opens out.*

BELOW *Veneered box made for a project at the London College of Furniture. This piece is another example of laminated veneering and is Post-Modernist in design. See how the form and the surface decoration come together to make a well-considered whole.*

RIGHT PROJECT PHOTOGRAPH *Steam-bent Shaker box. Also known as cheese or hat boxes, these containers were used for all general purposes. They were originally sold singly or in matched sets, and occasionally they were carved, named and dated.*

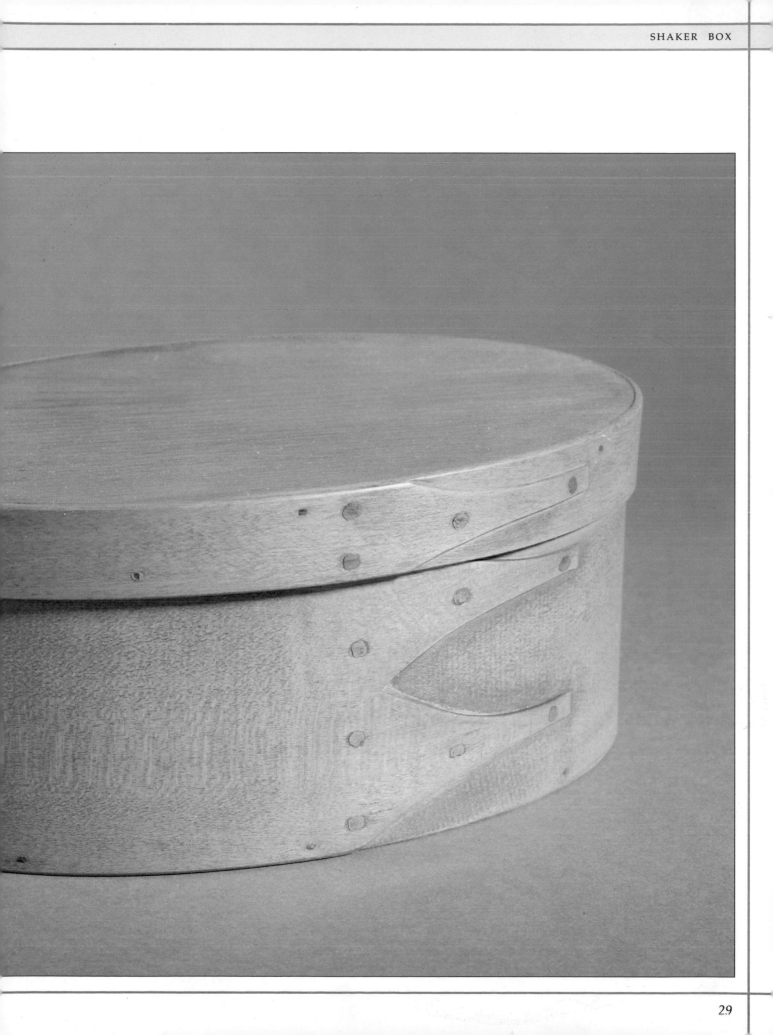

MAKING A TURNED BOWL IN THE SCOTTISH QUAICH TRADITION

THERE IS a Scottish tradition of making the most beautiful porridge and drinking bowls out of contrasting light and dark woods. Known variously as caups, cogues, coggies and quaiches (from the Gaelic word *cuach* meaning a small drinking dish or cup), these bowls are curious examples of decorative, domestic treen. Not only are they built like barrels out of alternating staves of different woods — usually sycamore and laburnum — but they are also turned. Even more interesting is the fact that traditionally these cooper-built bowls are held together by a decoratively structural feature known as 'feathering', and not by glue. If you look at the project photograph (see page 33) and concentrate on the interior of the quaich, you will see that the alternating staves of contrasting woods are linked by means of feathered or splintered hooks; gouge cuts on the sides of one stave are hooked into cuts on the sides of neighbouring staves. The whole bowl is strapped up with split willow in much the same way as barrel staves are held with iron hoops. Another characteristic feature of these bowls is their handles which are cut from the solid wood. These bowls, therefore, are not only stave-built and turned, but are also, in some part, carved.

TOOLS & EQUIPMENT

- Workbench
- Sandpaper
- String and wedge
- Measure
- Pencils
- Compass
- Craftsman's protractor
- Square
- Marking knife
- Hand saw
- Bow or frame saw
- Holdfast
- Vice
- Band clamp
- Scissors
- Clamps
- Screws and screwdriver
- Lathe and small face plate
- Callipers
- Sketchpad
- Long-handled fluted gouge
- Round-nosed scrapers
- Chisels
- Hammer

MATERIALS

- 4 cubes of wood measuring 4 × 4 × 4in (2 sycamore and 2 laburnum)
- 4in disc of 1in thick plywood
- PVA glue
- Brown paper
- Sketch paper
- Beeswax

The lefthand grid is scaled at two squares to 1in, and the righthand grid is one square to 1in. See how the grain needs to be carefully matched and arranged at the gluing stage.

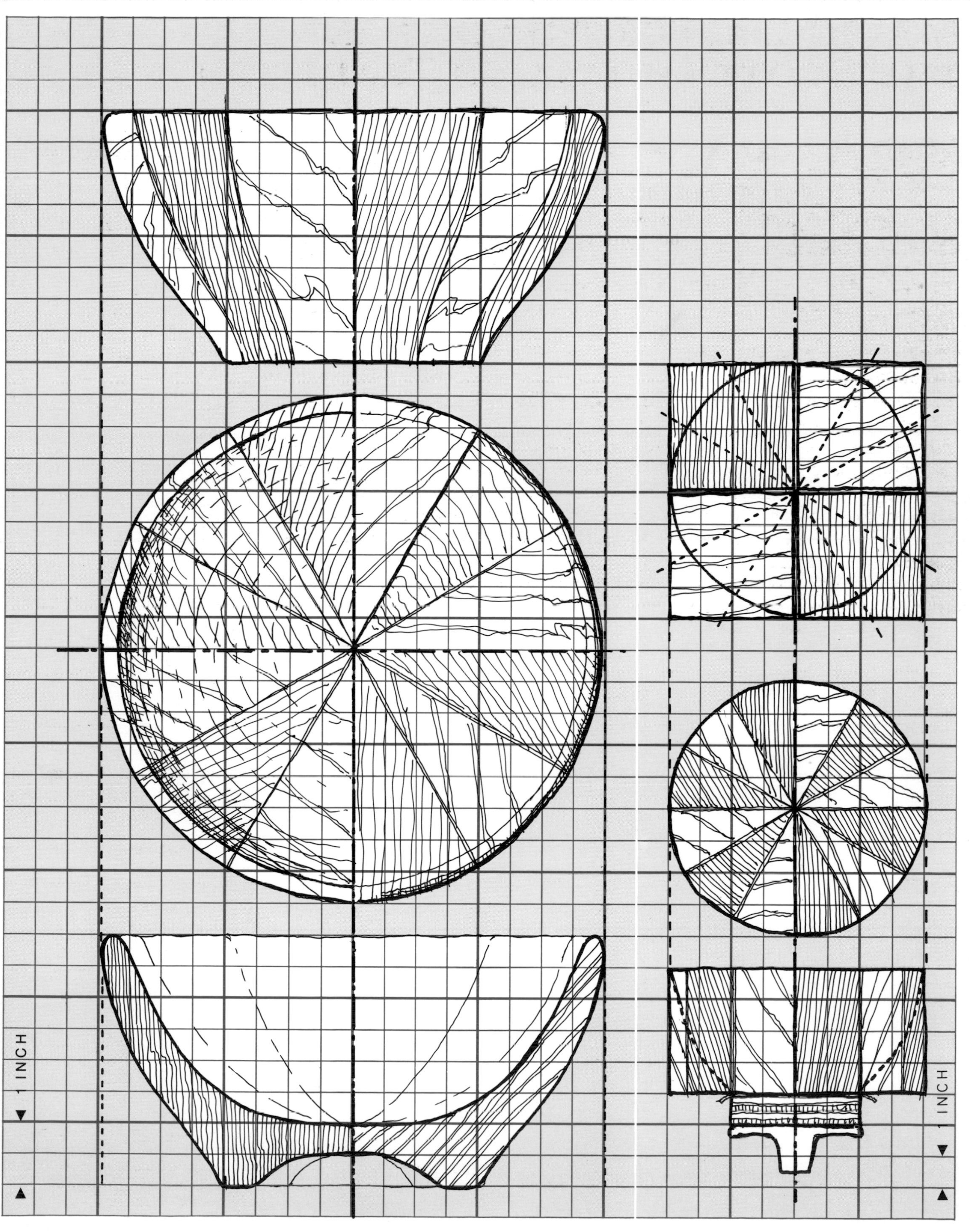
1 INCH
1 INCH

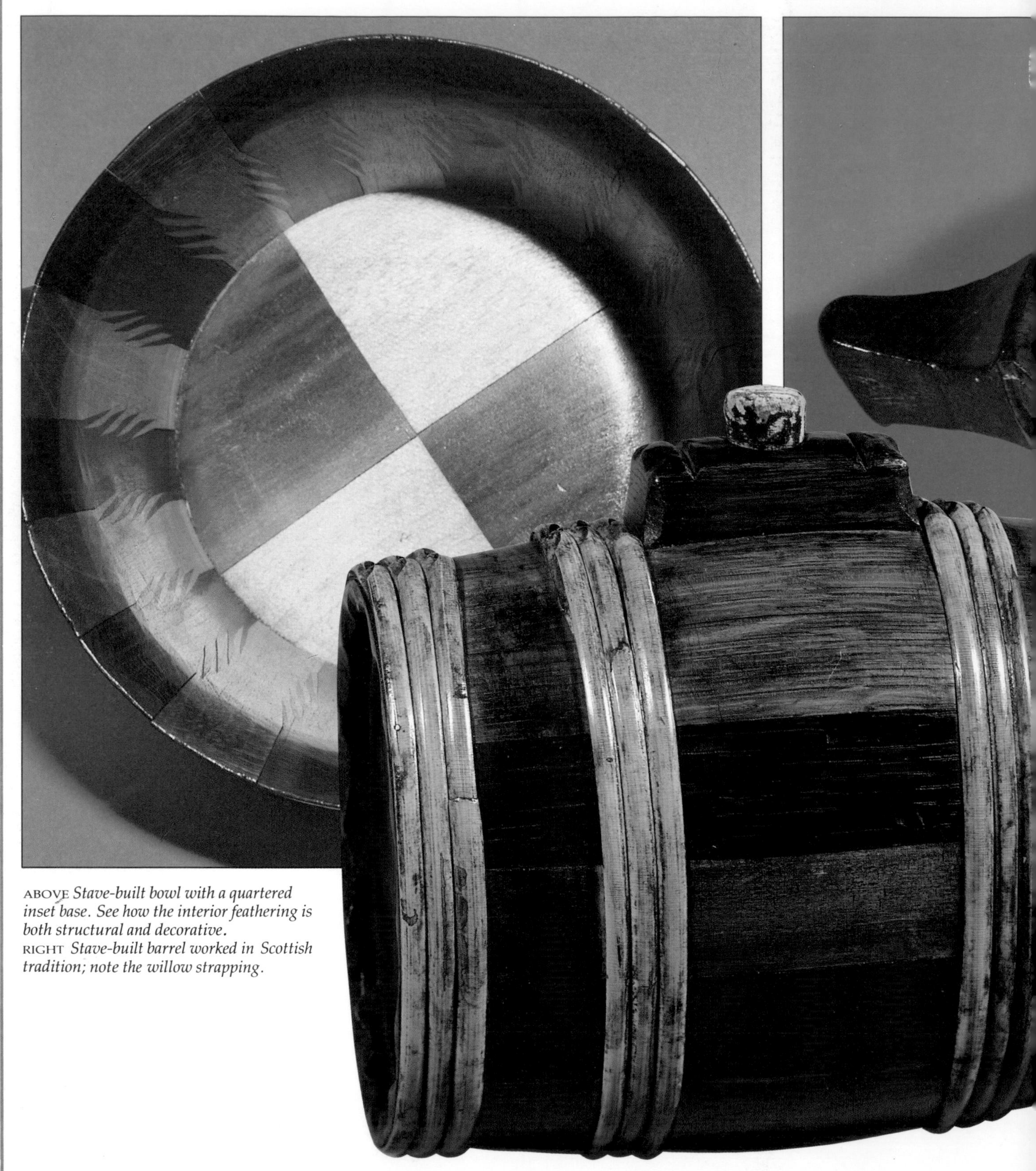

ABOVE *Stave-built bowl with a quartered inset base. See how the interior feathering is both structural and decorative.*
RIGHT *Stave-built barrel worked in Scottish tradition; note the willow strapping.*

ABOVE PROJECT PHOTOGRAPH
Scottish Quaich. The use of feathering and straps indicates that this bowl was made without glue, and is held together in much the same way as coopered barrels.

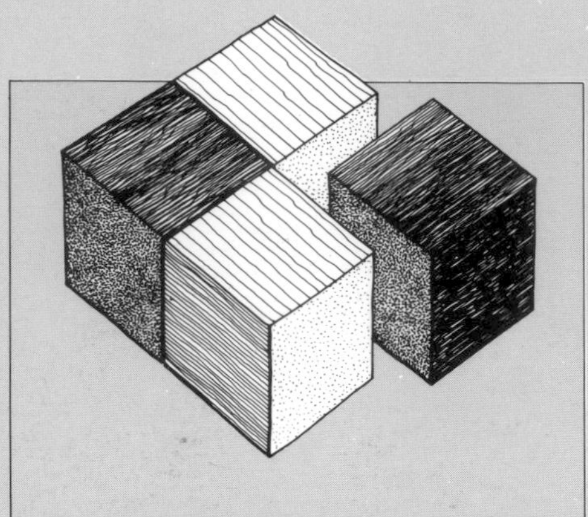

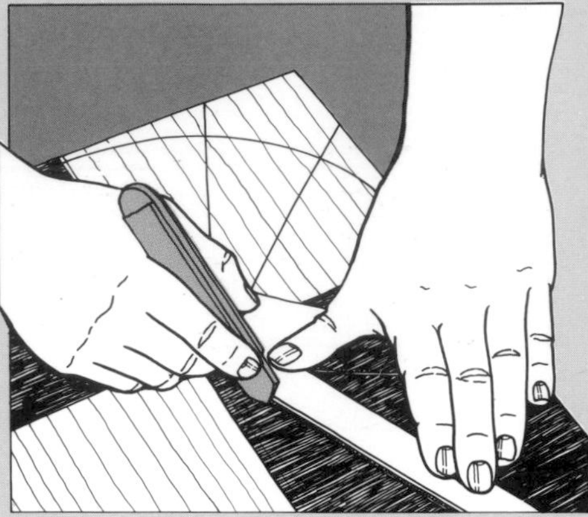

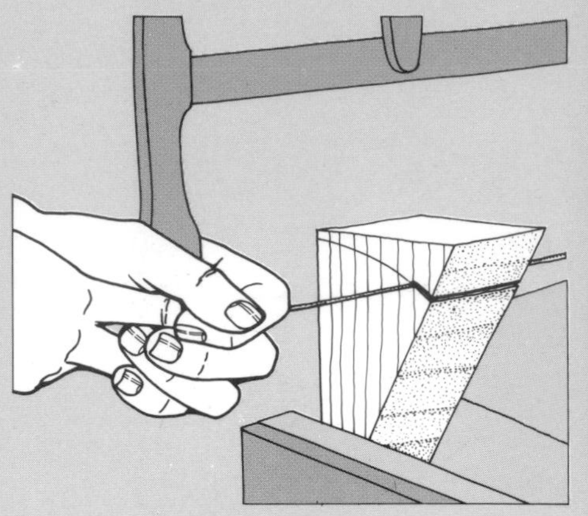

Considering the project and setting out the wood

Before you start this project, take a magnifying glass to the photograph of the Scottish quaich (see page 33) and see how it is built out of cooper-made staves of light and dark wood. Also note the hoops of split willow, the decoratively structural feathering and the integral handles.

Now, look at the working drawing and see how the project modifies the techniques — that is, the project still uses contrasting woods to make a lathe-turned bowl but it adjusts the design by not having handles and by using glue rather than strapping with willow. If possible, visit a folk museum and see examples of traditional domestic treen such as Welsh mazers or masarns (food bowls made of maple), carved platters, dipper spoons and, of course, Scottish quaiches.

Take your four blocks of wood — two of sycamore and two of laburnum — and set them out on the workbench. Have a close look at your wood and make sure that it is close- and straight-grained, and free from twists and dead knots. Finally, group the blocks (as illustrated) so that they come together to make a block with flush faces that measures 8 × 8 × 4in. If necessary, use a sheet of coarse sandpaper to work the various faces of the wood.

Setting out

Having achieved four flush-faced blocks, regroup them (as illustrated) and temporarily strap them up with a length of string and a wedge. Now, set out the measure, pencil, compass, craftsman's protractor and square. Fix the compass to a radius of 4in, and then mark out the wood with an 8in-diameter circle (it could be slightly smaller). Set the protractor to 30°, take the marking knife and divide the circle into twelve 30° segments or slices.

Gently turn the whole strapped-up block over and mark out the other side in the same way. Bearing in mind that the success of this project hinges on the wood being clearly marked out, work with extra care, double check all measurements, and score all lines with a marking knife. Having done this, extend the twelve radial lines so that they strike the edge of the 8 × 8in block. With a square and pencil, drop the radial lines down the side faces of the block.

Very carefully turn the wood over and check that the dropped radial lines meet the radial lines on the other side of the block. Now, label one side of the block A and the other side B. Note: it is important that every slice is marked.

When you have established all the lines with the marking knife, consider how best the slices might be arranged so as to make a contrasting light and dark blank.

Cutting, arranging and gluing

Once all the wood has been marked out and you have established all twelve slices, remove the twine and wedge. Set out the tools — the hand saw, the bow or frame saw, and the holdfast.

Start by taking the wood (one block at a time) and prepare to cut it into the identical 30° slices. Bear in mind how important it is that the sawn faces of the wedges are vertical and true. For this reason, secure the wood with a holdfast, hold the saw at 90° to the working face of the wood, and work with an unhurried, steady action. Do not worry too much if the wood at the point of the slices crumbles away slightly — at this stage settle for fractionally off-angle compromise cuts. Continue working until there are twelve near-identical slices.

Take the wood (one slice at a time) and put it in the vice. Use the bow saw to establish the circular profiles at the broad end of the wedges. Now, place a sheet of coarse sandpaper on the workbench and rub down all the sawn faces until they are true.

Bring all the wedges together on the bench and check and adjust for a good fit. Finally, glue the wedge faces, strap them up with a band clamp (or a stick and rope tourniquet) and put the whole work to one side to dry.

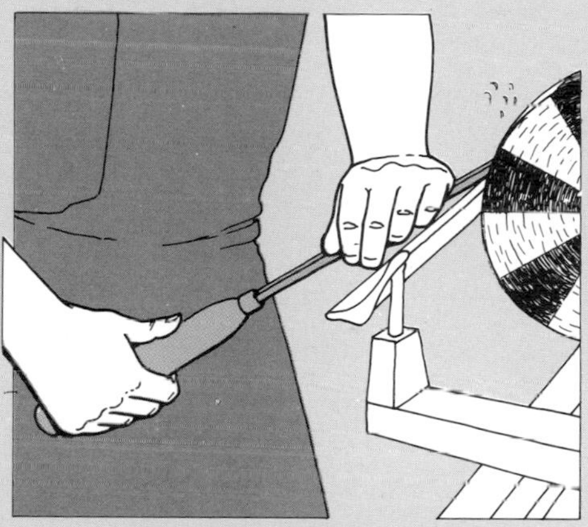

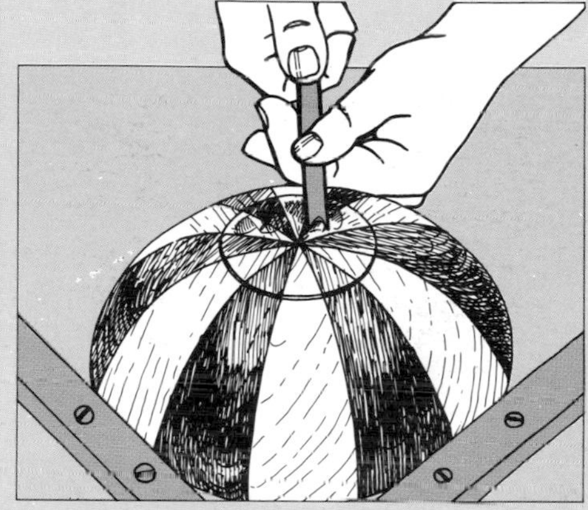

Gluing the blank and preparing for the lathe

When the PVA glue is dry, remove the clamps and check the composite blank for fit and stability. Now, set out the small plywood disc, a piece of brown paper, scissors, PVA glue and a pencil. Cut out a brown paper circle to match the plywood and, with glue and a clamp, sandwich the brown paper between the plywood and the wood to be turned. The correct sandwich order is — plywood, glue, brown paper, glue and finally the blank. Clamp the composite block and wait for 24 hours, until the glue is dry.

At this stage, screw the lathe face plate to the centre of the bottom of the plywood waster. Note: the screws must not be so long that they go into the blank. There are, of course, other ways of fixing the face plate to the blank but this method is easy to work and it leaves the piece to be turned free from screw holes. If this method is to be successful, all surfaces to be glued must be carefully prepared.

Finally, screw the face plate to the lathe. Having checked that the lathe is in good order, sit down with a pencil, callipers and sketch paper, and draw a series of possible bowl profiles and sections. If you want to stay within the tradition of Scottish quaiches, aim for a shallow dish — about 6–7in in diameter and 3–3½in deep.

Turning the outside of the bowl

Pin your working drawings, sketches and any collected inspirational material up so that they are within view. Set out the fluted gouge, a couple of round-nosed scrapers and a pair of callipers.

Bearing in mind that the grain of the composite blank will be constantly changing direction, set the lathe to run at a medium-slow speed, take the long-handled gouge and rough out the outside contours of the blank (as illustrated). Support the gouge on the tool-rest, hold the handle low at waist level or even slightly lower, and strip off the outside face of the blank with a series of shearing or sliding cuts. Run the gouge repeatedly along the side of the spinning wood until you have more-or-less established a smooth cylinder that relates to the outside diameter of the bowl rim. You need to work a cylinder that is about 6–7in in diameter. Continue working the wood until the face of the wood is true.

Now, still working with the fluted gouge and using the callipers to take readings from the working drawing, gradually shape the outside profile of the bowl. When you have achieved what you consider to be a good form, take a round-nosed scraper and work the outside of the bowl to a good finish. Hold the handle of the scraper slightly higher than the tool-rest and, with a gentle, stroking action, clean off the contours of the bowl. Do not dig the tool in — just 'kiss' the wood so as to remove the finest of shavings.

Turning the inside of the bowl and finishing

Once you have achieved a good outside profile, clear away the lathe waste and swing the tool-rest around so that it is over the bed of the lathe. First, establish the thickness of the bowl rim with the gouge and make a V-section cut.

Take the fluted gouge, run it into the rim-thickness groove and, with a gentle rolling action, sweep it across the inside of the bowl from side-to-centre. Hold the handle low (but not so low that it gets tangled up with the bed of the lathe) and continue to work the wood with a series of side-to-centre sweeps. As you are working, stop from time-to-time and check the bowl thickness against the working drawings using the callipers.

When you feel that you have achieved a good inside profile, take a round-nosed scraper and clean up the wood to a good finish. Finally, polish the spinning wood with a block of beeswax, take the face plate off the lathe and return to the workbench. Now, remove the face plate and set the bowl (rim-side down) on an easy-to-make block jig.

Take the chisel and hammer, and carefully ease away the ply veneers of the plywood disc. Work the ply little-by-little, being careful to avoid levering on the bowl, and skim off all the layers. When you have done this, take a wide chisel and pare away all the glue and brown paper. Work cautiously as you pare away the waste and be very careful to avoid damaging areas of short grain. Finally, take a U-section gouge and work the bottom of the bowl to a slightly 'dished' finish. Work from side-to-centre, just removing the finest scoops of wood.

MAKING A WEDGED MORTISE-AND-TENON JOINT

THE mortise-and-tenon joint is one of the most important and the most common joints used in woodwork. When one length of wood strikes another at right-angles and needs to be fixed, the mortise-and-tenon joint is the most suitable, the most efficient and probably the easiest to work. It is used particularly in structural woodwork such as windows and door frames, and furniture of all sizes, types and periods. The joint consists primarily of a tenon (a projection) on one piece of wood that fits into a mortise (a corresponding rectangular hole) in the other piece of wood. There are a great many variations on the basic joint. There are mortise-and-tenons with secret wedges, dovetail tenons, 'through' tenons that go right through the mortise, and blind or stubb tenons that go only part of the way through the mortise wood. Each of these variations has evolved over a long period in answer to a specific constructional problem. As regards correct tools for the job, you can use just about any chisel and saw and chop out a joint of sorts but for a first-class job you do need the correct tools. For a professional joint, the wood needs to be marked out with a two-pin marking gauge, a square and a marking knife. The tenon must be cut with both a hand and a tenon saw, and the mortise must be sunk with a mallet and a mortise chisel.

TOOLS & EQUIPMENT

- Workbench
- Pencil
- Mortise chisels
- Mortise gauge
- Vice
- Square
- Metal rule
- Marking knife
- Hand saw
- Tenon saw
- Bench hook
- Mallet
- Sandpaper

MATERIALS

- Piece of prepared oak measuring 6 × 2in (length to suit)
- Slab of 2in thick prepared oak (width and length to suit)
- White cartridge paper
- Linseed oil
- Wax polish
- Turpentine

The scale is two squares to 1in. When you are choosing the wood, make sure that the grain is true and free from knots at the point where the mortise occurs.

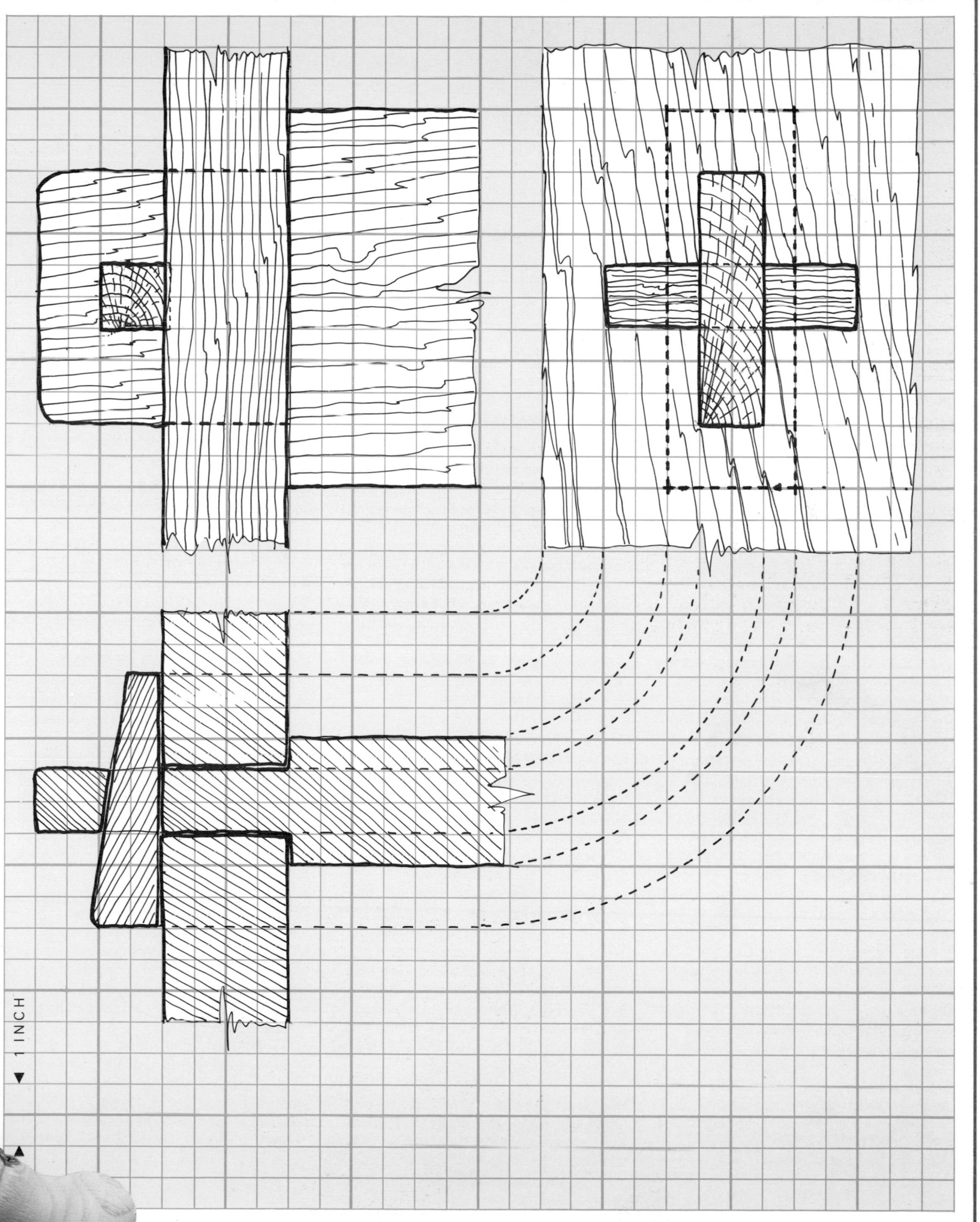
1 INCH

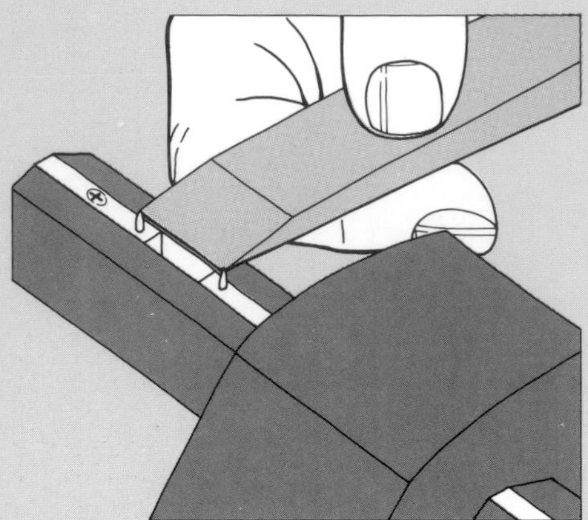

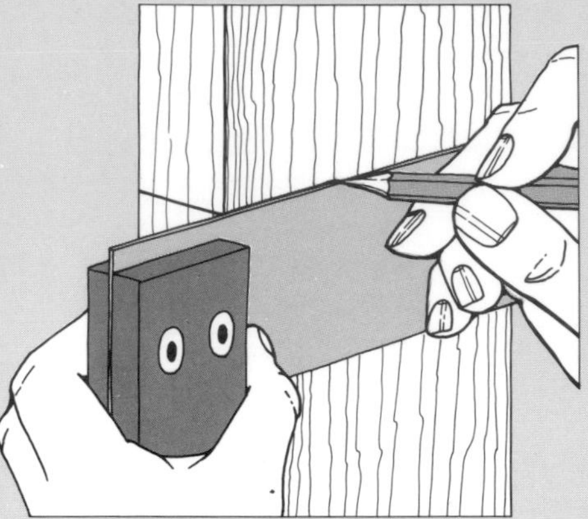

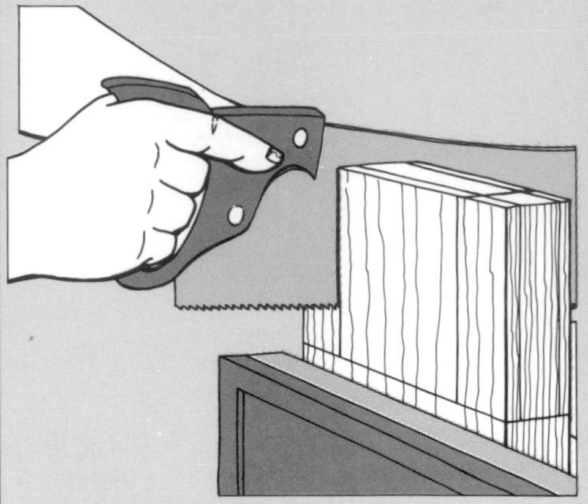

Considering the joint and setting the mortise gauge

Have a look at the working drawing and see how this project concentrates not so much on the trestle stool, but rather on the very efficient and decorative wedged mortise-and-tenon joint. These joints hold the trestle ends hard up against the shoulders of the stretcher. Note how the thick slabs of oak that make up the end boards are pierced and mortised to receive the stretcher, and how the seat slab is mortised to take the top of the end slabs.

Take a magnifying glass to the photograph and see how the shoulders of the tenon are pulled tight up against the inside faces of the end slabs and are then held in place with wedges. When you have studied the photograph in detail and you appreciate all the subtleties of the mortise-and-tenon joints, take a sheet of white cartridge paper and a pencil, and make a working drawing to scale. With a piece of work of this character it is most important that the drawing is set out with all the sizes, details and sections marked out.

Note the width of the mortise, the thickness of the tenon, the sizes of your mortise chisels, and then set the points of the mortise gauge accordingly. Note: there are any number of different types of marking gauges, some with flat cutters and others with two pins and two beams. For this project you should use ideally a single beam gauge with two pins for marking out mortises and a single pin on the underside of the beam for general marking out (see the illustrations).

Setting out the wood

Lay the pieces of wood out on the workbench. Put the stretcher piece in the vice so that one end is uppermost. Now, take the square, measure and pencil (or marking knife) and strike off tenon shoulder lines around all four faces of the wood. See how this line is at least 4in away from the end of the stretcher to allow for the thickness of the end slab and the wedge. Also note how the line firmly establishes the tenon shoulders.

Now, take the marking gauge, check that it is set to the tenon and chisel thickness, and then run the spikes from one 'shoulder line' over the end of the wood and then back to the other. When you have done this, reset the gauge and mark the tenon width. You should now have four lines that run over the end of the wood and mark out the tenon profile (see the working drawing). Mark the other end of the stretcher in the same way.

When you have set out the tenon, take the slab of wood – the wood through which you want to cut the mortise – and arrange it on the workbench. First, establish the position of the mortise hole. Adjust the gauge to suit the wood size, and then set out the mortise accordingly. Run lines around the wood with the square, and then strike off the width of the mortise with the gauge.

Once all these lines have been struck, take a pencil and clearly label the wood 'mortise', 'tenon' and 'waste'. Generally mark the wood so that there is no doubt as to which is the waste side of a line and which is the good or right side.

Cutting the tenon

Put the marked stretcher in the vice end up (as illustrated) and place the hand saw, the tenon saw and a chisel so that they are to hand. Now, take the hand saw and proceed to cut down on the waste side of each of the gauge lines until the teeth of the saw are level with the tenon shoulders. This procedure is straightforward as long as you make absolutely sure that the kerf (or cut) is on the waste side of the tenon. Note: if you cut on the good side of the gauge lines, the tenon will be a loose fit. As the old saying goes, look three times, check twice, and cut only once.

Re-position the wood in the vice, and cut the other four kerfs that make the four sides of the tenon. When you have done this, take the wood out of the vice and put it up against a bench hook or in a clamp. Take the tenon saw and hold it square with the wood. Check that the cut is going to be on the waste side of the shoulder line, and then saw down into your initial cut.

Continue sawing and re-positioning the wood in the vice until you have cleared all the sides and shoulders of both tenons. Note: if you are a beginner, it is advisable to saw well on the waste side of all gauge lines and then bring the wood to size with a chisel. However, if you do decide to work the joint in this manner, support and guide the chisel with one hand, and push and manoeuvre it with the other – always pare the wood at a slight angle to the grain.

Cutting the mortise

Once you have set out the trestle slab as described and you have checked that the size of the cut tenon matches up with your marked-out mortise and the size of your chisels, you can clamp the wood to the bench. Using the mallet and mortise chisels, work the mortise from centre-to-end with a series of chip-cuts. As you work, space the cuts about ¼in apart and make each cut successively deeper than the one before.

When one half of the mortise has been worked, take the chisel back to the first central cut, set the blade at a low angle and clear or dig out the sliced wood. Having done this, turn the chisel around and clear the other half of the mortise – ie cut a succession of chips and then clear them with an angled cut.

Turn the wood over on the bench and approach the mortise from the other side. Work in precisely the same manner until the hole has been pierced. If you have worked systematically as described, there should be only a small core of wood at the centre of the mortise and this can be cleared with a few swift cuts. However, if you have been over cautious and the core is bigger than expected, then pick it out gradually with a smaller mortise chisel. Note: if you are a beginner, be cautious and cut the mortise to a good fit at the fitting stage.

Cutting the mortise for the wedge

When you have cut both the tenon and the mortise, bring the two pieces of wood together for a trial fitting. Tap the tenon home and adjust to an easy, not too tight, fit. If possible, get a helper to push the stretcher into the end slab while you have a close look at how the shoulders of the tenon meet the mortise surround. If there are any problems, such as the joint being too tight or the shoulders not being quite square, dismantle the joint and adjust the wood with a few strokes of the chisel.

Once the joint is a good fit, get a helper to hold the stretcher hard up against the end slab while you take a pencil and mark around the tenon projection. Dismantle the joint and set the stretcher out on the workbench.

Take the gauge, square and pencil, and set out the mortise for the key wedge. Work the wood with a suitable mortise chisel (as already described), cut chips from centre-to-end and then clear the chips. Do this to both ends and on both sides of the wood until the two tenons have wedge holes. Assemble the joint and, if all is well, the wedge hole should be slightly set back from the outside face of the trestle slab and be just a fraction inside the thickness of the slab wood (see the working drawing and details). Taking an off-cut, make two key wedges with a saw and chisel.

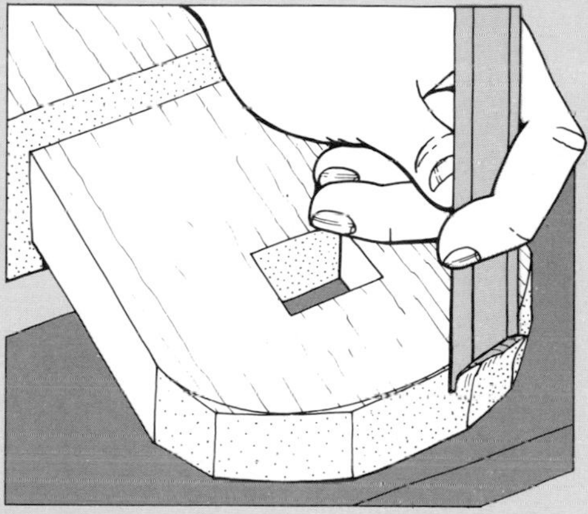

Fitting, fixing and finishing

If you are working more than one joint, it might be as well at this stage to mark the joints of mating members so that the wood can be worked for a matched fit. When the joint is assembled, tap the key wedges home with a light blow of the mallet so that the tenon shoulders are drawn up against the slab ends. If you have worked all the wood as described, the mortise-and-tenon joint should be tightly clenched, and the union between the stretcher and seat stable.

If all is correct, tap out the key wedge, dismantle the joint, and then put the stretcher in the vice end up. Now, with a tenon saw and chisel, knock off the corners of the projecting tenon and take the wood to a smooth, rounded finish (see the project photograph and the working drawing). Re-assemble the joints and clench them with the wedges.

Take a piece of medium-grade sandpaper to the wood and remove all hand marks and pencil lines. Finally, consider how you want the wood to be finished. For example, you might want a 'seasoned' effect, in which case the wood can be rubbed down with linseed oil. The wood could be left natural and just waxed or it could be slightly darkened with a linseed oil and turpentine mixture (1 part turpentine to 3 parts oil), left to dry and then waxed.

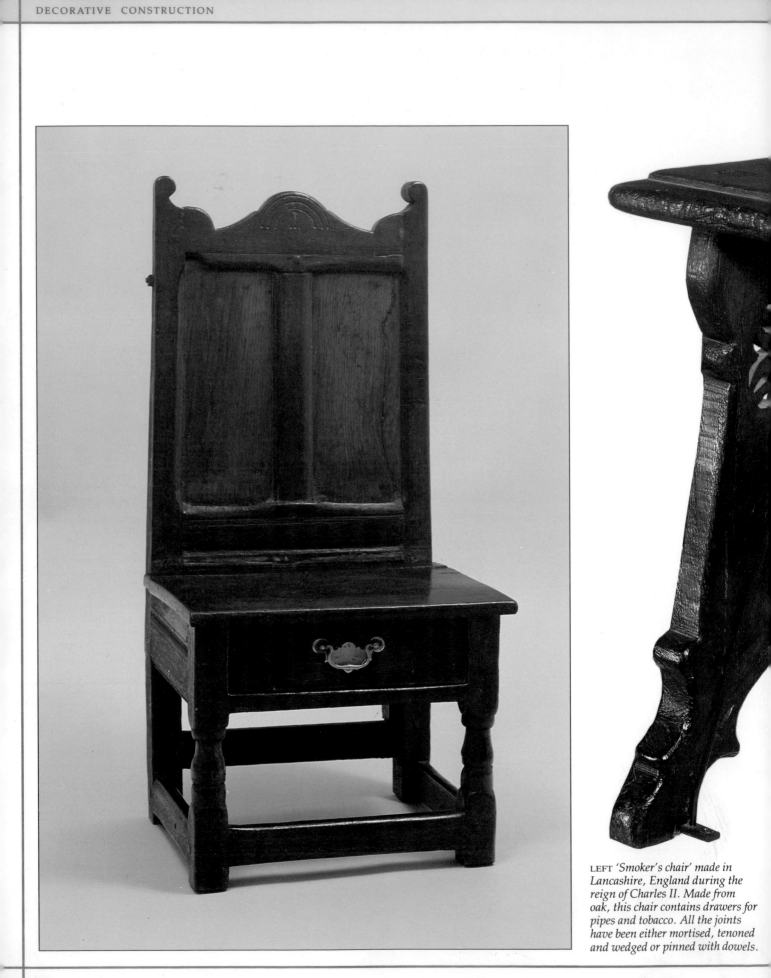

LEFT *'Smoker's chair' made in Lancashire, England during the reign of Charles II. Made from oak, this chair contains drawers for pipes and tobacco. All the joints have been either mortised, tenoned and wedged or pinned with dowels.*

LEFT PROJECT PHOTOGRAPH *Fifteenth-century Gothic stool. The seat has been beautifully worked with mortise-and-tenon joints whereas the stretchers have been fixed with wedged mortise-and-tenon joints. Furniture of this basic construction came to be called 'country' or 'kitchen hearth', and was made well into the nineteenth century.*

ABOVE *Eighteenth-century stool. Oak and elm have been used for this stool. All the mortise-and-tenon joints have through dowel pins that are both structural and decorative.*

MAKING A WINDSOR CHAIR

THE Windsor chair has always been a piece of country cottage or kitchen hearth furniture – the sort of chair that might be found in a simple, unsophisticated environment. Basically, chairs of this character have carved saddle-shaped seats, lathe-turned splayed legs, bow or straight backs and an infill of sticks, spindles and pierced splats. Developed in the early years of the eighteenth century, the Windsor chair is archetypal – that is, it probably started life as a slab-and-stick stool and gradually evolved into the chair that we know today. This theory is supported by the fact that the chairs are actually built up as stools and that the arms and back are separated from the legs by a thick slab seat. Another unusual feature of the Windsor chair is that the various parts are traditionally made of different woods by a variety of craftsmen. Traditionally, for example, the elm seat may have been worked with a bow saw and adze by the village carpenter whereas the turned and shaved beech-wood parts such as the legs, stretchers and stumps were produced by the forest 'bodger'. Finally, all the parts were sent to the chair-maker who steamed and bent the ash arm and back bows, and put the whole chair together. As to why the chairs are called Windsor, it is possible that George III ordered a set for Windsor Castle but it is much more likely that the name relates to the fact that the area in and around Windsor was, at one time, the main distribution centre for these chairs.

The scale is one square to 2in. With a project of this type – that is, making a rather sculptural 'country' chair – there is room for any number of individual features. For example, you can increase the size of the seat slab, splay the sticks and spindles, or you can simplify the turnings.

TOOLS & EQUIPMENT

- Workbench
- Beetle and froe
- Vice
- Drawknife
- Spokeshave
- A pair of lathe callipers
- Pencils
- Lathe
- Gouges
- Skew chisel
- Parting tool
- Bow or power band saw
- Long-handled adze
- Clamp
- Rasp
- Cloths
- Brace
- 3 Forstner drill bits (5/8, 3/4, 1in)
- Measure
- Bending rig (see page 47)
- Large steamer (see page 27)
- Mallet
- Graded sandpapers

MATERIALS

- 9 billets of green beech measuring 18 × 2½ × 2½in
- 17 billets of green beech, 9 measuring 38 × ¾ × ¾in and 8 measuring 12 × ¾ × ¾in
- A slab of well-seasoned elm measuring 19 × 19 × 1½in
- 2 lengths of green, straight-grained ash measuring 60 × 1 × 1in and 66 × 1¾ × 1in
- Workout paper
- Tallow or grease
- Beeswax
- Tracing paper
- White PVA glue

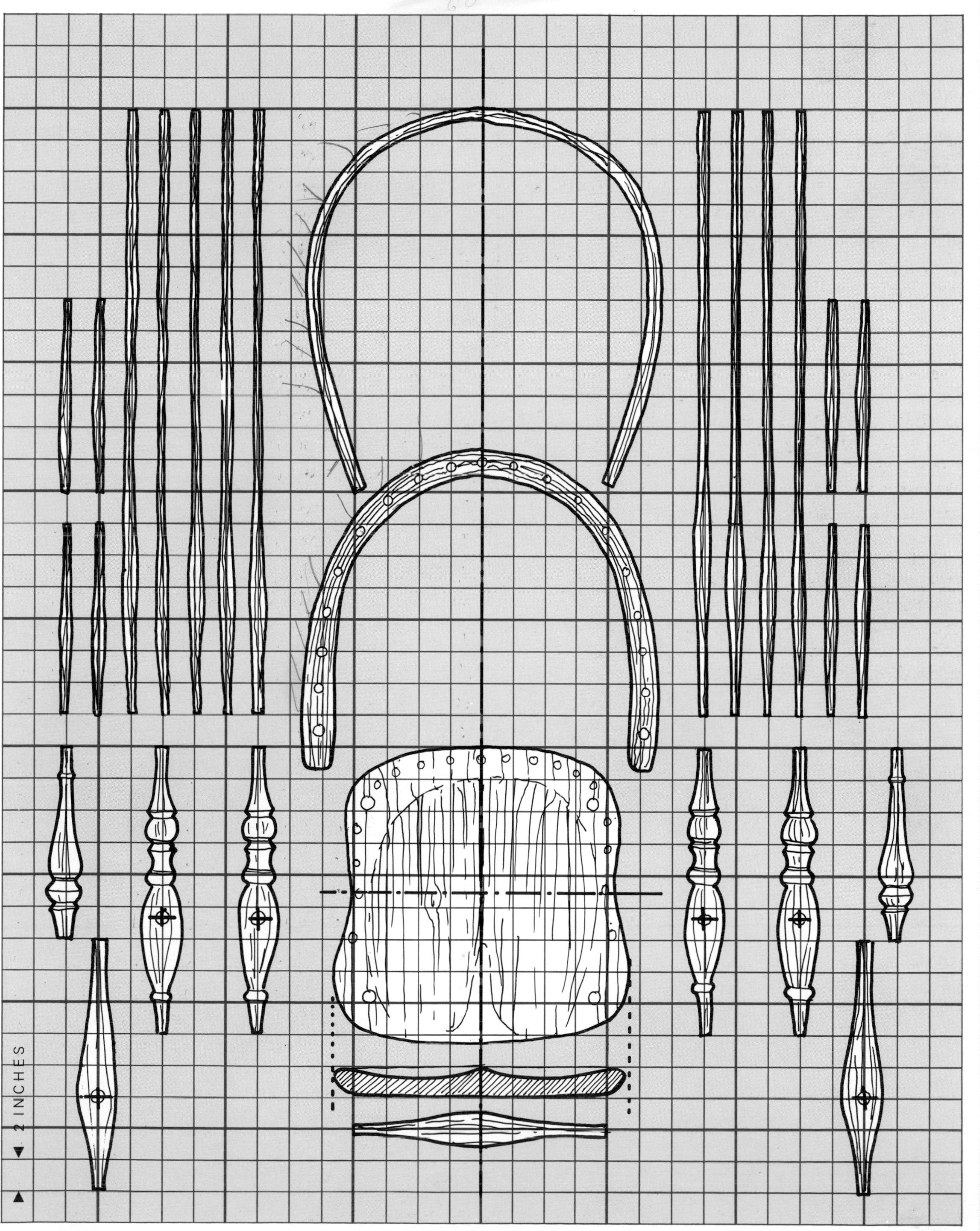
2 INCHES

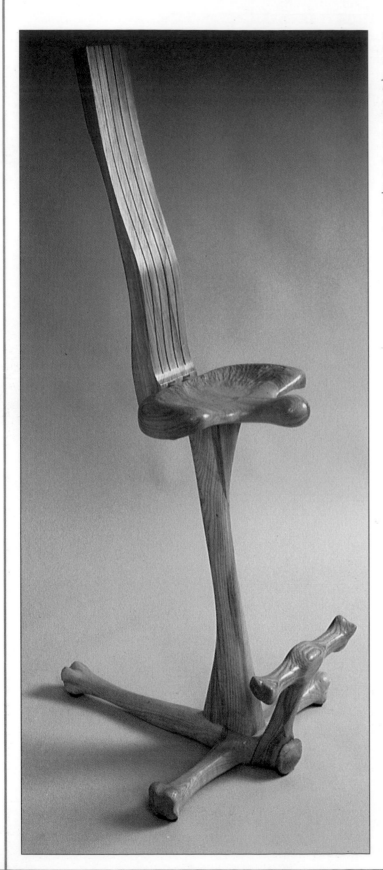

LEFT *Sculptured chair by Thierry Chessum. Ash was used to make this chair, a material that is known for its strength, resilience and aesthetic characteristics. This piece cleverly combines a fluid sensuous line with functional form.*

RIGHT PROJECT PHOTOGRAPH *Windsor chair. Made in the eighteenth century, this stick-back chair has all the characteristic features – steam-bent back and arm bows made of ash, an elm seat worked with an adze, and an 'H' leg stretcher.*

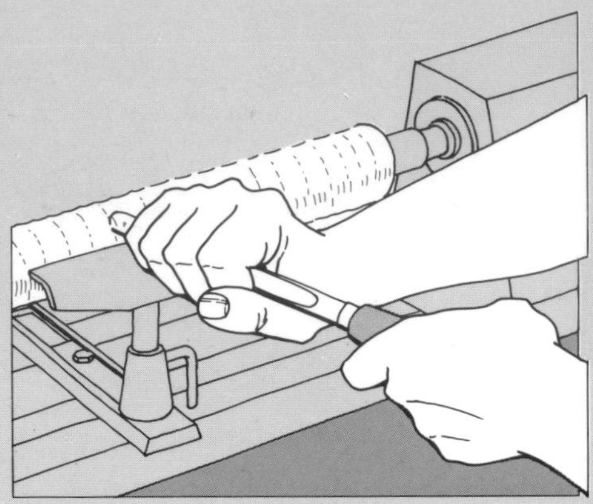

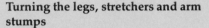

Making the back sticks

Study the working drawing and see how the chair back is made up from 17 'rising rods', sometimes called spars or sticks. Notice how these sticks delicately taper and see how they are set in the back bow at different lengths and then run down the chair to pierce both the arm bow and the seat.

Now have a close look at your billets of green beech wood, and note their characteristics – the run of the grain, the size of the knots and the quality of the growth rings. Select and group the back-stick billets, and set some aside for the chair turnings.

With a beetle and froe, or a dull wedge and a hammer, reduce the quartered wood further until you have 17 suitable, radially split sticks. Set these sticks in the vice, one at a time, or better still in the jaws of a low work-horse, and then, with the drawknife and spokeshave, knock off all the corners. When you have done this to all the sticks, go back to the working drawing and note the approximate lengths of the various sticks.

Having grouped and cut the half-shaved sticks to size, put them back in the vice and continue working with the drawknife and spokeshave. Work from the centre swell of the wood and draw the tools forward with a firm, even stroke. Continue working until you have achieved 17 smooth, sensitively tapered sticks.

Turning the legs, stretchers and arm stumps

Take a pair of callipers and some workout paper, and draw up several working details to scale. Now take the green beech billets that you set aside and group and label them – legs, arm stumps and stretchers. Having done this, check over the lathe and set out all your tools, materials and working drawing so that they are within view and close at hand.

Take the first billet of wood and dab a little tallow or grease onto the end that is going to pivot on the 'dead centre'. Place the wood between the lathe centres and screw up until the 'driving centre' bites into the wood. Now ease the lathe off slightly so that the wood spins freely and adjust the tool-rest so that it is placed just above the axis of the wood. When all is set and centred, start turning by swiftly running the shallow gouge the length of the billet. Do not attempt to remove all the waste in a single thrust; just cut away the rough parts. Temporarily stop the lathe after the first cut and take the callipers to the wood and check for size.

When you have achieved a rough size, take a skew chisel and take the wood to a smooth finish. This done, stop the lathe again and mark out the position of the various swellings, rings and curves that go to make up the turning. Now with a parting tool and various gouges, take the wood to a good finish. Finally, with the lathe still running, burnish the wood with a handful of ribbon shavings and polish it with beeswax. Repeat this procedure with all the pieces.

Cutting and shaping the seat

Make a full-size drawing and tracing of the chair seat, and transfer the drawn lines onto the top side of the slab of well-seasoned elm. Note: the grain of the seat can run from back to front or from side to side – the choice is yours.

Now take the bow saw or a power band saw and cut out the seat blank. When the blank has been cut, take a pencil and mark out the areas of the seat that are to be bottomed – that is, the part of the seat that is to be hollowed out and saddled.

Place the wood on the workshop floor, stand astride and pinion it with your feet, and begin to hollow out with the curved adze. Work across the grain, and swing the adze between your legs with a smooth, controlled action like a pendulum, letting the weight of the heavy blade do the work. Aim to hollow the saddle so that the central mound is nicely proud and rounded.

When you have achieved a well-saddled, comfortable and attractive-looking seat, clamp it to the workbench. Now with a rasp and drawknife, chamfer the top and underside edges so as to give an illusion of thinness. Next, take a shallow gouge and go over the whole seat – top, bottom and edges – giving the wood a delicate dappled and scooped texture. Finally, take a soft cloth and give the wood its first waxing. Do not burnish at this stage, but allow the wax to soak in.

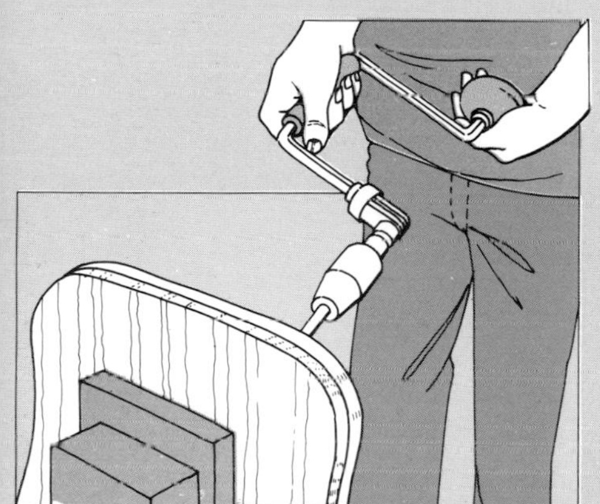

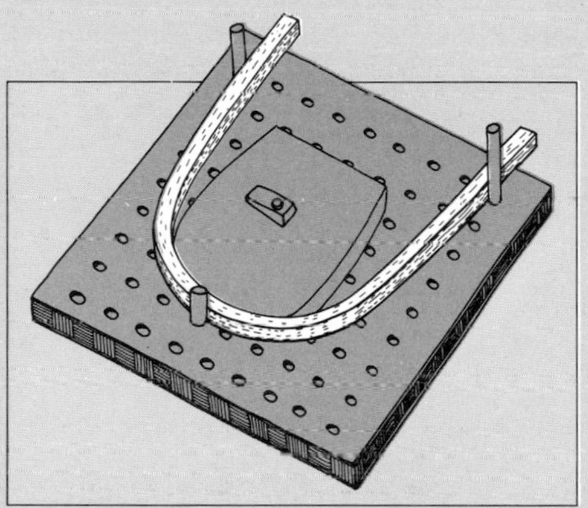

Boring holes in the seat

If you look at the photograph (see page 45) and working drawing you will see that in the seat plank there are 23 holes in all – 17 for the riser sticks, two for the turned arm stumps and four on the underside for the turned legs. Starting with the leg holes, flip the seat over so that the underside is uppermost. Set out and mark the position of the holes, as shown in the working drawing.

Now set the 1in diameter drill bit in the brace, and note the angle of entry and the depth for the front and back leg holes. Work the brace with an even action, keeping the brace steady and stop when the holes are about 1in deep. Turning the seat face up, set out and mark the position of the ⅝in diameter back-stick holes, and the two ¾in diameter arm-stump holes, according to the working drawing.

When the seat has been correctly marked out, clamp it to the bench and take all 19 holes straight through the wood thickness using the appropriate drill bit. Note: if you look at the working drawing you will see that the back sticks angle out from the edge of the seat plank at about 10–15° off vertical; you can adjust and modify this angle to suit your own needs.

Bending the arm and back bows

Run a measure over the working drawing and work out the finished length of the two bows (add on 3in for fitting wastage, end splits and building take-up). Now look at the bending rig details and set out a former rig to suit your own workshop conditions. You can use a patent steel strap bow-bender or you can make your own template and bending bed (as illustrated). Note: the template and bed are both made out of laminated layers of marine ply.

The steamer needs to be a larger version of the kettle and plastic bag used in the Shaker Box project (see page 27). Start by taking your prepared pieces of ash and check them for faults and flaws. Mark the pieces halfway along their lengths and put the back bow in the steam for about an hour, or until it can be easily bent and flexed.

When the wood is pliable, swiftly take it from the steamer, place it on the bending bed, line up the centre point with the former template and bang in the key wedge. Still working as fast as possible, take the levers and wedges, and persuade and coax the wood around the contours of the former template. When all wedges are in place, let the wood cool and set. Repeat this procedure with the arm bow. Note: once out of the steamer, the wood must be bent and worked as quickly as possible, in approximately 1–2 minutes.

Putting together

Clear your working area and set out all the parts of the chair for the first 'dry run' fitting. Start by taking the four legs and pair them off. Measure, drill and fit the side stretchers. Knock the legs into the seat holes and then measure, drill and fit the single cross stretcher. Stand the chair on its legs and tap home the arm stumps, and the side and back sticks.

Now position, mark and drill the arm bow, and slide it over the back sticks until it comes to rest on the side sticks and arm stumps. When the arm bow is in place, take the back bow and line it up by eye, marking on its underside the position of the nine back sticks. Mark and drill the two points where the ends of the back bow strike the arm bow. When this has been done, take the ⅝in bit and work the holes on the underside of the back bow making sure that you do not drill too deep. After all the holes have been worked, cut back the top of the back sticks to fit so that the ends of the back bow can be seen on the underside of the arm bow.

When the whole chair has been fitted and adjusted, knock it down, glue all sticks and holes with PVA glue and re-assemble. (You may need to use a mallet to hit the pieces home.) Next, turn the chair upside down and wedge, glue, cut back and trim the ends of all sticks and stumps as well as the ends of the back bow. When the glue is dry, take a fine-grade sandpaper and rub down the work. Bring all the wood to a smooth finish with wax polish.

CHAPTER 2

VENEER, MARQUETRY AND TUNBRIDGE WARE

MARQUETRY, Nonesuch, boulle, parquetry and Tunbridging are in general terms all methods or techniques of fixing thin sheets of exotic decorative wood onto a more common wood base. The idea of laying a precious, visually exciting wood into, or on, a base wood is perhaps one of the oldest of the decorative woodcrafts. The Egyptians made coffins that were built up from various layers of wood; in the fourteenth and fifteenth centuries European craftsmen used inlay techniques to achieve glorious combinations of materials — wood, ivory, shell, precious metal and gems; and the great master woodworkers of the Renaissance enriched all manner of furniture with the most beautiful intarsia and marquetry designs.

The craft, in its various forms, is thought to have had its roots in the East, in China, Japan and India. Small items such as chests and caskets were traded from east to west until gradually knowledge of the craft found its way via Venice and other parts of Italy into Germany, Holland and England. Nevertheless, it was not until the seventeenth century that the craft became fashionable. The catalyst of this popularity was improved communications and easier travel. Suddenly, within the space of just a few years, strange, beautiful, wonderfully figured and grained woods were coming into Europe from such places as the East and West Indies and the Americas. The pity of it is that as this popularity increased, so the use of applied woods became more and more excessively florid and indulgent.

By the end of the eighteenth century, no longer were decorative marquetry designs restricted to delicate and subtle panels and motifs; all manner of chests, boxes, tables and cupboards were being swamped with ill-considered applied decoration. And so it continued until the nineteenth century, when the inlay and marquetry crafts just about burned themselves out.

Now the term 'veneer' is used in a disparaging way to describe something that is not quite what it seems — a veneer is often thought to be a surface that conceals. Since the early 1960s, however, there has been a worldwide revival in marquetry and inlay, and the techniques are now used not so much as a means of covering up poor base woods, but as a service to artistic and craft expression. Craftsmen are now using varied materials from delicate, restrained wood inlays to hard-edged, brilliantly coloured plastics in an effort to achieve unique, self-expressive pieces.

Inlay and marquetry techniques can be used to give expression to objects of just about every taste, style, design and purpose. If you want to 'paint' a picture with coloured woods, then veneers are inexpensive and relatively easy to work; if you want to cover a synthetic wood base, the techniques are equally suitable. Inlay, intarsia, parquetry, Tunbridging — all wonderfully decorative woodworking techniques.

MAKING A MARQUETRY DESIGN

MARQUETRY is the name given to the process of cutting fine sheets of wood – all of an equal thickness – and bedding them in glue on a base wood. It is thought that the craft is a final extension and development of the much older crafts of thick-wood inlay and intarsia. No doubt, the inlay craftsmen, for reasons of economy, would always have been looking for ways of cutting rare, exotic and expensive woods thinner and thinner. This way of working, followed to its logical conclusion, would naturally result in marquetry.

The craft is traditionally one of taking figured and patterned fancy veneers and sticking them directly onto a prepared surface – there is no need, as with inlay, for the base wood to be recessed. During the fifteenth century marquetry expressed itself only in rather formal and elaborate architectural perspective designs on boxes and bench seats. However, by the seventeenth century it had evolved into a style of furniture decoration that is characterized by its free-flowing lines and profusions of figurative motifs – flowers, ribbons and swags. It has been said that the craft reached its peak in Europe in the seventeenth and eighteenth centuries when it found expression in full-bodied designs, sumptuous colours and amazingly intricate and exaggerated displays. Modern marquetry, by comparison, is restrained and considered by many to be a hobby rather than an all-consuming profession.

TOOLS & EQUIPMENT

- Work board
- Metal rule
- Surgical scalpel
- Cutting board
- Pencils
- Sharpening stone
- Craft knife
- 4 G-clamps
- 2 clamping boards
- Battens
- Soft brush
- Cabinet scraper
- Cork sanding block
- Pack of graded glass/ garnet papers
- Cotton cloth

MATERIALS

- Selection of veneers to suit your design
- Brown paper tape
- Tracing paper
- Masking tape
- Base board
- A large sheet of compensating veneer
- Newspaper
- White PVA glue
- Grain sealer
- Methylated spirits
- Wax polish

Adjust the scale to suit the size of the project that you have in mind. Before you start this project, trace the working drawing and modify the design. Spend time laying out the veneers and choosing interesting grains and colours.

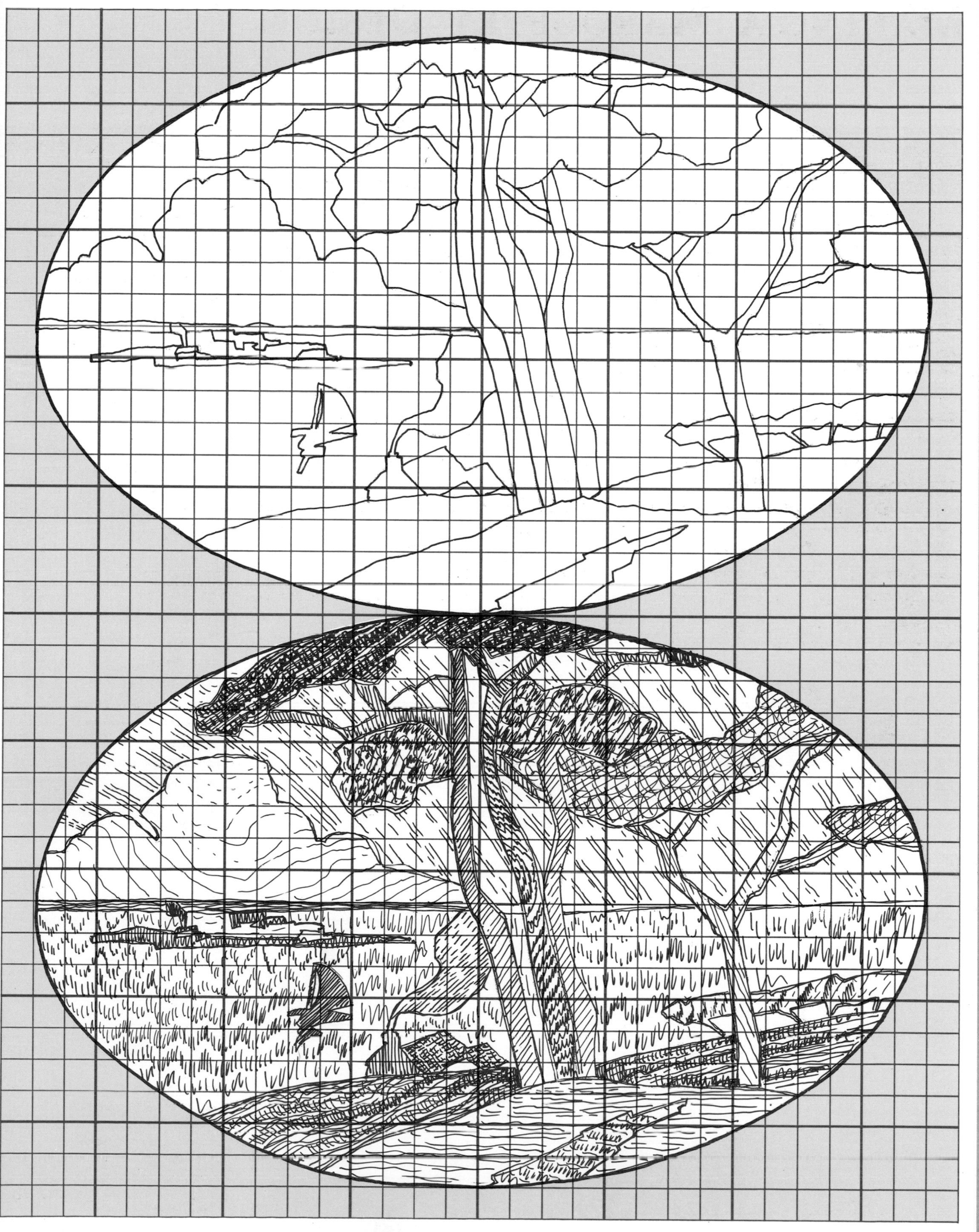

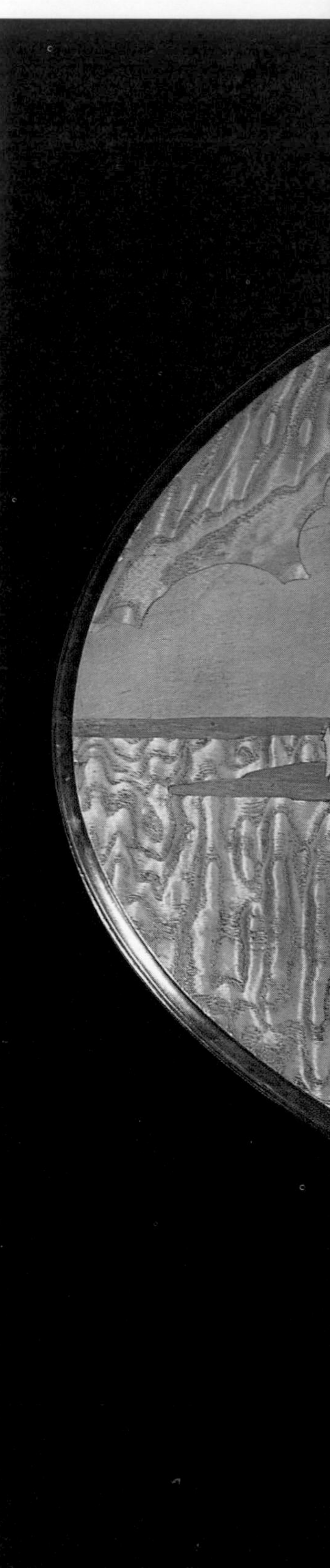

ABOVE LEFT *and* RIGHT *Abstract marquetry made by students at the London College of Furniture working to the design theme 'Autumn Leaves'. The piece on the left has been worked from natural and stained veneers using hot-pressed resins, whereas the piece on the right concentrates on the use of more formal straight-line parquetry techniques.*

LEFT CENTRE *Detail of an English marquetry box of about 1670. Worked with scorched walnut wood, notice how the forms of this design have been arranged so that there is a well-balanced 'mirror-imaged' pattern.*

RIGHT *Detail of a Chippendale secretaire dating from about 1770–1773. The ebony ground, onto which ivory has been applied, has been worked so that the grain always runs towards the centre of the design.*

FAR RIGHT PROJECT PHOTOGRAPH *Two-tiered marquetry table by Emile Gallé of the late nineteenth century. This piece of Art Nouveau craftsmanship has been worked with a variety of veneers. Marquetry of this style set the scene for the bold designs of the early twentieth century.*

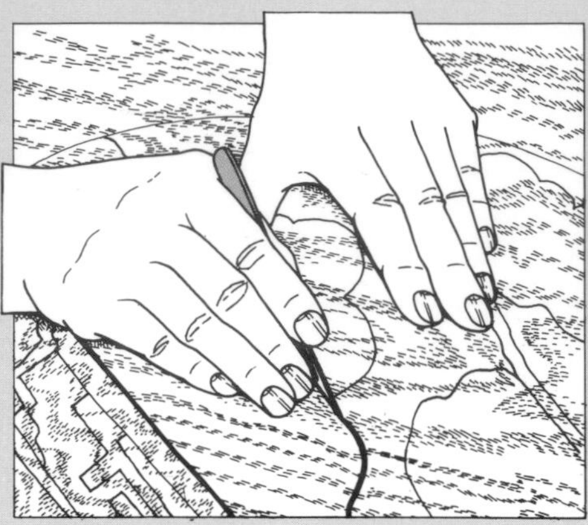

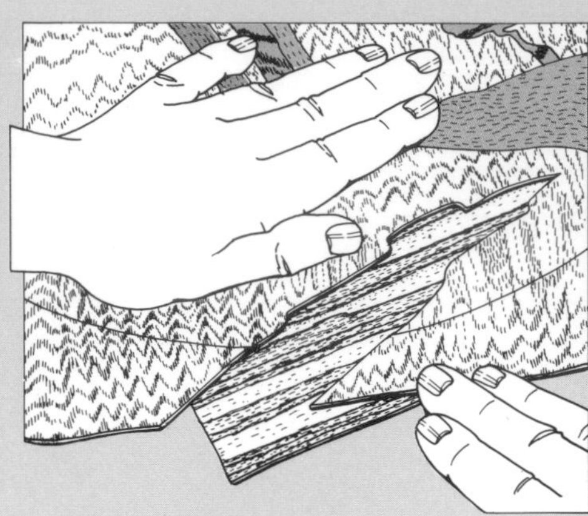

Considering the design and laying the waster veneer

If you look at the working drawing and the photographs you will see that in very general terms this design can be broken down into two well-defined areas; the sky and the sea. Begin by choosing two suitable veneers – maybe sycamore for the sea and soft obeche or Swedish birch for the sky. Bearing in mind that a large part of these two ground veneers will eventually be sacrificed as 'wasted windows', choose veneers that are easy to cut and suitably patterned and textured.

Take the two veneer sheets, relate the run of the grain and the figuring to the design and shift them around until they fit into a suitable scheme. Having done this, take the metal rule, the scalpel and the cutting board, and cut the two veneers so that they can be butt-jointed, edge to edge. Check the joint carefully, and adjust and manoeuvre the sheets until the joint is a close, well-considered fit.

Flip the two veneers over so that they are face down and then tape them together using gummed brown paper tape. Wait a few minutes for the tape to dry and turn the veneers face up. Meanwhile, make a tracing of the master design. Pencil press the lines of the design through to the front face of the veneer and go over the whole design labelling with a pencil the drawn windows, ie the boat, tree, house, etc. Finally, to stop the veneer cracking and splitting, take the brown paper tape and reinforce all the outer edges.

Cutting and working the first window

Place the two butt-jointed sheets of ground veneer face up on the cutting board. Look at the master design and then decide which of the larger areas is to be the first window. With the razor-sharp scalpel cut the chosen window out of the veneer ground.

When you have cut and removed this first window, slide various other veneers behind the hole and shift them around until the grain, colour and figure show to best effect. Now fix the chosen veneer to the back of the window with a couple of tabs of masking tape and turn the design over so that it is face up. Having done this, take the scalpel and score the motif outline through to the new piece of veneer using the window profile as a guide. When the window outline has been transferred, the veneer can be taken from behind the window and cut to a perfect fit.

When you are working the veneer, cut the wood thickness in several over-scored stages rather than trying to cut in a single heavy-handed sweep. As you are cutting, hold, control and manoeuvre the veneer with one hand so that the scalpel is presented with the next line of cut. If you find that the wood tears or cracks, then replace or sharpen the blade with a sharpening stone. As each new piece is cut, fit it into the appropriate window and hold it in place at the back with brown paper tape. Continue working systematically through the design, cutting out windows and then replacing the cut-outs with new pieces of veneer.

Working the total design

As you work slowly through the design cutting motif windows out of the waste ground and then filling in the holes with new veneer, the initial pencil guide-lines will gradually break down and disappear. When this happens, re-align the tracing with the marquetry so that the motifs fit, and re-establish the drawn lines by pencil pressing the design through.

At this stage have a look at the working drawing and the master design, and see how the smaller features – the tree trunks and the foliage – cut across several veneer types. When the paper tape at the back of the design becomes bulky and gets in the way, dampen it slightly, remove the build-up with a craft knife and re-tape. Gradually the picture will fill out and take shape, and the original sky and sea veneer will in some parts be replaced by smaller, more complex veneer forms.

From time to time throughout the project, sit back and distance yourself from the design. Consider the quality and tone of the various veneers and the overall placing of grain and figure. If at this stage you feel that a piece is badly placed and less than perfect or a colour is too crude, now is the time to cut it out and try another.

Finally, when you have cut and fitted all the windows, made good all the faults and checked with the master design that all is correct, put the marquetry to one side and clear the working area of all clutter.

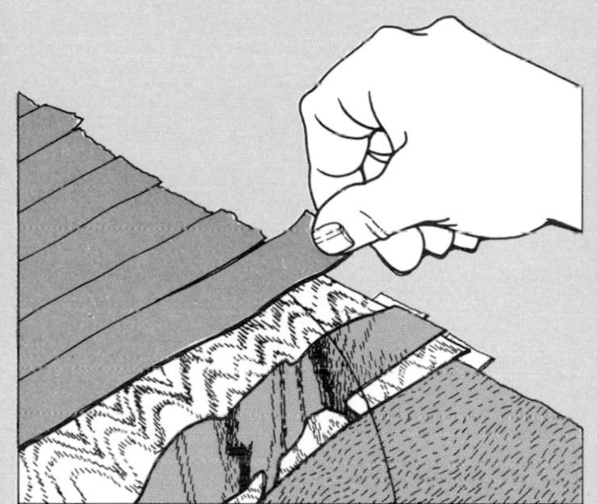

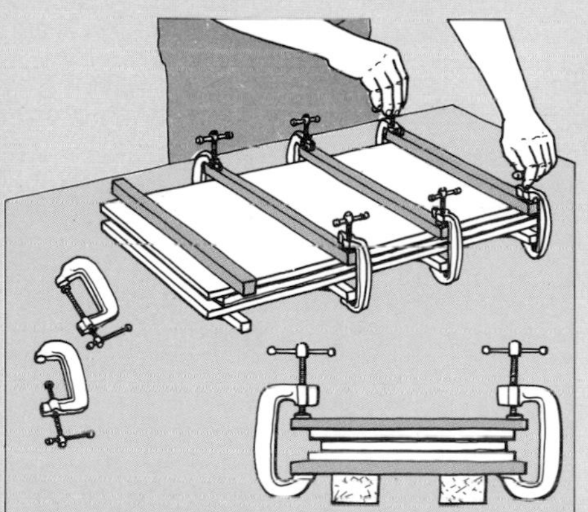

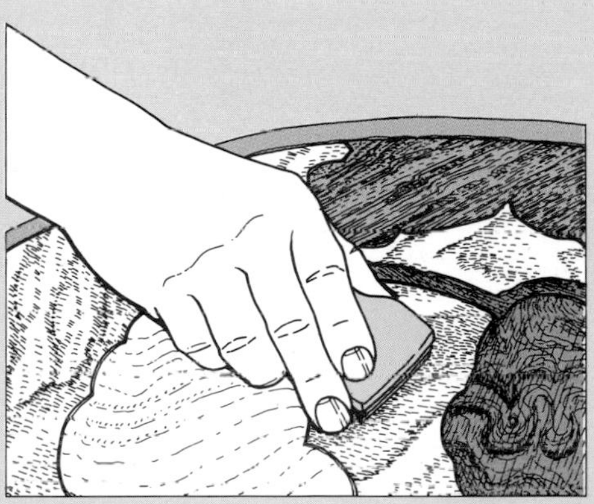

Laying the marquetry and preparing the base board

When you consider the design finished, place it, face up, on the work surface and cover the front of the picture with strips of brown paper tape. Having done this, wait a short while for the tape to dry off and then flip the design over so that it is face down.

Very carefully dampen down the scraps of gummed tape at the back of the picture so that you can ease them off with the craft knife. Do not soak the whole area, but start at one corner and work a small area at a time. When all the tape has been removed, place the picture under weighted boards and leave it to dry.

While the marquetry is drying out, consider the base board on which it is to be mounted. If the design is not being fixed onto an existing piece of furniture but is to be mounted like a picture then it is most important that the base board material is well chosen. Avoid using thin, poor grade, sheet wood such as hardboard, thin plywood or chipboard. It is much better to use a good quality, heavy duty laminated material such as ¾in plywood or blockboard.

Finally, note that the base board must be structurally balanced – that is, if the marquetry is to be glued on one side then it must be compensated by having a sheet of cheap grade veneer glued to the other side. Failure to use a compensatory veneer could result in the base board's being thrown off true and the marquetry lifting.

Gluing and pressing

Clear the workbench and set out your tools and materials (the clamps, clamping boards, the newspaper and glue) so that they are close to hand. Start by having a 'dry run' – that is, place all the parts to be glued, and the equipment involved in the gluing, in sandwich-like order on the bench.

First, set a clamping board down on the work surface and put on top of this the newspaper, the compensating veneer, the base board, the marquetry picture, a few more sheets of newspaper and, finally, the other clamping board. Check that you have enough clamps and make sure the PVA glue is fresh, smooth, lump-free and at the correct temperature. Having done this, start the gluing and placing. Glue the compensating veneer and position the base board on top of it. Glue the topside of the base board and then, with the greatest of care, place and position the marquetry picture. Now cover the marquetry with newspaper, position the other clamp board, have a final check that the marquetry has not moved, and clamp-up the boards with battens and G-clamps.

After about 24 hours, remove the clamps and boards, and peel away the newspaper. If all is well the marquetry should feel smooth and free from buckles and blisters. However, if part of the marquetry feels blistered, ease that portion up with the point of the craft knife, introduce a little more glue into the cavity and then re-clamp.

Finishing

When the PVA glue is dry (this may take three or four days) dampen down the marquetry and remove all traces of brown paper tape. Take a brush and a little grain sealer and give the marquetry a light coat. When the sealer is dry, run your fingers over the design and feel the various steps and thicknesses of the veneer.

Take the cabinet scraper and remove thin shavings until the whole marquetry feels at the same level. Make sure that the scraper does not dig into the wood and try, all the while, to manoeuvre the tool so that you cut at an angle to the line of the veneer grain.

Once the various woods are all at the same level, take the cork sanding block and the pack of graded glass/garnet papers, and work the marquetry surface until it is completely smooth to the touch. Sand the wood with a regular, side to side action until all the steps and joins have been flattened out.

Work through the graded papers from rough to smooth until the surface of the wood takes on a burnished, dull sheen. When you consider the marquetry finished, remove all the bench clutter and wood dust, and wipe the veneer down with a soft, fluff-free cloth and methylated spirits. Finally, give the whole marquetry several coats of plain wax polish and burnish it to a fine finish.

Making a Marquetry Design in the Boulle Tradition

Boulle, boule or buhl describes a type of marquetry that was very popular in France in the seventeenth and eighteenth centuries. The technique was named after the French cabinetmaker Charles André Boulle (1642–1732) who produced his best-known and most characteristic work when he was employed by Louis XIV to work at Versailles. The main feature of the boulle technique is the layering of sheets of wood, brass, silver, tortoiseshell and other materials, and then cutting a design through all the layers and changing the pieces around. This method of marquetry is very economical in its use of materials but, at the same time, it calls for a considerable amount of preconceived design work.

A careful study of the piece of Boulle's work shown in the photograph reveals that the large central motif – that is, the floriated brown tendrils on the white/silver ground – is made up of eight identical repeat cuttings. If Boulle used 16 alternating brown and white sheets of veneer to create the design, then, in fact, he would also have been able to produce another identical motif that had white floriated tendrils on a brown ground. It is this economical use of materials together with the repeat or mirror-image design that sets boulle work apart from most other marquetry techniques.

Adjust the scale to suit the size of the project that you have in mind. See how the contrasting veneers are interchanged and 'mirror-imaged', and note also how it is possible to build two negative/positive identical designs.

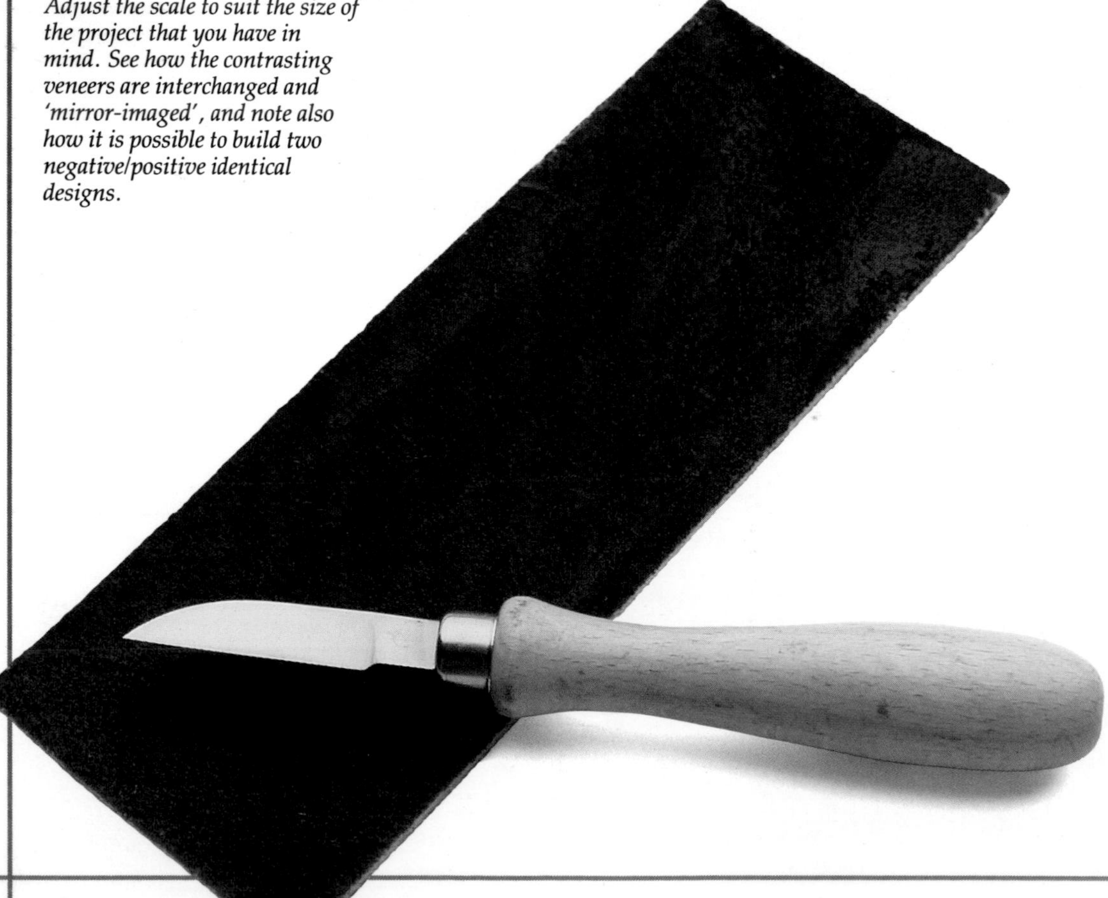

TOOLS & EQUIPMENT

- ◆ Workbench
- ◆ Selection of pencils
- ◆ Drawing board
- ◆ Fine-point pen
- ◆ Light hammer
- ◆ A pair of wire clippers
- ◆ Vice or fret-saw cutting table
- ◆ A fret saw with a pack of 4/0 and 6/0 jewellers' piercing blades
- ◆ Hand drill
- ◆ Fine-point craft knife
- ◆ 2 clamping boards
- ◆ Battens
- ◆ G-clamps
- ◆ Metal rule
- ◆ Cabinet scraper
- ◆ Cork sanding block
- ◆ Glass/garnet papers
- ◆ Cotton cloth

MATERIALS

- ◆ 16 contrasting wood veneers (or a wood veneer and a thin inlay brass) of size to suit
- ◆ 4 'waste' veneers
- ◆ White cartridge paper
- ◆ Black waterproof ink
- ◆ Sheets of fine, long-fibred mulberry paper
- ◆ A sheet of compensating veneer
- ◆ Masking tape
- ◆ Water-based starch/flour paste
- ◆ Vegetable oil
- ◆ Veneer pins
- ◆ Tracing paper
- ◆ Brown paper tape
- ◆ White PVA glue
- ◆ Base board
- ◆ Newspaper
- ◆ Grain sealer
- ◆ Methylated spirits
- ◆ Wax polish

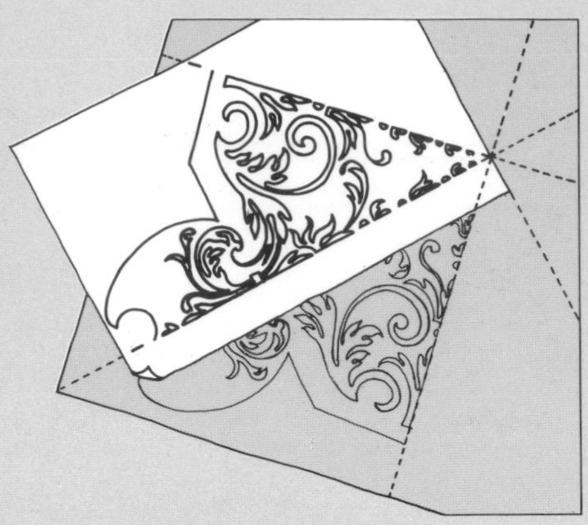

Considering the boulle technique and tracing the master design

Study the photograph (see page 60) and see how in this particular piece of boulle work the design has been quartered and mirror-imaged. Note, for example, how the central motif has been built up from eight identical repeats.

Now take a pencil and some paper and analyze the design and working implications. Look at the working drawing and the step-by-step illustrations and note how the project concentrates on a small part of the total design – the central motif. At this stage it might be useful to follow through the design analysis and technique appreciation by visiting a museum and searching out examples of other boulle works.

When you feel that you have a good understanding of the boulle technique in general, and this project in particular, go back to the drawing board and work out your own design modifications. With black ink, a fine-point pen and white cartridge paper, draw up two full-size design grids and consider how the positive/negative interchange of the various motifs can be achieved. When you have done this, take the long-fibred mulberry paper and make careful ink tracings of the master designs. Note the motif areas and clearly label them so that they correspond to labels on the master design.

Setting up the veneers for the multiple cut

Bearing in mind that this piece of boulle work was conceived as a counter-match (it has a reverse colour twin), and taking into account that within the motif there are eight identical repeats, it is necessary to use 16 veneer thicknesses. However, as the project is to be worked with a fret saw, the design must be broken down into two identical eight-sheet cuttings.

Begin by taking the contrasting veneers and arranging them in two stacks of eight alternating colours. Add 'waste' veneers to each side of the stacks and strap the whole blocks with masking tape so that all the sheets are well contained and stable. Having done this, give the mulberry paper and the waterproof-ink tracings, a generous brushing with the water-based starch/flour paste. Wait a few minutes for the paper to stretch and then place, arrange and smooth the tracings onto the topmost veneer of the strapped-up sandwiches.

Wait until the paste is completely dry and then rub the pasted-on design with the few drops of light vegetable oil until the paper becomes transparent and the ink lines can be seen clearly. Take the light hammer and the fine veneer pins and, with the greatest of care, nail the layered slabs through the waste margin around the edge. Finally, take a pair of clippers and nip off the pins so that they are flush with the veneer.

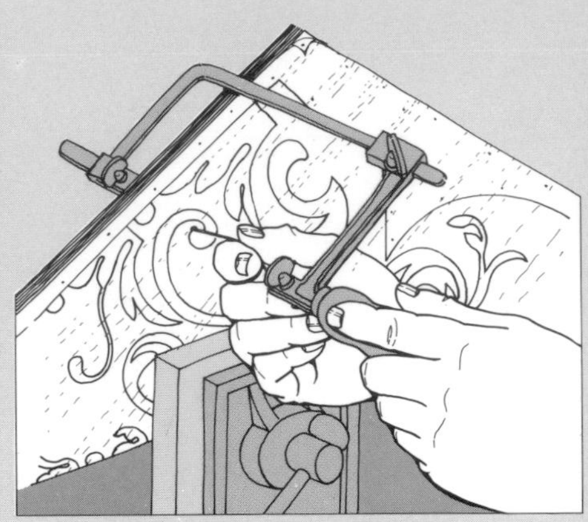

Multiple sawing

Clear the workbench of all clutter, pin the reference drawing and the master designs up around the working area, and set out all the tools and materials so that they are close to hand. Having done this, place the first of the multiple-layered slabs in the jaws of a vice or on a fret-saw cutting table.

Before you start cutting, have a look at the fret saw and notice how the saw blade is fixed and tensioned. See how the blade can be removed and refitted, and note that the teeth of the blade point towards the handle so that the cut is achieved on the pulling stroke of the saw.

Begin by drilling a small pilot hole on one of the lines to be cut. Pass the blade of the saw through the slab and tension it in the frame. Work the saw with a steady action, cutting along the drawn guide-lines, and keep the saw blade at 90° to the working face of the wood.

Continue sawing, slowly manoeuvring the veneer stack so that the saw blade is always presented with the line of the next cut. When you come to a tight corner, keep the blade moving and the veneer turning but try not to force the pace or twist the blade as it may break. As each little motif is cut out, place it in a cardboard box and move on to the next area to be cut. Finally, when both eight-sheet stacks have been worked, cut the waste margins off.

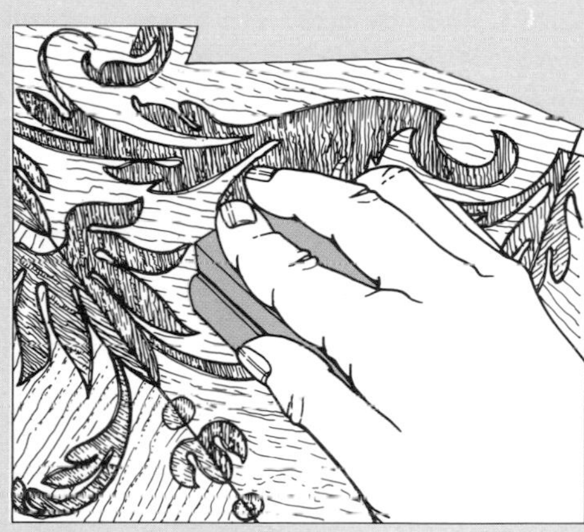

Setting the veneers

Take the craft knife and ease the various veneer cut-outs apart. Group them according to type, shape and colour. Now study the working drawing and see how all the pieces fit together to make up the two mirror-image motifs – that is, two complete designs; one positive and the other negative. Having done this, take two tracings of the master design and fix them to the drawing board with masking tape.

Start assembling the whole jigsaw puzzle design by setting out the main blocks of ground veneer. As each piece is found and identified, place it on one or other of the tracings and butt-joint it to its neighbouring piece with the brown paper tape. Continue working until you have found all 16 pieces of veneer, and the ground for both designs has been established and fixed. Now, select one of the design windows and fill it with a piece of reversed-out veneer of a different colour.

Work through all the windows of the ground in turn; reversing, changing, fitting and taping the veneer infill until the whole puzzle is complete. Note: each piece of marquetry infill has eight possible placings so try each in turn and settle for the best fit. When the two designs have been completed trim them to size and adjust the paper tape so that the surface is free from build-up. Put them under weighted boards and leave them to one side to dry out.

Laying, gluing and pressing

Clear the working area and set the two boulle designs out on the workbench. Collect together the glue, the base board, the clamp boards, the battens, the G-clamps, some newspaper and a pencil and a measure. Begin by measuring up and placing the two designs so that they are square with the base board.

First, set out one clamping board, and stack on top of it a few sheets of newspaper and the sheet of compensating veneer. Check that you have enough clamps. Spread an even, lump-free layer of PVA glue on the compensating veneer and the base board; then bring them both together and place them (veneer-side down) on the newspaper and clamping board.

Generously glue the top of the base board and carefully lower the boulle design into position on top of it. When you are sure that the placing is correct and as described, gently cover the design with more newspaper and the other clamping board. Using the G-clamps, clamp all the layers up. Do not over tighten the clamps as there is a risk of twisting the veneers off true; just screw up the clamps until the surplus glue oozes out between the various layers.

Finally, after about 24 hours or when the glue is dry, carefully remove the clamps and boards and view the work. Note: if you do not have clamps, you can modify this stage by using a suitable impact adhesive.

Finishing

When the glue is dry, dampen the brown paper tape and clean off the face of the work. Once the veneer is both clean and dry, give it a light coat of sealer. When the sealer is dry, take the cabinet scraper and work the face of the marquetry until all the variations and steps have been removed. Work with a firm but delicate touch, making sure that the corners of the tool do not drag, and being careful to remove only the finest wisps of wood.

Now take the cork sanding block and the graded glass/garnet papers and rub down the working face with a regular, smooth action. Do not scrub around but settle for either a vertical or horizontal texture, and then work the sanding block rhythmically backwards and forwards. Continue until the wood feels completely smooth and looks slightly burnished. Note: it is critical throughout the sanding stage to stop from time to time and inspect the working face. Check that the thinner veneers have not been worn through.

When you consider the rubbing down complete, wipe the marquetry with methylated spirits so as to bring out the colours and texture, and check the work over for possible faults and blemishes.

Leave the work for a day or two and, when you go back to it, hold it up to the light to make sure that the veneers have not lifted or buckled. If all is correct, give the wood a generous polish with a plain wax and a smooth cotton cloth. Finally, burnish the whole work to a good finish.

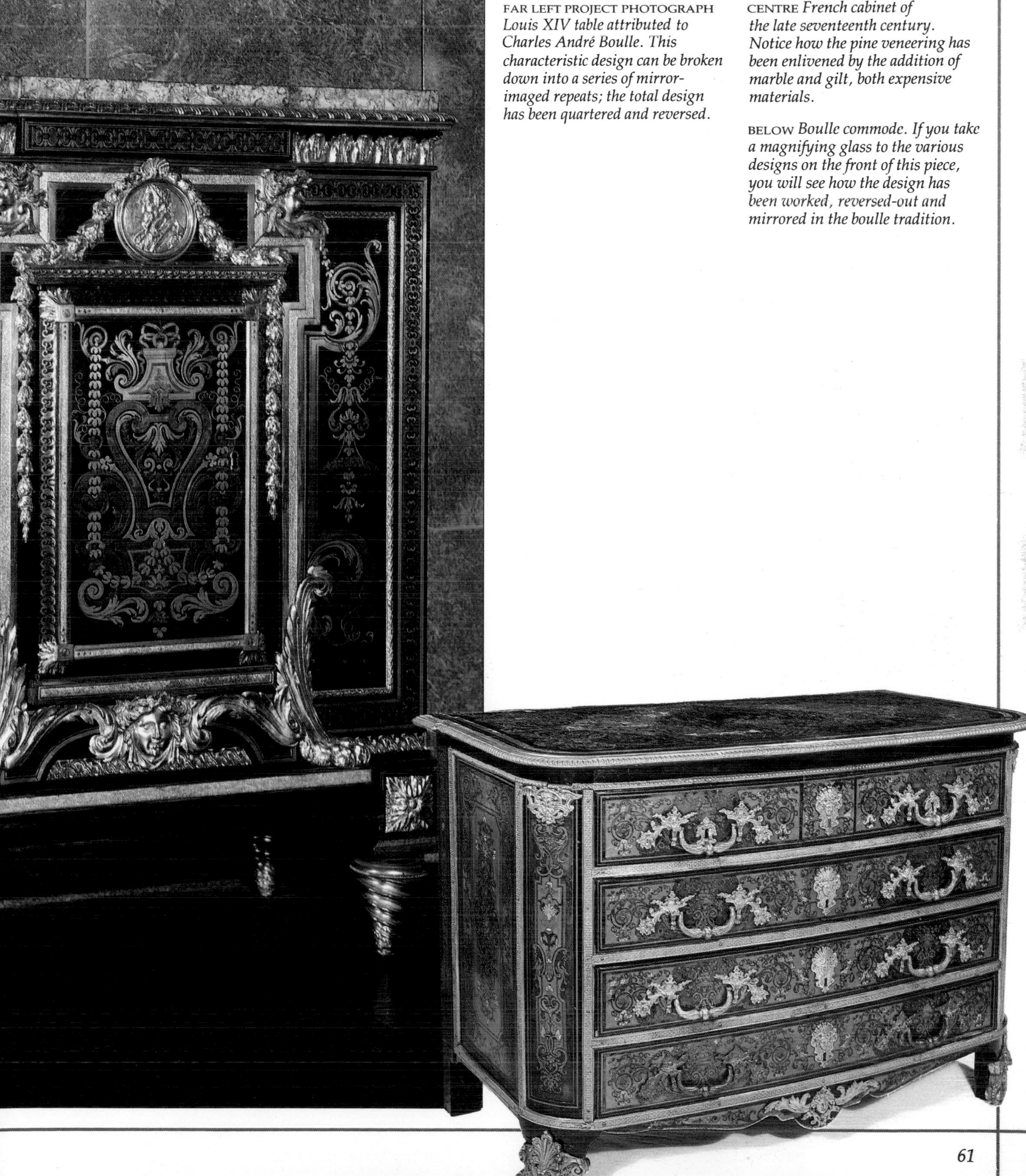

FAR LEFT PROJECT PHOTOGRAPH *Louis XIV table attributed to Charles André Boulle. This characteristic design can be broken down into a series of mirror-imaged repeats; the total design has been quartered and reversed.*

CENTRE *French cabinet of the late seventeenth century. Notice how the pine veneering has been enlivened by the addition of marble and gilt, both expensive materials.*

BELOW *Boulle commode. If you take a magnifying glass to the various designs on the front of this piece, you will see how the design has been worked, reversed-out and mirrored in the boulle tradition.*

MAKING A PARQUETRY GAMES BOARD

PARQUETRY is the name given to a type of marquetry that is made up out of cut and arranged formal geometrical shapes – squares, triangles, diamonds, tessellated lozenges, etc. Technically, parquetry differs from marquetry only in that the designs and motifs relate to interlocking forms rather than, for example, floriated patterns and pictorial scenes. Parquetry techniques have in the past been used to decorate all manner of furniture, although in the early part of the twentieth century the craft was largely forgotten.

However, parquetry is not dead and buried and the technique is now seeing a revival in America where it is being used to good effect to decorate modern furniture and high-tech interiors. Basically, the technique involves the use of straight-grained veneers cut with knives, a special cutting jig and an understanding of basic geometry. With great precision, veneers are cut into strips; the strips are rearranged, taped together and cut into squares, the squares are rearranged, taped together and cut into triangles, the triangles are then in turn rearranged, taped and cut, and so on *ad infinitum*. By cutting, reversing and alternating colour sequences, it is possible to achieve any number of characteristic parquetry designs and motifs.

TOOLS & EQUIPMENT

- ◆ Cutting board with a batten jig
- ◆ 1½in wide metal rule
- ◆ Surgical scalpel
- ◆ Set-square
- ◆ Oilstone
- ◆ Selection of pencils
- ◆ Broken hack-saw blade
- ◆ Selection of cloths
- ◆ Soft brush
- ◆ 2 clamping boards
- ◆ G-clamps
- ◆ Cabinet scraper
- ◆ A pack of graded garnet/glass papers
- ◆ Cork sanding block

MATERIALS

- ◆ 2 sheets of contrasting veneers measuring 12½ × 6in
- ◆ ¾in thick sheet of multi-ply for the base board
- ◆ Brown paper tape
- ◆ Masking tape
- ◆ A sheet of compensating veneer
- ◆ White PVA glue
- ◆ Newspaper
- ◆ Grain sealer
- ◆ Methylated spirits
- ◆ Wax polish

The scale is four squares to 1in. Note that this drawing shows only a quarter of the total design. When you are choosing the veneers, select those that have a straight grain, and also, of course, those that are of the same thickness.

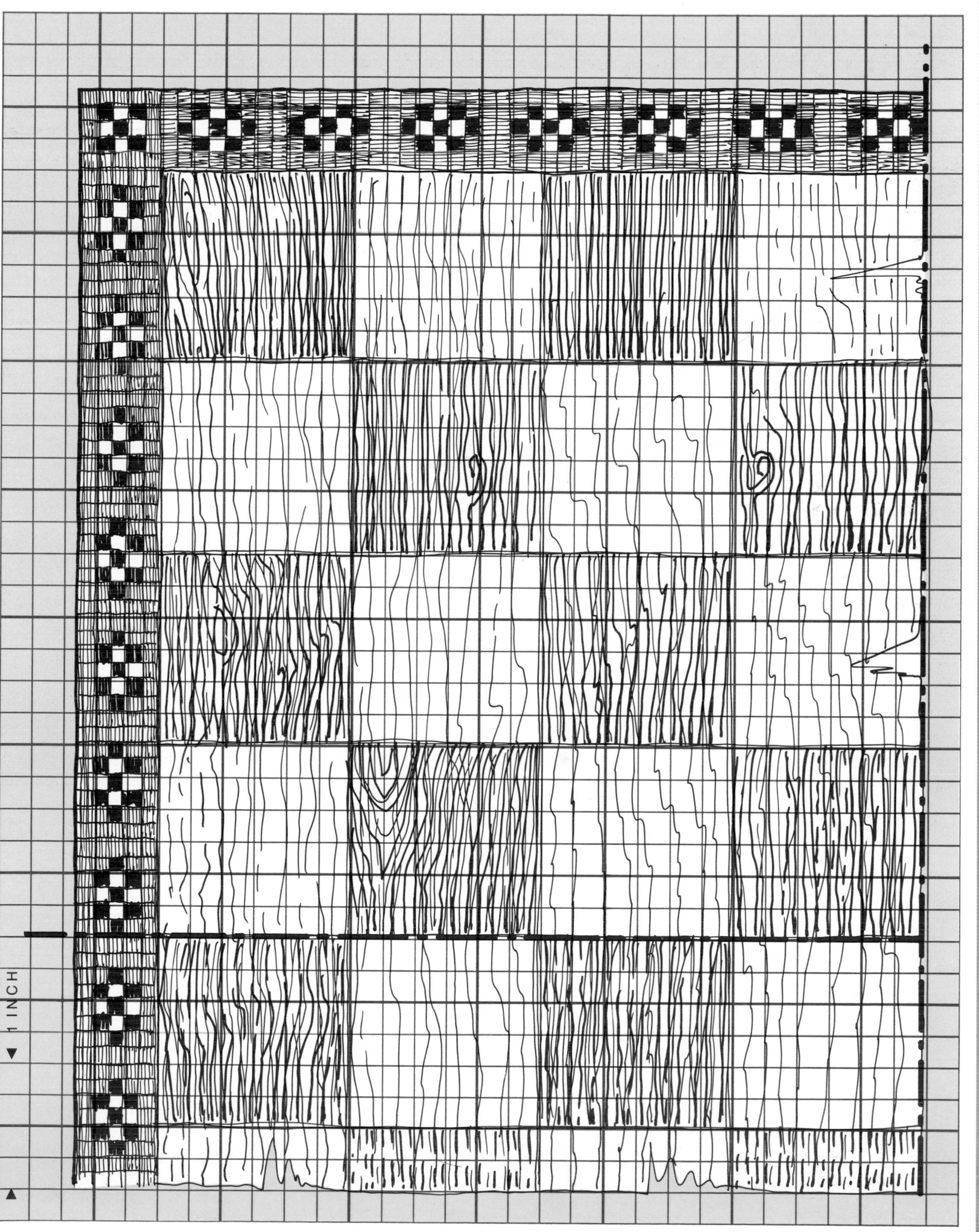
1 INCH

ABOVE LEFT *Writing desk made by a student at the London College of Furniture. Worked in ash and inspired by the Arts and Crafts movement, this writing desk includes a games board which is concealed under the central top section.*

LEFT *and* BELOW LEFT *Two marquetry projects made by Peter Niczewski. In his skillful use of natural and stained veneers, this craftsman has got away from the more traditional use of marquetry.*

ABOVE PROJECT PHOTOGRAPH
Parquetry games board with Tunbridge ware details and features dating from about 1830. The parquetry centre has been skillfully worked: note the perfection of the butt-jointing and the run of the grain – two very attractive features.

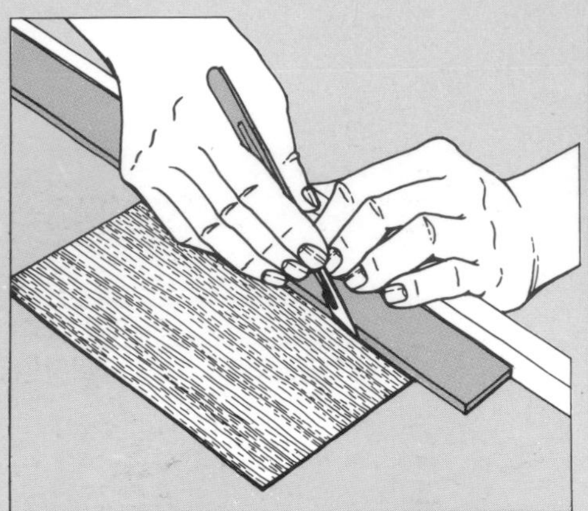

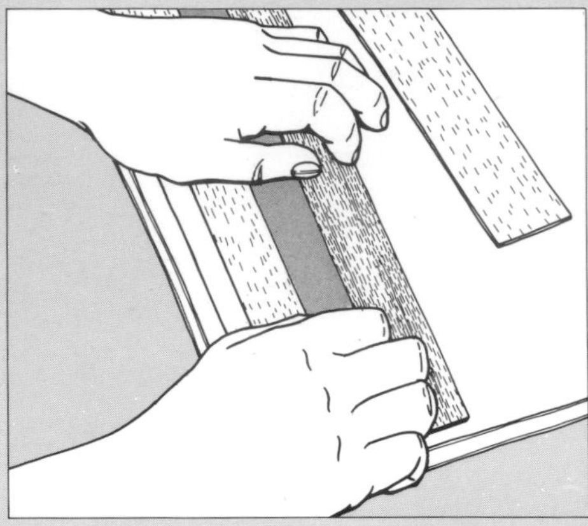

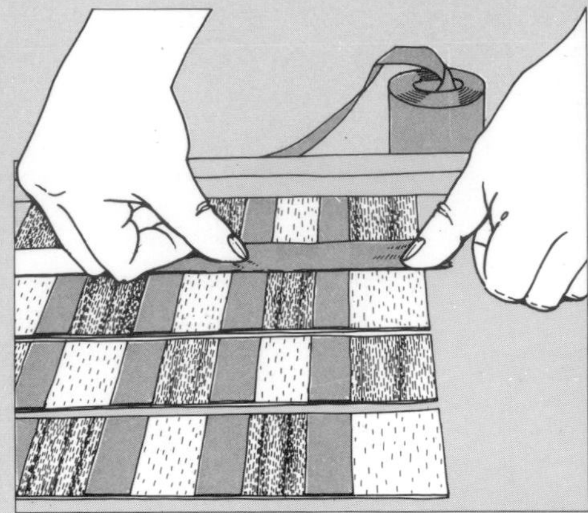

Considering the veneers and the initial cuts

Have a look at the photograph (see page 65) and the working drawing and see how this project concentrates on the simple, central checkered element of the games board. Note: the decorative border techniques are covered in Tunbridge Ware (see pages 74–79) and Marquetry (see pages 50–55).

Begin by looking through a veneer supplier's catalogue and spend some time considering the various options. Ideally, you need veneers that are free from knots, straight-grained and easy to work. Of course, the two chosen veneers must set each other off to give a light and dark contrast.

Bearing in mind that you only require two relatively small sheets of veneer, you can choose light-coloured woods such as sycamore, birch, obeche, or alternatively a delicate pink rosa peroba or a brilliant red padauk. Off-white ash and greyish-brown mansnia are also suitable. In fact, there are literally hundreds of veneer types to choose from.

When you have made your selection, take the batten-edged cutting board and the metal rule, and trim both sheets along one grain edge with the scalpel. Take the veneers, one sheet at a time and butt the true edge against the batten jig. Hold it in place with the metal rule which must also be butted against the stop and then cut the veneer along the edge of the rule. Continue cutting until there are eight strips measuring 12½ × 1½in.

Taping and cross-cutting

Begin by arranging the 1½in wide strips of veneer so that the colours contrast and the long-grain edges are butt-jointed. Now take the gummed paper tape and, making sure that the edge-to-edge fit of the strips is as near perfect as possible, build a composite sheet that measures 12½ × 12in and stick the sheets carefully together on the underside.

When the tape is dry, take the set-square and the scalpel, and trim one end of the sheet across the grain, ideally at 90° to the grain edge. When you have checked that the sheet is square by measuring the angles, butt it against the jig, hold it in place with the metal rule and cut strips across the grain. Keep the scalpel blade sharp, and work the veneer with a series of carefully considered and controlled cuts.

As you are working – that is, holding the veneer and the rule against the jig with one hand and guiding the knife with the other – make sure the knife is held at 90° to the working face of the wood. When you feel the knife blade drag or notice that the cut lines look a little crushed, stop work and bring the blade to a keen edge on the oilstone. Note: with edge-to-edge precision marquetry of this character, it is most important that each and every cut is crisp and clean – the scalpel blade will need to be stroked on the oilstone after every dozen or so cuts.

Reversing and taping

Clear the work surface of all clutter and wipe it down with a clean cloth. Set out the colour-alternating veneers and see that there are eight strips, each with four dark and four light squares. There should be 64 1½ × 1½in squares in total. When all is correct, arrange the strips so as to achieve the characteristic draughts board or checker board design.

Still working on the jig-board, butt the first cut strip against the batten stop and fix it to the board with a strip of gummed paper tape. When the first strip is in place, take the next strip and then butt it against the first strip, making sure that the colour sequence is reversed. Check that all the veneer squares are perfectly aligned and fix the two strips edge-to-edge with the gummed tape. Run the set-square over the two strips making sure they are well placed and then secure the second strip to the workboard.

Work the whole design until all eight strips are aligned, butt-jointed to neighbouring strips and fixed with gummed paper tape. When the gummed tape is dry, take the scalpel and cut the checker sheet clear of the workboard. Flip the sheet over and hold it up to the light to see possible joint faults. Finally, put it to one side to dry out.

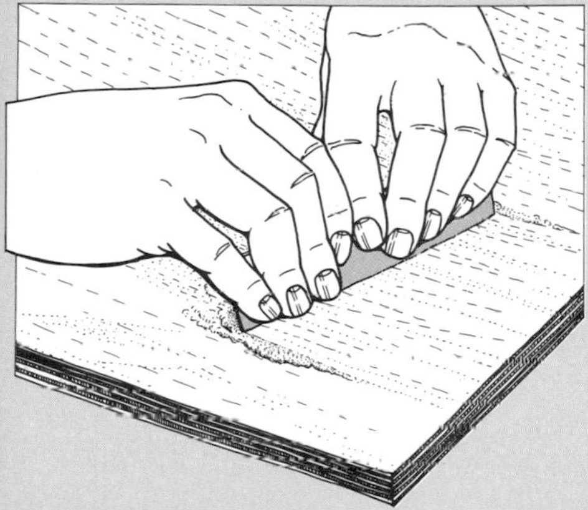

Preparing the base board

Take the ¾in thick sheet of plywood and make sure that it is free from warps, loose knots, fungal decay, insect bore holes and stains. Reject any wood that looks to be less than perfect. When you have checked on the condition and quality of the wood, take the pencil, metal rule and set-square, and set out the base board so that it relates to the overall design of the games board. Remember to allow enough room for border decoration, marquetry infill, Tunbridge patterns etc.

Now have a look at the compensating veneer and see that it is sound and has a good colour. Having done this, take a piece of broken hacksaw blade and go over the base board giving it a roughened, 'keyed' surface. Work the board from side-to-side and corner-to-corner until every surface is evenly scored and textured.

Take a damp cloth and a brush, and clean down the work board, the veneers to be glued and the whole working area. When all the wood dust has been removed, gather the elements to be glued and have a 'dry run' fitting to check that they all fit together. Before you start, see that the glue is fresh, smooth and at the correct temperature. Check that the clamping boards are free from blobs of hard glue, and generally go over all the equipment making sure that it is clean and ready to use.

Laying, gluing and pressing

Set the first clamping board down on the work surface and cover it with several sheets of clean newspaper. Now spread a thin, even layer of PVA glue on the compensating veneer and set it, glue side up, on the newspaper. Having done this, glue one side of the base board and place it, glue side down, square on the glued compensating veneer. Check that the veneer has not slipped out of true and then spread glue generously over the base board.

With care and caution, position the checkered veneer so that it is tape-side up. Now spread newspaper over the veneer and top the whole stack off with the other clamping board. When you have checked that every part of the sticky sandwich has been well set, gently slide the G-clamps into place and tighten them. After 24 hours or when the glue is dry, remove the clamps and inspect the work for faults.

It is well worth noting that even the smallest fragment of hard glue or the finest splinter of veneer waste can dent the face of the work. Always carry out checks before clamping up to make sure the various layers are free from dust and dirt. However, if the veneer is dented, fill the depression with water and press with a medium-warm iron: this treatment will expand the wood fibres and correct the fault.

Finishing

Once the work has been taken out of the clamps and generally looked over, clear away the clamps, boards and newspaper, and set out the cabinet scraper, the rubbing down papers, the cork sanding block, the sealer and the various cloths. Begin by dampening down and removing all the paper tape. When this has been done, take the scraper and work the face of the veneer with a firm, dragging action. Draw the blade across the wood, making sure that the corners of the tool do not dig in and lift the veneers.

Continue scraping until the whole surface of the games board feels level and unstepped. At this stage, clear away all the shavings, take a soft brush and give the veneer face a coat of sealer.

When the sealer is dry, you can begin the sanding. Use the garnet/glass paper and the sanding block, and rub down the face of the board until it feels completely smooth to the touch. Work through the range of graded papers, starting with, for example, a medium 4/0 and finishing with a superfine 9/0. When you are happy with the results, wipe the wood with methylated spirits and check for dents and scratches. When you consider the veneer sufficiently rubbed down, wipe it once again with methylated spirits and re-seal. Wait for the sealer to dry and then give the face a final cutting-back with a piece of 9/0 garnet paper. Finally, use a plain wax polish and a fine cotton cloth and bring the wood to a smooth, burnished finish.

Making a Nonesuch Inlay

NONESUCH is the name commonly given to a group of sixteenth-century inlay chests. These chests are characterized by having as their central design theme a fantastic architectural motif that supposedly represents Henry VIII's pleasure palace of Nonesuch. However, it is now thought that perhaps these chests are not English but were made in Germany. It follows that the name probably has its roots in the archaic meaning of the word nonesuch or nonsuch – a matchless thing, nonpareil, or nothing similar.

Nonesuch chests are uniquely beautiful examples of the inlay craft. Inlay is what the term suggests – it is the laying of one wood into another. Unlike marquetry, inlay is primarily a woodcarver's craft because it is necessary first of all to carve out and lower a ground pattern into which small pieces of coloured wood can be bedded. In early European inlay work the designs tend to be geometrical and, as with Nonesuch boxes, the patterns and motifs gain much of their effect by having curious perspective illusions. As the craft became popular in the seventeenth century and the craftsmen used more and more expensive and exotic imported woods from the East Indies and the Americas, the woods were cut thinner until gradually the inlay techniques were replaced by those of marquetry.

The scale is four squares to 1in. When you are working a project of this type, spend time at the design stage getting the proportions and layout just right. Keep the number of different inlay shapes to a minimum.

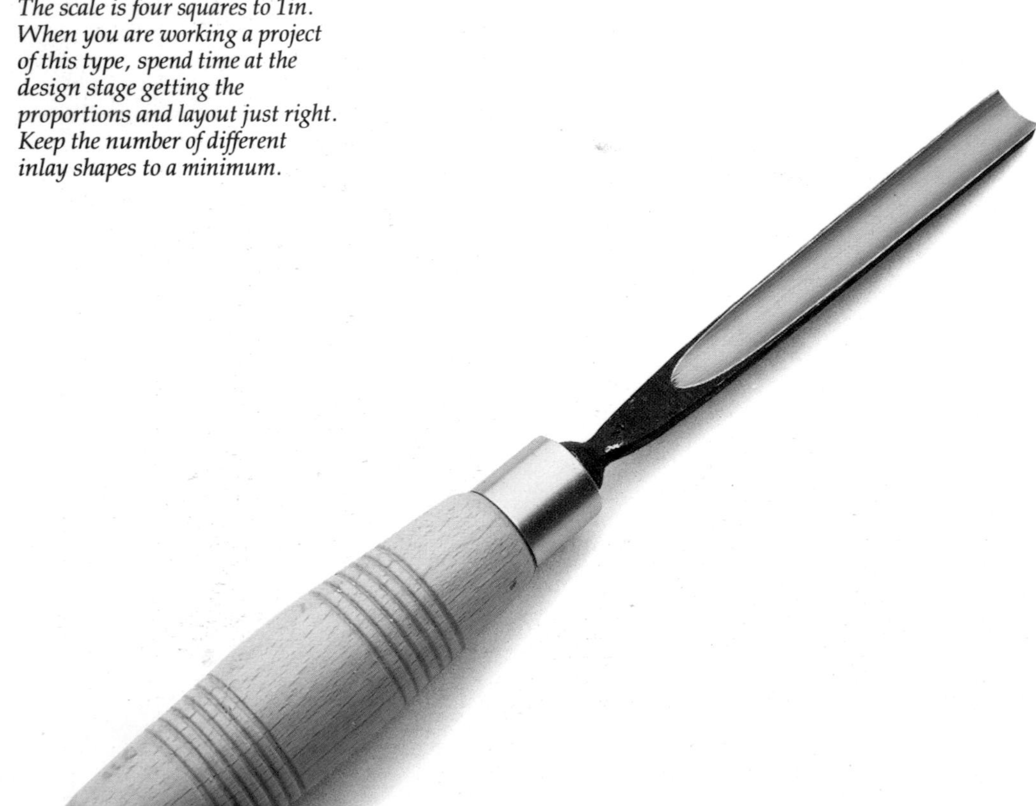

TOOLS & EQUIPMENT

- Workbench
- Metal rule
- Pencils
- Drawing board
- Scissors
- G-clamps
- V-section parting tool
- Deep gouges
- Macaroni chisel
- Dog-leg chisel
- Straight chisel
- Vice or cutting board
- Gent's or fine tenon saw
- Coping saw
- 2 clamping boards
- Plastic sheeting and carpet felt
- Battens
- Rasp
- Plane
- Sanding block
- Large cabinet scraper
- Graded glasspapers
- Cotton cloth

MATERIALS

- 1in thick slab of straight-grained knot-free wood (of size to suit)
- A selection of ¼in thick coloured inlay woods
- Workout paper
- Glazed tissue paper or fine long-fibred mulberry paper
- Waterproof ink
- Water-based flour/starch paste
- Vegetable oil
- PVA glue
- Newspaper
- Wax polish

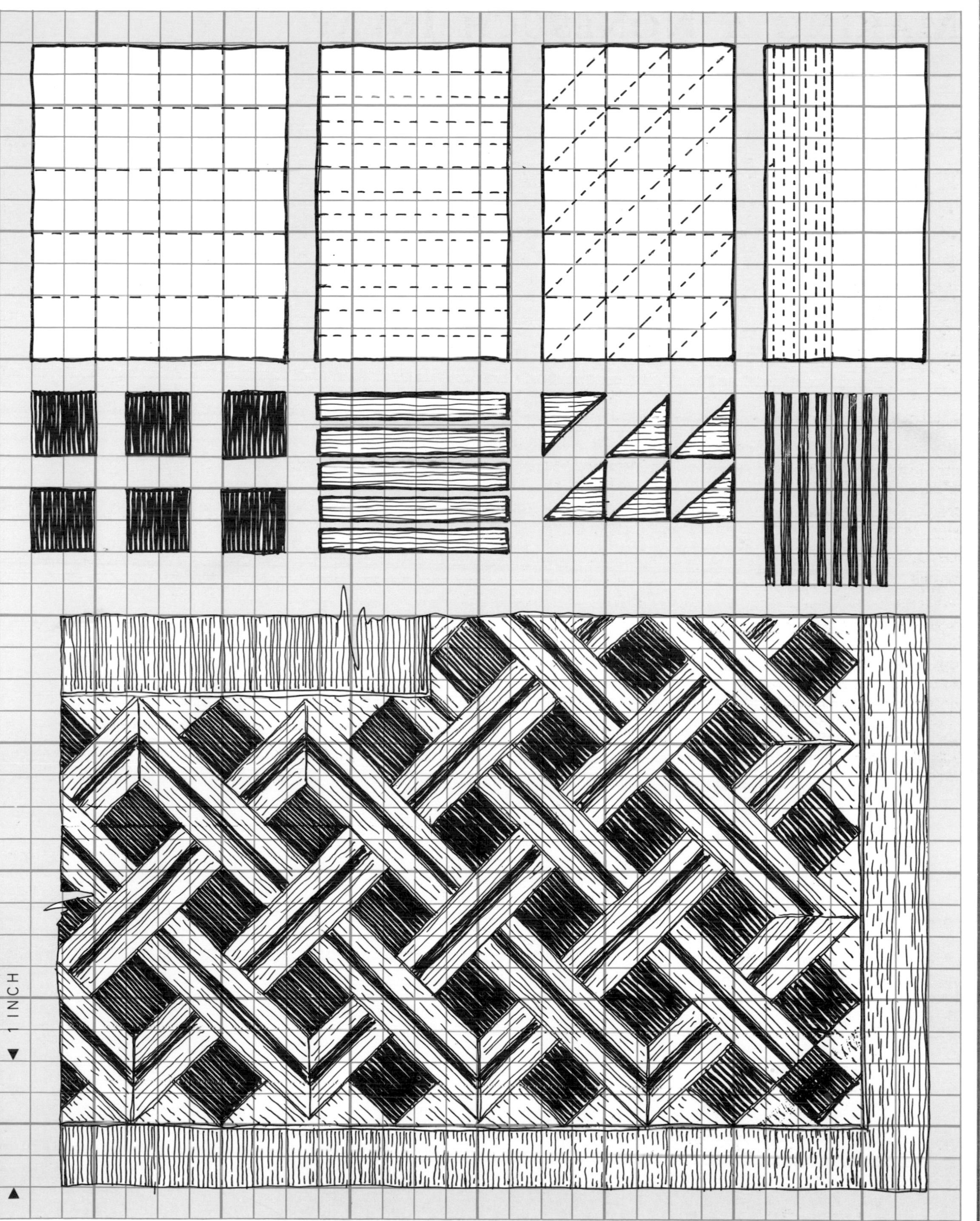
1 INCH

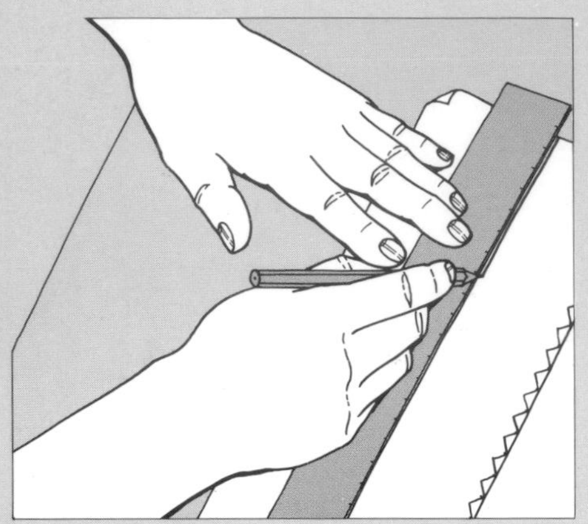

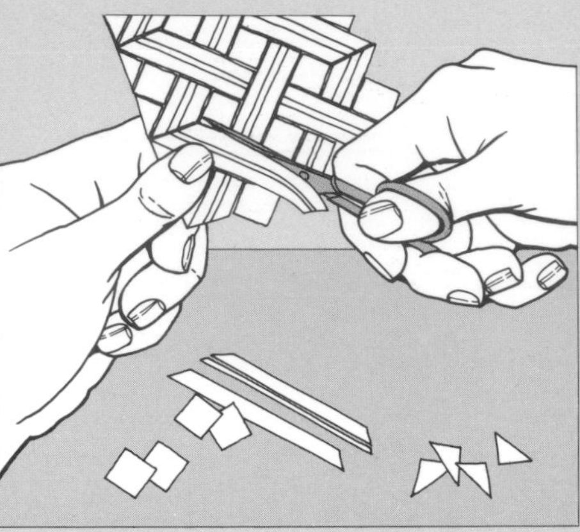

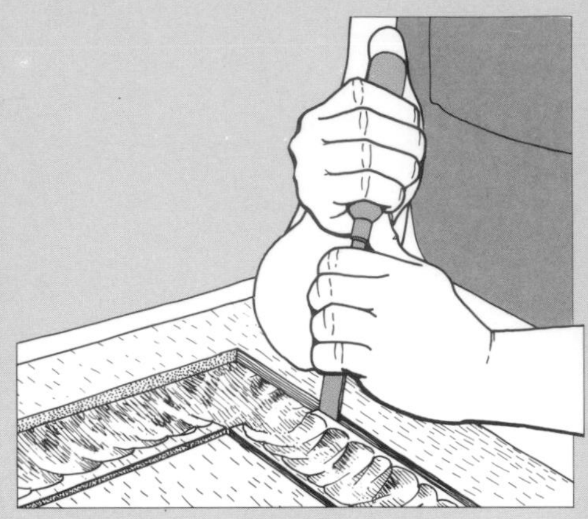

Considering the techniques and drawing up the design

Study the photographs and the working drawing, and note how the Nonesuch design is characteristically made up of small straight-cut pieces of inlay. See how the outer borders, the inner margins and even the central Nonesuch palace motifs are all, to a greater or lesser extent, worked from little geometrical repeats – squares, triangles, diamonds, lozenges, bars and crosses.

Take a magnifying glass to some small part of the design, for example one of the borders of alternating colours, and note how individual elements look loosely fitted although overall the work is of good quality. With a work of this size and character this flexibility is desirable if the unrestrained and enthusiastic ethnic feel of the design is to be achieved.

When you have a good understanding of the inlay technique and the Nonesuch design, take the rule, a pencil and workout paper, select some small part of the total inlay motif and draw it to size. After you have drawn out the various design and pattern details, make a fully worked-up master drawing and label the various inlay areas with wood names or reference numbers that relate to the inlay woods that you have selected.

Transferring the design

When the master design has been fully worked and is to size and labelled, take the sheets of wet-strength glazed tissue paper or the mulberry paper and make several waterproof ink tracings. Now take the slab of 1in thick ground wood, trim it to size and set it on the workbench. Note: the ground wood needs to be relatively easy to work – you can use a wood such as lime, a straight-grained pine or a dark wood such as mahogany.

Give one of the tracings a brushing with the water-based flour/starch paste. Allow the pasted paper time to expand and slacken, and smooth it over the working face of the ground wood. Put it to one side to dry out.

Now spread the various sheets of coloured inlay wood over the work surface and then refer back to the master design. Decide how the coloured woods are going to fit and, taking a pair of scissors, cut up the traced sheets accordingly. Group the little tissue cut-outs and match them up with the sheets of wood. When you have done this, double check that all is correct. Take note of the wood grain and colours, and then stick the cut-outs onto the working face of their allotted sheets of inlay wood.

Finally, when the paste is dry, take a few drops of vegetable oil and rub it into the paper until it becomes transparent and the lines of the design are clearly visible.

Lowering the ground

Place the slab of ground wood, face up, on the bench and secure it with a G-clamp. Now set out the various woodcarving tools – a V-section parting tool, a couple of deep gouges, a macaroni chisel, a dog-leg chisel and a straight chisel, and make sure that their cutting edges are keen.

Start by identifying the areas on the ground wood that need to be cut away and lowered. Having done this, take the V-section tool and, with care and caution, outline the drawn motifs. Working on the waste side of the ground and keeping about ⅛in away from the drawn lines, cut a V-section trench around the whole of the design.

As you work the tool along the drawn lines, you will be cutting both across and with the grain of the wood. Always hold the tool with both hands, one guiding and the other pushing and manoeuvring. Cut to a uniform depth of about ¼in, working the wood with short, shallow, controlled strokes. Always be ready to stop short and brake if the tool starts to dig too deeply or runs away into the grain.

When the design has been set in, take a medium-deep gouge and the macaroni chisel, and skim and chop out the unwanted ground wood. Cut a broad trench on the inside of the design outline and establish the level of the lowered ground. Once the depth has been set, lower the whole unwanted ground area and leave it so that the right-angle between the low ground and the raised design is free from burrs and rough edges.

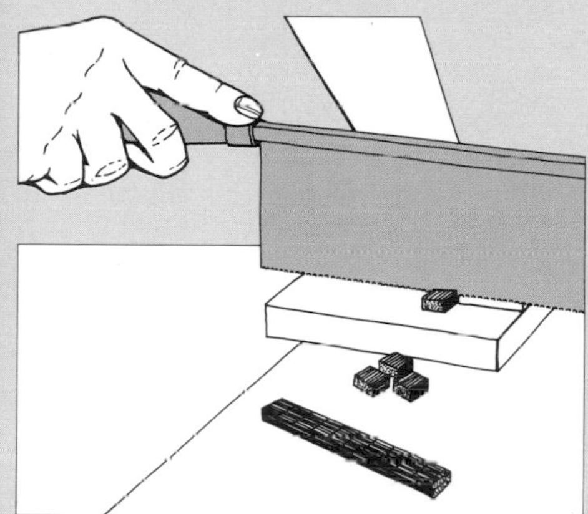

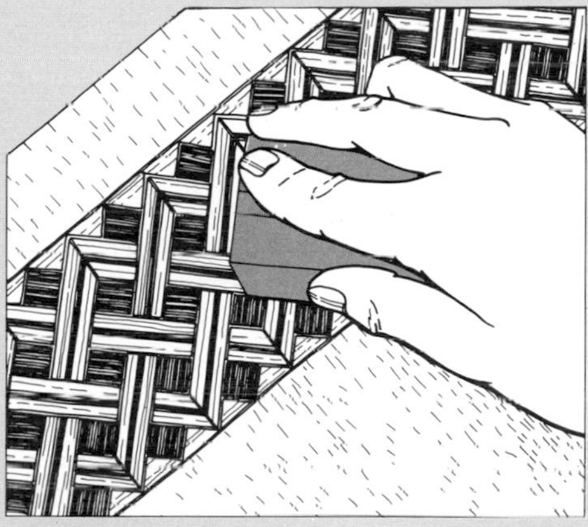

Cutting and fitting the inlay

Once selected areas of the ground wood have been set in, lowered and cleaned up, you can begin to work the individual pieces of inlay. Start by looking at the master design and matching up lowered ground areas with the various sheets of inlay wood.

When you have identified all the pieces of wood, put them in the vice or on a cutting board, one at a time, and set to work with a gent's or tenon saw and a coping saw. Follow the paper-pattern guidelines as closely as possible and, as each little shape is cut out, refer back to the master design and then place it in the lowered ground.

Continue sawing the ¼in thick sheet wood, adjusting the ground, placing inlay pieces and generally building up the design. As the work progresses and inlays are arranged and set, be flexible. The pattern should be followed but at the same time be prepared to 'fill in' and make good, as and when the need arises.

Gluing, placing and pressing

At this point, all the pieces of inlay should be a good close fit although, at the same time, they should be slightly proud of the ground or base wood. When this stage has been reached, remove the inlay very carefully and set it to one side on a tray.

Now take the PVA glue and flood the lowered ground areas of the base wood to a depth of about ⅛in. Having done this, take another look at the master design, the working drawing and the inspirational photographs in order to get the feel of the inlay. Then start to set the individual pieces of wood in the glue. Work systematically across the design until all the elements are in place.

Have a last minute check to make sure that the glue has flooded in and around all the individual pieces that go to make up the design.

When this has been done, you can start to build the clamping 'sandwich'. Place the first clamping board down on the bench and cover it with one of the plastic sheets.

Next, cover the plastic with a generous layer of newspaper and carefully arrange the slab of ground wood and inlay. Cover the inlay with more newspaper, put the other sheet of plastic over the newspaper and finally place the thick felt and the other clamping board. When all this has been done and is secure, put the battens in place and clamp the boards together.

Finally, wipe up any glue ooze and put the sandwich to one side to dry out. Note: do not over tighten the clamps as there is a risk of the ground wood splitting, and make sure that the clamping boards are well covered with plastic sheet.

Finishing

After about 48 hours or when the glue is dry and the puddled inlay pieces well set, ease off the clamps and remove the clamping boards. Then, with care, peel away the various layers of plastic, felt and newspaper, and reveal the face of the inlay.

Once this has been done, check that the glue is completely dry and the pieces of inlay fit securely. If all is well, clamp the base board to the workbench and set out the rasp, the plane, the sanding block, the cabinet scraper, the graded glasspapers and wax polish. First, take the flat rasp and swiftly cut-back the hard glue and newspaper. Next, working with great care, cut back the proud inlay so that it is flush with the main body of the base board.

Continue working with the rasp and plane until the whole inlay face is crisp and true. Having done this, take the cabinet scraper and drag it backwards and forwards across the inlay until the wood gleams and feels completely smooth to the touch.

Finally, work through the full range of glasspapers from coarse to fine, and then bring the whole project to a good finish with a soft cotton cloth and a plain wax polish.

RIGHT|*Elizabethan Nonesuch chest. Worked in oak and fruit woods, compare this chest to the project chest and notice how similar they are. The designs certainly come from the same pattern book and they may even have been worked by the same hand.*

RIGHT PROJECT PHOTOGRAPH
Elizabethan Nonesuch chest. This piece of furniture has all the characteristic Nonesuch features including fruit-wood inlays, arched panels and the rather curious Nonesuch Palace motif. This chest is slightly unusual in that the arched forms have actually been built out from the front of the chest.

LEFT *'Symbols' board made by a student at the London College of Furniture. Unusual and visually stimulating, this piece sets out to explore the use of plastics and inlay-inspired angular forms.*

MAKING A TUNBRIDGE WARE DESIGN

ALTHOUGH over the last two or three hundred years the term 'Tunbridge ware' has been used to describe all manner of treen and woodware decoration – everything from transfers to inlay – it has more recently come to mean a form of sliced veneer mosaic marquetry. The ware is characterized by having panels, pictures and bandings that seem to be worked with delicate, intricate and minute tessera inlay. However, the Tunbridge mosaic technique is neither true inlay nor is each piece unique and individually worked. In fact, Tunbridging is a method of mass-producing identical mosaic veneer designs.

The patterns are first of all worked out on grid paper, rather like embroidery sheets, so that the various elements of the design relate to little squares of colour. Coloured woods are then sliced and laminated, re-sliced, re-positioned and finally re-laminated, until they look like bundles of coloured spills. It is the sliced section through the bundles that relates to the original squared-up design. When the bundles are so worked and the glue is dry, they are placed in a guillotine or disc saw and cut into very thin veneer slices. Like slices cut through the trunk of a tree or through a Swiss roll, each and every slice carries a near identical design or motif. With traditional Tunbridge ware, the motifs and patterns are organized so that the slices can be interlocked and bedded in glue to form a complete design. This technique was used to decorate all manner of fancy ware including small pieces of furniture, ink stands, picture frames, snuff boxes and games boards.

TOOLS & EQUIPMENT

- Workbench
- Large G-clamps
- 5 clamping boards, 6 × 3in
- Plastic sheets
- A pack of graded glasspapers
- Marking gauge
- Small-toothed gent's saw
- Bench hook
- Rasp
- Cork sanding block
- Soft brush
- Cotton cloth

MATERIALS

- The item you want to decorate (Games Board, see pages 62–67)
- 20 veneer slips measuring 5 × 2 × ⅛in, 13 of medium brown mahogany, 4 of black oak and 3 of white holly (the grain must run across the width of the strips)
- PVA glue
- Newspaper
- Grain sealer
- Wax polish

There are two scales for this working drawing: the main drawing is eight squares to ½in, and the detail is one square to ⅛in. When you are choosing the veneers, make sure that the grain runs across the width of the strip.

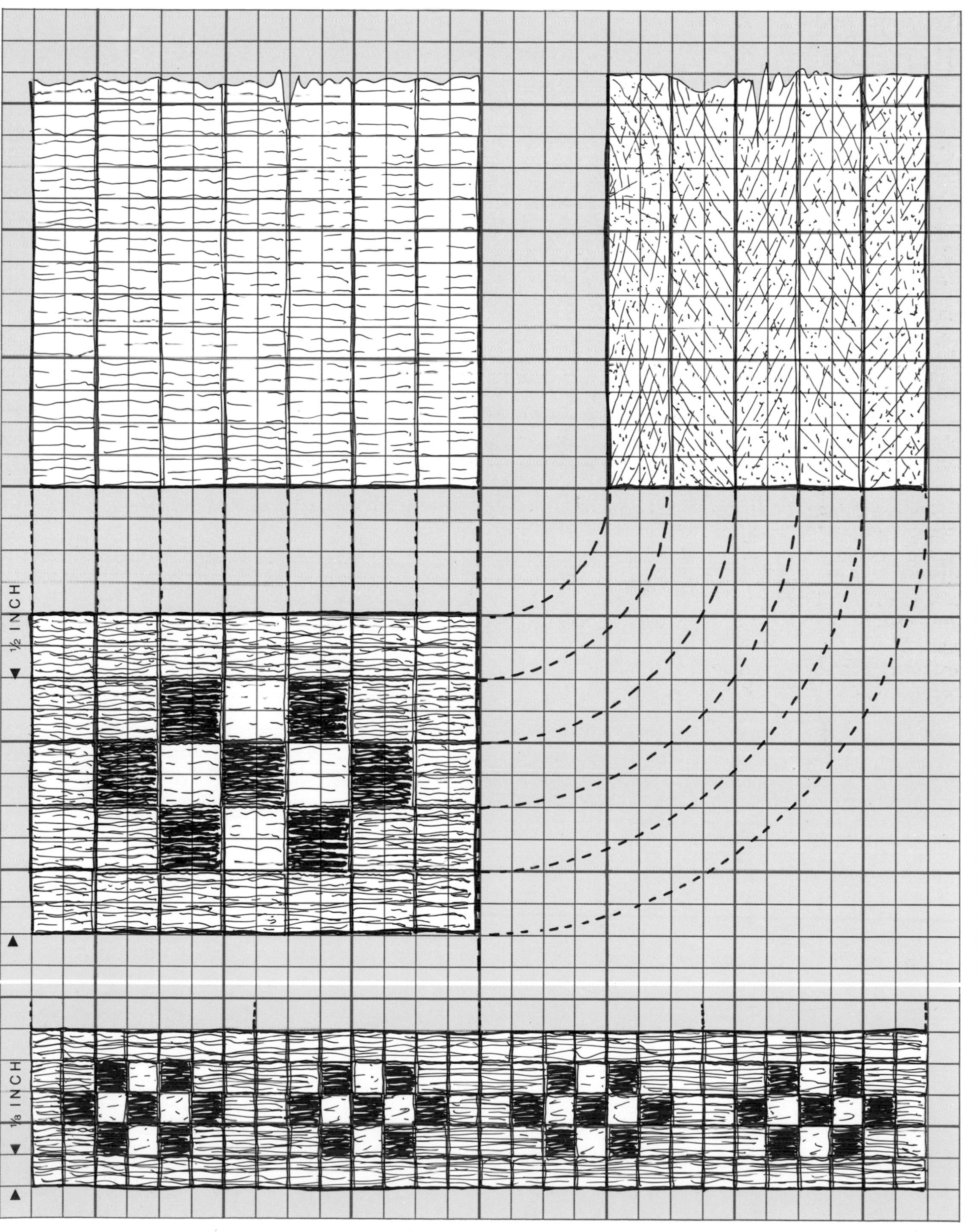
½ INCH
⅛ INCH

BELOW *Regency Marquetry and painted boxes. These boxes were probably made in the Tunbridge Wells area, and works of this nature inspired the nineteenth-century craftsmen of Tunbridge ware decoration.*

ABOVE PROJECT PHOTOGRAPH *Characteristic Tunbridge ware box with a mosaic central motif and border. In some instances the lid blocks of similar boxes were built up and laminated, and then sliced. In this way it was possible to mass-produce hundreds of identical lid motifs.*

RIGHT *A beautiful mirror frame made by a student at the London College of Furniture. Made up from plywood and veneers, the raised circle surrounding the mirror has been cooper-built and turned, and the veneers have been glued with hot resin. The delicate chevron banding was bought ready-made.*

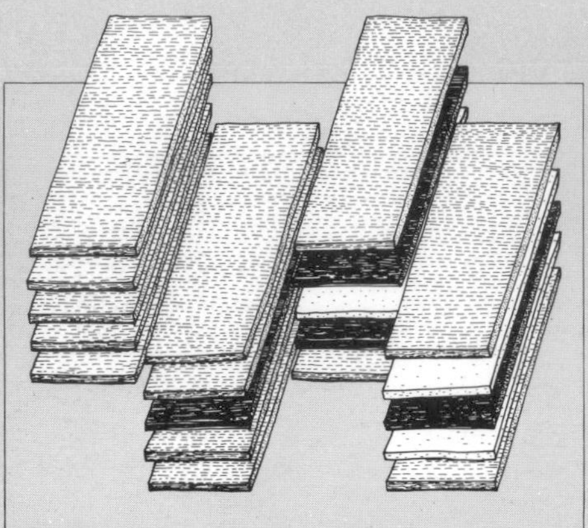

Considering the design and the technique

Have a look at the working drawing and take a magnifying glass to the photograph (see page 77) to see how the characteristic Tunbridge ware design has been worked and put together. Note how the large central motif has been made up from two identical reversed and turned mosaic slices.

Focus your attention on the border, count the squares and see how, in the main, the running design has been built up from two slightly different motif repeats. This project concentrates on the smaller of the two designs. Count the squares that make up the motif and note that three colours are used: a light-yellow buff, a medium brown and an inky black.

You may want to use types of wood other than those recommended. Any variety of wood is suitable as long as the chosen veneers are straight-grained and are of contrasting colours.

Check over the wood for quality and possible faults and choose the 20 suitable slips: 13 medium brown, four black and three white. Group the veneers in four stacks of five slips (as illustrated above). Arrange the stacks from left to right so that the first stack has five brown slips, the second stack has four brown and one black, the third stack has two brown, two black, and one white, and the fourth stack has two brown, two white and one black. The colour composition relates to the colour order of the vertical lines of squares within the motif (see the working drawing).

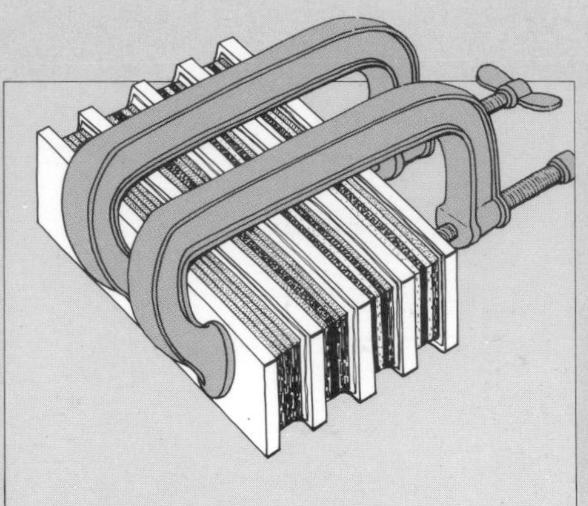

Stacking, gluing and clamping

Set out the PVA glue, the four stacks to be glued, the G-clamps, the five small clamping boards, the newspaper and a plastic sheet. Taking each stack at a time, spread glue on the veneers, stick them together, cover them with newspaper and plastic sheet, and then sandwich them between the clamping boards. Having done this, bring the four glued stacks and the five clamping boards together, and build one sandwich out of all the stacks, ready for clamping.

When you have double checked the colour order and composition of each stack, position the clamps and screw them up until the surplus glue is squeezed out. Wipe up the surplus glue with a damp cloth and then put the work to one side to dry out thoroughly.

After 24 hours or when the glue is dry, unscrew the clamps, carefully ease the stacks apart, and remove the plastic sheet, newspaper and clamping boards. Now clear the work surface of all clutter and arrange the four stacks side-by-side so that they relate to the colour order as shown in the working drawing. Number the stacks from left to right for reference.

Set a sheet of medium-grade glasspaper on a smooth surface face-up, and rub down all six faces of each laminated stack. Continue until they are smooth and free from hard glue, bits of newspaper and rough wood. Finally, if necessary, re-number the stacks and wipe them clean with a damp cloth.

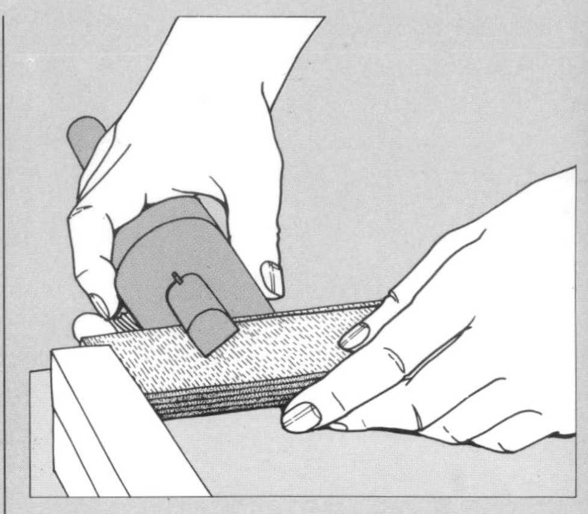

Initial sawing and assembling the pattern

First, set out all the tools: the marking gauge, the small-toothed saw and the bench hook, and have another look at the working drawing and inspirational illustrations. Take the marking gauge and fix it at ⅛in. Set out the first glued stack across the grain and along its length so that a slice is clearly marked.

With the greatest of care, support the laminated stack against the bench hook and then saw through the laminations so as to remove a single striped slice. When you have done this, take the marking gauge, set out the second slice and saw it off. Work through all the laminated veneer stacks until you have four sawn stacks of twelve or so ⅛in thick striped slices. Note: this sawing needs to be done with care and you may want to use a fine-blade power saw.

When all the slices have been longitudinally cut across the grain, select various colours and group them in stacks of seven slices so that the end-grain patterns match up with the motif (see the working drawing). When six stacks have been built, put the spare slices to one side. Finally, check the order of the wood colours and then glue and clamp them up using boards, G-clamps, plastic sheeting and newspaper.

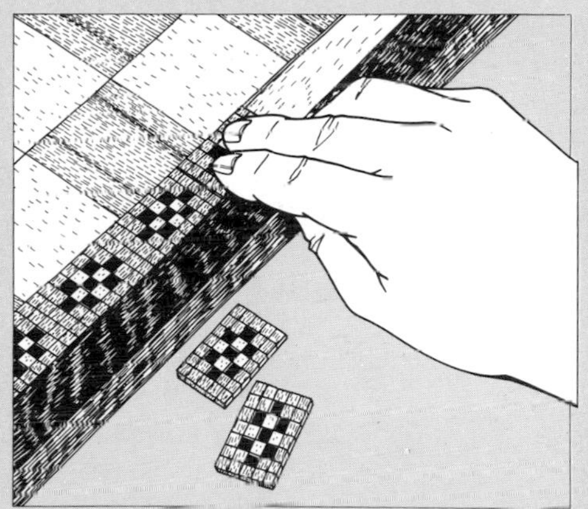

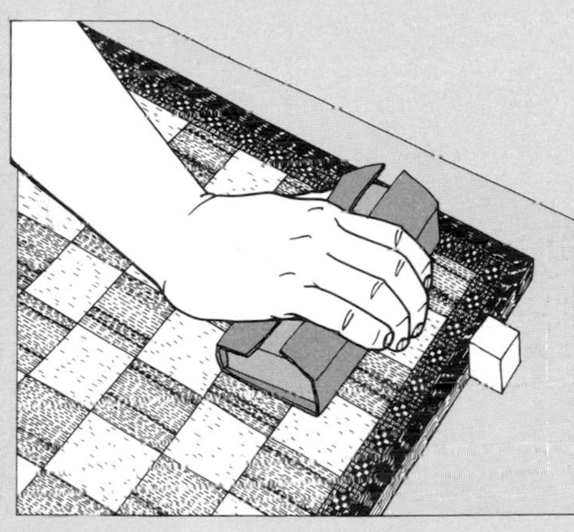

Slicing and arranging the pattern

Once the glue is dry, remove the clamps, clamping boards, plastic sheet and newspaper and arrange the six patterned sticks out on the workbench. Now, with a medium-grade glasspaper positioned face-up on the bench, bring all the faces of the pattern sticks to a smooth, clean finish.

When this has been done, take the marking gauge – still set at ⅛in – and mark off the first pattern slice. Set the marked-off wood against the bench hook, take the gent's saw and slice off the patterned veneer. Continue slicing the sticks and cutting off identical tessera mosaic motifs.

When a stockpile of veneers has been cut, set them out on the work surface and arrange them according to your master design. You may wish to cover a small item like a cigar box or a picture frame or, alternatively, they might be used to decorate the border of a games board (see pages 62–67). Look at the various inspirational photographs and then consider how it is possible to group the motifs so as to build up the most complex or interesting pattern.

Traditionally, Tunbridge mosaics have been used to decorate all manner of items – everything from work boxes and writing cabinets to table tops, tea trays and caddy ladles. It is even possible to lay the mosaics over convex and concave surfaces.

Laying and gluing

When you have settled on a suitable surface to decorate, be it an existing item like a box or a games board, have several dry-run fittings to see how the mosaic module relates to the dimensions of the base ground. Have a look at the various photographs and see how the designers of these pieces have had to either trim back or to fill in so as to make the mosaics fit the item to be decorated. Bearing this in mind, you may have to use slightly off-balance motifs if a corner or shape is difficult to work. If you do need to pad out and fill in a difficult area you can use the spare laminates.

Clear the workbench and set out the PVA glue, newspaper, plastic sheets and the various boards and clamps.

Start by carefully placing the arranged mosaics to one side and setting out the base ground with a guide-line grid. Having done this, spread a thin layer of lump-free PVA glue over the surface to be decorated, and then, with great care and caution, systematically bed the little repeat veneers in the glue.

When the whole design has been set, cover it with several layers of newspaper, place it between the damping boards and clamp-up. Finally, when the glue is dry, remove the boards and clamps, and peel away the newspaper. Note: it is most important that the clamps are not too tight as this may cause the veneers to twist off true. If possible, get a helper to hold and secure the board sandwich while you clamp-up.

Finishing

Clear the bench and arrange the various tools – the rasp, the graded glasspaper, the sanding block, the sealer and the wax polish – so that they are close to hand. Begin by setting the mosaic face-up against the bench stop. Start by giving the face of the work several swift strokes with the rasp, just enough to cut back all the hard bits of glue and newspaper. Having done this, take the graded glasspaper and the sanding block, and rub down the Tunbridging with an easy but firm backwards-and-forwards action.

Bearing in mind that there will probably be considerable differences in mosaic thickness – anything from ⅛–3⁄16in – work methodically through the full range of papers. Cut back the whole stepped surface until it feels completely smooth to the touch.

When you consider the work finished, take a soft brush and a grain sealer, and give the wood a thin coat. Wait for the sealer to dry, then cut back with the finest of papers and re-seal. This sequence of grain-sealing and cutting-back needs to be done three or four times until the wood is silky smooth.

Finally, take a plain wax polish and a cotton cloth, fill the wood grain with the wax and burnish the work to a rich, shiny finish. Note: if the decorated surface is to be used frequently as, for example, a coffee table or perhaps a decorative feature on the edge of a piece of furniture, then it might be as well to protect the mosaic with a plastic varnish instead of wax.

CHAPTER 3

RELIEF WOODCARVING

RELIEF carving includes every type of flat, or semi-flat, carving from simple knife-worked incised line and chip carving, through to whittling, low reliefs and applied fretted panels. Woodcarving of this type is the oldest of all the crafts.

Primitive groups in America, Africa and the South Pacific; iron age Celts, the Vikings, and ancient peoples in China and India — all have traditions that relate to this type of carved decoration. Red Indians on the north-west coast of America amazed early European travellers with the scale and range of their woodcarvings; in Africa and Oceania the carvers worked unbelievably complex chip-carved designs; and the Vikings in pre-Christian Europe produced huge low reliefs on their ships and buildings. If you could go back to the deepest dark corners of the oldest and most primitive cave dwellings you would almost certainly find evidence of low-relief carving.

In the context of this book the terms 'folk', 'primitive' and 'naïve' are in no way disparaging judgments of craft levels or skills — they simply describe the source of the works. Traditionally, low-relief carvings were achieved with the simplest of tools — the small single-handed adze, the straight knife and the curved, hooked or crooked knife. First, the works were shaped and roughed out with the adze, then the surface was decorated with incised lines, stylized chip carving and low reliefs. Patterns and designs in folk and primitive woodcarving always relate directly to available materials and to the performance and efficiency of the tools.

Early carvings tended to be no more than scratched lines over found forms, then, as more efficient cutting edges were introduced, so the patterns became deeper and the carvings more three-dimensional. The development of woodcarving can indeed be thought of as a series of steps following logically one from another. First came the incised lines, then these patterns were filled in with chip carving, and then later, when better tools were introduced, the wood was set-in, wasted and, finally, worked in relief.

It is helpful to beginners in woodcarving to work through the developmental stages of the craft. Thus a beginner might start by whittling, say, a love spoon, one with plenty of incised line and chip carving, then work through various projects until he or she is attempting more complex reliefs. Working in this way, the beginner will gradually increase his or her knowledge, expertise and craft confidence and at the same time learn about the tools and materials. The beginner could well start with a penknife and a piece of found wood, and then work towards a time when choice woods are selected and worked with a good range of gouges and chisels.

As to the wood itself, there is no such thing as a perfect piece; the best you can do is look out for problem indicators to help you spot flaws at an early stage. Wood is not a predictable material like, say, plastic. In growing it has developed a character, and it is this character that the woodcarver needs to assess. In the first instance choose a bland, easily worked wood such as lime, and then work through to more complex and visually exciting woods like oak, walnut and yew. When choosing your wood, look out for imperfections such as soft, sappy, wany edges, unexpected grain twists, dead knots, decay and blemishes. Choose woods that are straight-grained, of good colour and knot-free.

WORKING A MEDIEVAL CHIP-CARVED ROUNDEL

OF ALL the decorative woodcarving techniques, chip carving is the oldest, the most basic and perhaps the most beautiful. It is a relatively simple process in which the surface to be decorated is gridded and geometrically patterned so that the main elements of the design are seen as triangular, 'three-cut' pockets. The carver uses a few basic tools – a knife, a straight chisel and a shallow-curve gouge – and works the triangular pockets of the design with simple stab-slice-chip cuts.

European chip-carved designs are characterized by stylized sharp-edged triangular and petal-lozenge cuts that are set within circles and hexagons. Of circular motifs, one of the most effective is the English 'rose-hex' or roundel, as found on many medieval pieces of slab furniture including chests, tables and benches. These roundels are nearly always intricately worked with a compass, stepped off and subdivided so as to form the hexagonal three-cut pocket forms. The beauty of traditional chip carving lies not so much in the designs being deeply worked, undercut or in any way original, but rather in the work being imaginatively gridded and efficiently carved. The best designs and motifs are simple, circle-based and well-balanced but, above all, they are crisply and rhythmically cut.

TOOLS & EQUIPMENT

- Workbench
- Large compass
- Metal rule
- Pencil
- G-clamp or bench holdfast
- 1in shallow-curve gouge
- Small V-section gouge
- Mallet
- ¼in straight chisel
- 1in straight chisel
- Soft-haired brush

MATERIALS

- Slab of quarter-sawn wide board oak measuring 18 × 18 × 2in
- Workout paper
- Linseed oil
- Turpentine
- Beeswax polish

The scale is two squares to 1in. When you are choosing your slab of oak, make sure that the wood is free from curious grain twists and knots. See how the whole roundel can be set out with a compass.

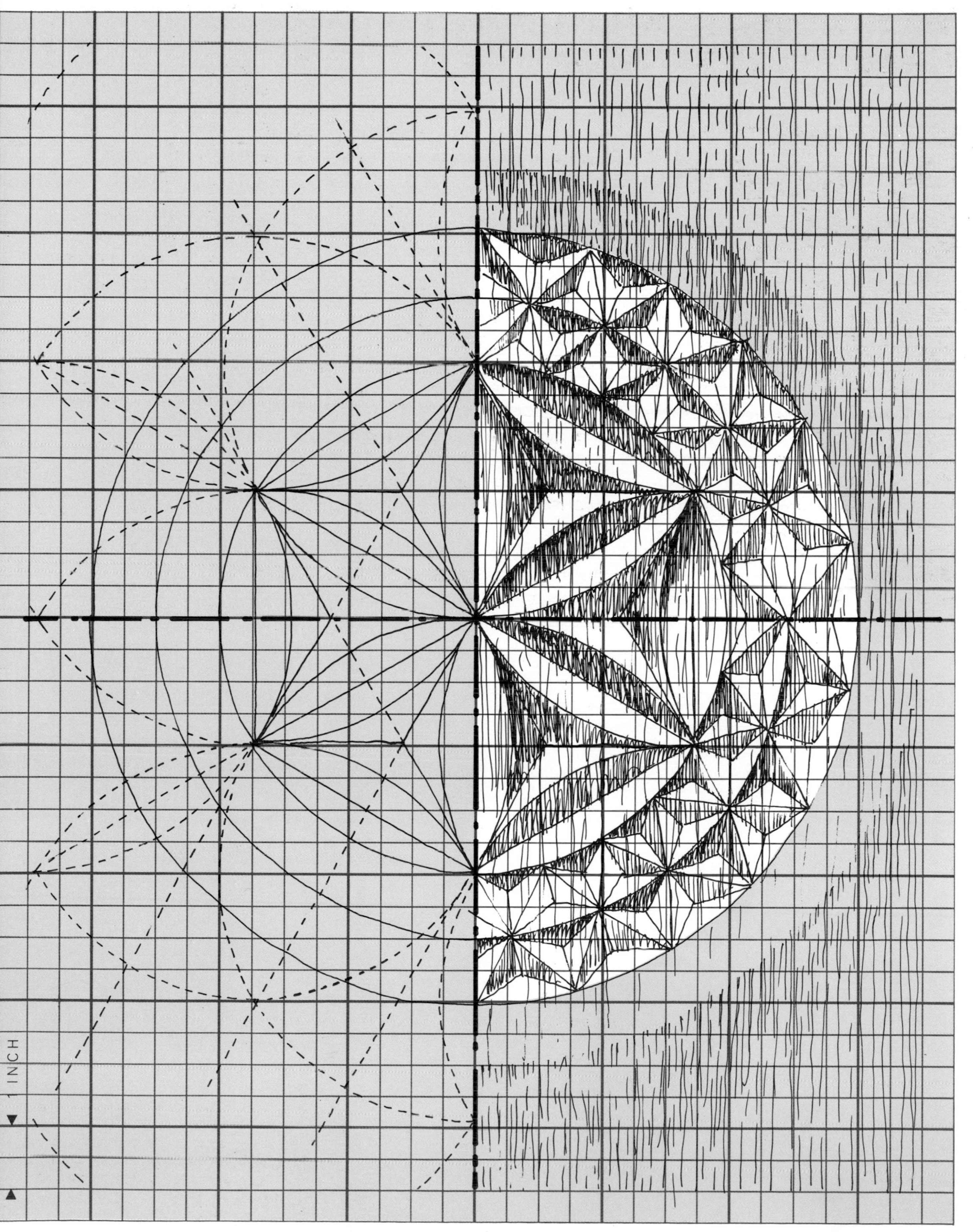
1 INCH

BELOW PROJECT PHOTOGRAPH *A thirteenth-century chest. Thought to have come from a church in Hampshire, England, this chest measures 1ft 8in high, 3ft 7in wide and 1ft 7in deep. Inside the chest are grooves into which was fitted a tray or money till.*

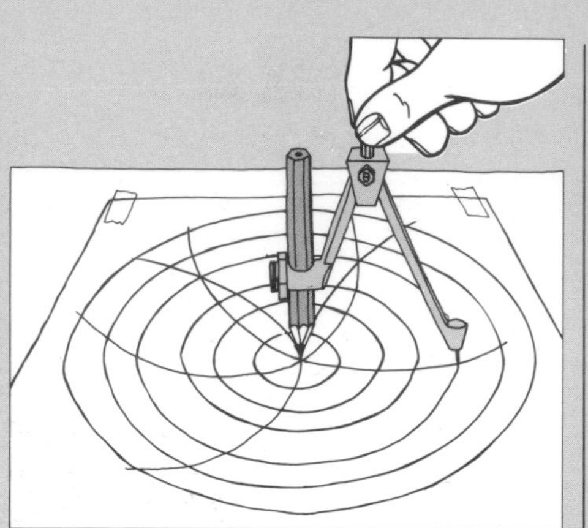

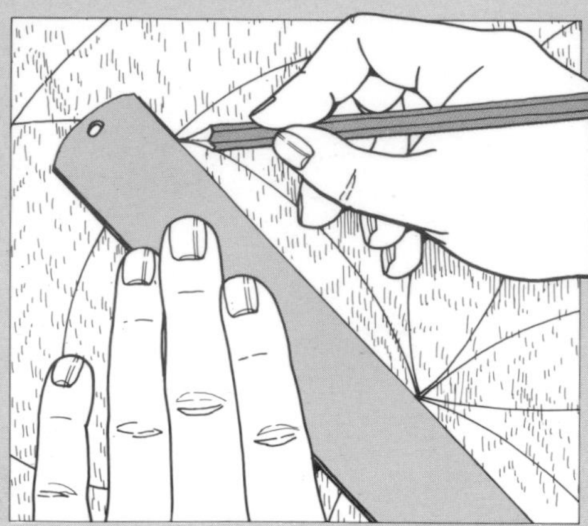

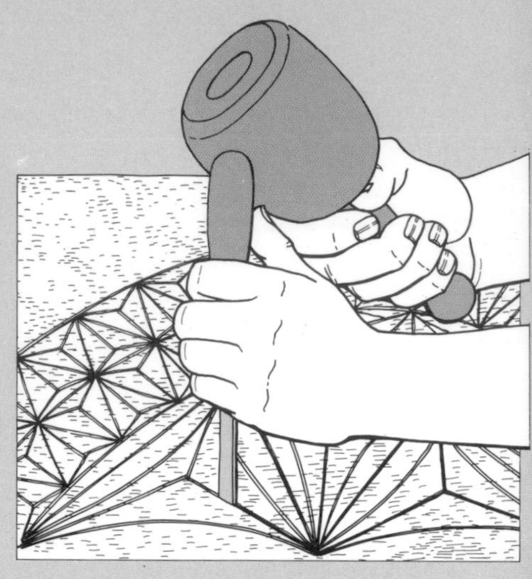

Considering the roundel design

This project uses a slab of oak, chisels and gouges, but, if you prefer, you can use a light softwood such as pine or lime and use knives to cut out the design as the basic techniques are the same as described.

Take a look at the circle shown in the far left of the photograph (see page 85) and consider how, in the main, the design is built up from radius-length arcs making a large hexagon set within a circle. Notice how the central six petal-lozenge forms are made by setting the compass point on the angles of the hexagon and repeatedly striking off radius-length arcs. See how these arcs pass through the centre of the circle to meet and create the petals.

Take some sheets of workout paper, the compass, metal rule and pencil, and again have a long look at the three medieval chip-carved roundels shown in the photograph. Draw up several practice patterns on the paper.

Although this project concentrates on the first of the three roundels, there is no reason why you should not modify the design and the working order, and carve either of the remaining roundels.

In fact, all three roundels in the photograph are either compass-drawn hexagons within circles with petal-lozenge divisions, or circles with compass-arc spirals.

Setting out the roundel motif

Set the slab of quarter-sawn oak on the workbench and secure it with a G-clamp or a bench holdfast. Now, take the shallow-curve gouge and go over the face of the wood with it, bringing the worked surface to a smooth, slightly rippled finish.

When this has been done, fix the compass at a radius of 6in. Find the centre of the slab and then set out a 12in diameter circle. Still using the same centre point, set out two more circles reducing the compass radius first to 5in and then 4in. Set out the two outer zigzag border circles according to the working drawing. Keep the compass radius set at 4in and strike six circumference arcs around the inner 8in diameter circle.

Take a metal rule and a pencil, and draw lines from the six outer petal points to the circle centre. Having done this, use a compass and ruler to fix the centre point of each of the six equilateral triangles that go to make up the hexagon. When these centre points have been established, take the metal rule and draw the three corner-to-centre lines that divide each of the triangles.

Now have a close look at the photograph and the working drawing, and see how the two outer border circles are filled with small triangles. Consider how there are seven triangles in both the inner and outer zigzag borders between the petal-lozenge points. Notice how the triangles increase in size the nearer they get to the outer edge of the roundel. These triangles are best drawn by eye.

Setting in the first cuts

When the roundel motif has been drawn out and all the lines of the design are clearly established, clamp the slab of oak to the workbench and arrange the tools so that they are comfortably to hand. Now, take the small V-section tool, and very gently set-in the drawn lines of the design with a shallow V-cut or trench. Work with a feather-light touch, just skimming over the pencil lines and removing the finest of slivers. If you now look at the working drawing and the details, you will see that this cut not only emphasizes the total design but also marks out what will be high ridges or deep chip-cuts.

As you work along the drawn lines, you will be cutting both across and with the grain of the oak. With this in mind, always hold the tool firmly with both hands, one guiding and the other manoeuvring. Work with well-controlled skimming strokes and be ready to stop short if the tool starts to run into the grain or slips across the proud surface of the wood. If the cutting edge is kept sharp, you will not need to use a mallet – just keep the weight of your shoulder behind the thrust of the tool.

When the whole design has been cut and set-in, take a light mallet and a straight chisel, and make sure the wood is secure. Now select one of the pyramidal pockets, identify the three corner-to-centre lines that mark out the facets and chop in the lines with a corner-to-centre angled cut. Continue working until all the lines that mark out the deepest part of the triangles and the petal-lozenges have been set-in.

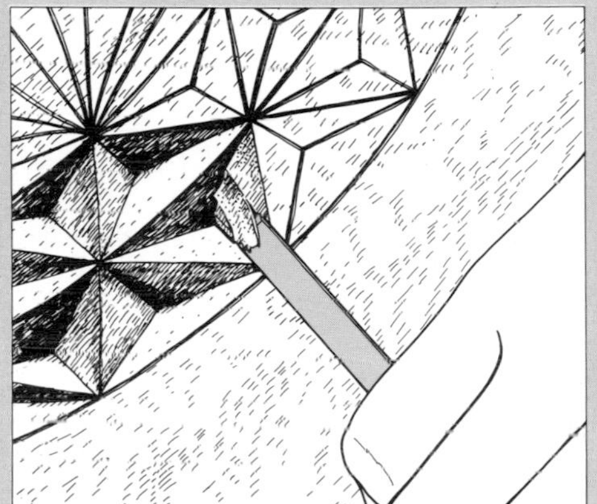

Working the triangular chip cuts

Make sure the slab of oak is held firmly by the G-clamp or holdfast and then set out a mallet and a couple of keen-edged straight chisels such as a ¼in and a 1in. Once again have a look at the various photographs and working drawings, and draw a distinction between the two types of chip-carved forms. Clearly identify the triangular cuts and the elongated petal-lozenges – maybe even shade in one of these types with a pencil.

Start the work by chip carving the triangular pockets. Select one pocket, for example, one of the larger triangles that go to make up the hexagon and then, taking the 1in straight chisel, rework the three corner-to-centre cuts. Chop with the chisel at an angle so that one corner of the blade enters the wood first. When this has been done, hold the chisel so that it is at the same angle as one of the three facets of the pyramid and slide it into the wood, chopping out a single, clean-cut chip. Do this with each of the three facets that go to make up a pocket.

Always try to work each pocket with three clean, swift cuts. However, if the wood is hard or your chisel is not so sharp, then they may have to be worked in several successive stages. It can be done in this way as long as the end result looks clean-cut and crisply worked.

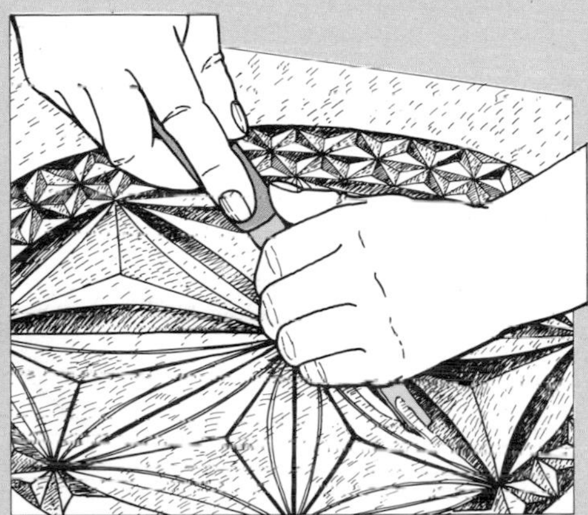

Working the curved petal-lozenge chip cuts

Once all the triangular chip-cuts have been worked, check that the slab is still held firmly. Brush away all the shavings and chips, and then set out the 1in straight chisel and a 1in shallow-curve gouge. Start by taking the straight chisel and reworking the straight lines that link the ends of the petal-lozenge forms. Avoid stabbing straight down into the wood, but rather slide the blade, corner first, so as to establish the curved bottom, or keel, of the petal-lozenge pocket.

Next, take the shallow-curve gouge and slide it around the two facets of the petal with long sweeping cuts at an angle. In the first instance, do not try to remove all the wood with one or two cuts, but start from the initial centre cut and gradually work outwards and downwards until the slightly curved faces of the petal-lozenge form have been achieved.

In a similar manner, work all twelve of the curved pockets – that is, all the pockets that are contained within the two zigzag borders. As you work, be aware of the direction of the wood grain and try not to split short-grain areas or leave the wood looking scraped and overworked.

When all the pockets have been cut, spend time getting the tools really sharp and keen-edged. Finally, swiftly clean out the various cuts, angles and ridges – aim to leave the whole roundel looking crisp and tool-burnished.

Finishing

When you feel that the carving is nearing completion, stand well back and give it a super critical inspection. Look at the subtle ridge lines and the various curved facets, and run your fingertips over the face of the wood. Search out faults and imperfections, and, if necessary, take a fine-edged tool and deepen angles or sharpen ridges.

Once you consider the carving finished, clean out the various pockets with a soft-haired brush and then clear the bench and the working area of all tools, shavings, wood dust and clutter. Having done this, consider how the wood might be finished or otherwise treated. In the past, oak has been variously painted, stained, varnished, fumed, weathered, bleached, and given all manner of chemical washes. How you wish to finish the piece is a matter of personal preference. However, it is desirable that the finish or final treatment should emphasize the tooled surface of the wood and the swirl of the grain. Oak can be darkened slightly with oil – 3 parts linseed oil to 1 part turpentine – and then polished with beeswax. Alternatively, if you want a fresh, light finish, the wood can simply be waxed.

The finish of the final piece of work will always, of course, relate to your initial choice of wood. The choice of quarter-sawn wide board oak for this project should ensure that there is no warping or shrinkage.

WHITTLING A PIECE OF TREEN: BALL-IN-A-CAGE

THE WORD 'treen' comes from the old English *'treowen'* and *'treow'*, meaning of wood or made of trees. Although in its broadest sense the word is still occasionally used to describe any object that is made of wood, it is now more often used to describe small pieces of woodware – anything that is small enough to be picked up in one hand. It can be used to describe something as delicate as a snuff box or as large as a food bowl or milking stool. The word 'whittle' also comes from the old English and is derived from *'thwitel'*, meaning to cut and pare with a belt-slung knife. It has come to mean just about any small wooden item that has been carved with a knife. Although the term 'whittled treen' by dictionary definition refers to folk, ethnic and period items such as nutcrackers, distaffs, corset busks, butter rollers and back scratchers, it is now more often used to describe small, not very serious wooden objects that have been made and worked in the American folk tradition. They include small, 'fun' items such as trick chains, caricature animals and balls-in-a-cage.

This project has been inspired by an old English knife-worked knitting sheath. These sheaths, rather like love spoons and corset busks, were made by lovers and presented to their sweethearts. Beautifully worked and delicately carved, these unique treen items are certainly labours of love. No special tools or skills were needed – just a good sharp knife, a knot-free white wood and the desire on the part of the carver to do better than the next man.

TOOLS & EQUIPMENT

- Workbench
- Sketchbook
- Pencil
- Penknife
- Compass
- Metal rule
- Scalpel
- Oilstone and strop

MATERIALS

- A piece of lime measuring 6 × 1 × 1in
- A block of modelling wax
- Wax polish

There are two scales for this working drawing: the lefthand detail is at four squares to 1 in, and the righthand detail is four squares to ½in. Note that although most of the measurements can be adjusted, the size of the ball in relationship to the size and spacing of the bars is critical.

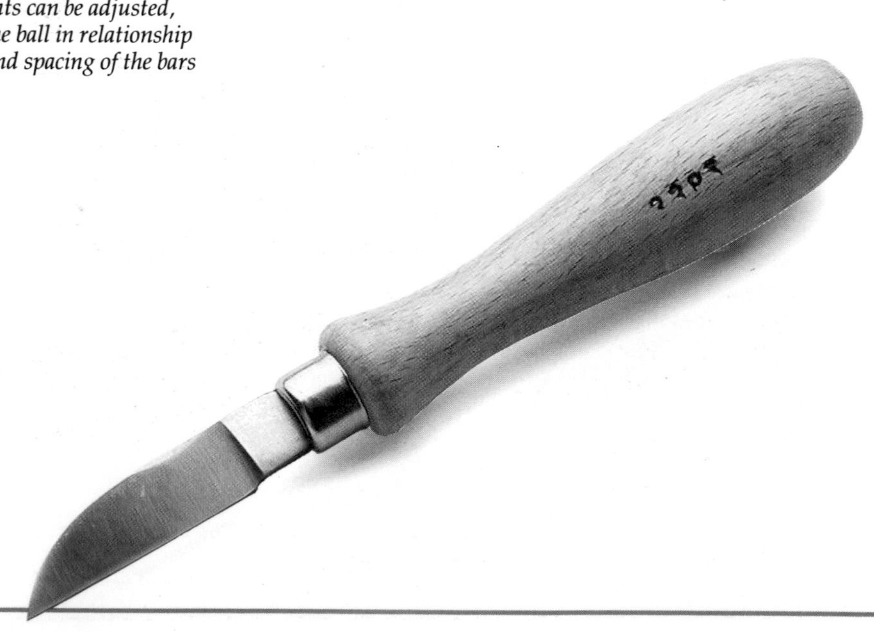

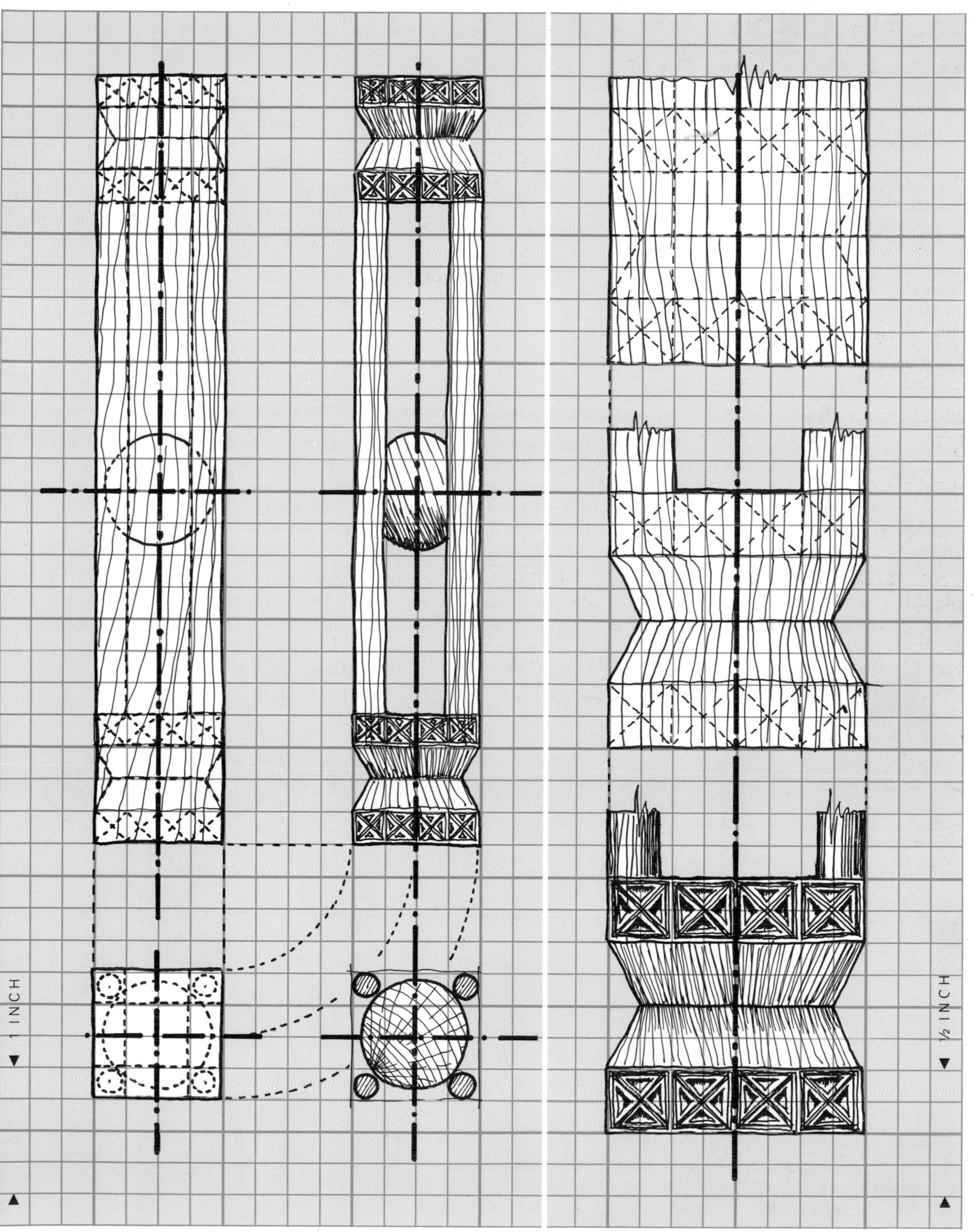
1 INCH
½ INCH

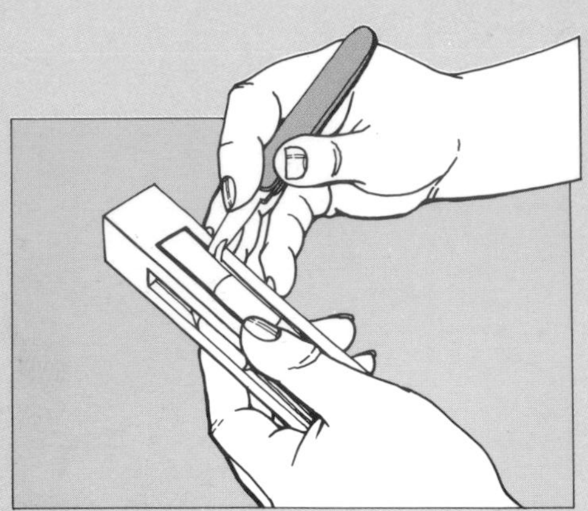

Considering the technique and making a wax maquette

Place the project photograph (see page 93) under a magnifying glass and study all the details. Take note of the total form including the tapered point, the slot for the needles and the 'neck'. Also notice the beautifully delicate incised and chip-carved surface decoration. Most important of all, focus your attention on the traditional and characteristically whittled ball-in-a-cage. Decide how you might modify the design to make a useful modern object such as a letter knife or a paper weight.

When you have studied all the photographs and the working drawings, try to visit a museum and search out the treen section – see if you can have a close-up look at some small item that includes a ball-in-a-cage feature. Make a series of design sketches and consider how the whole ball-in-a-cage has been whittled from one piece of wood.

Take a block of hard modelling wax and a penknife, and have a trial run at making the ball-in-a-cage. Follow the project through the various stages and sort out all the possible problems and snags. Work through the step-by-step sequences as described, and establish in your own mind how best you feel the ball-in-a-cage ought to be worked.

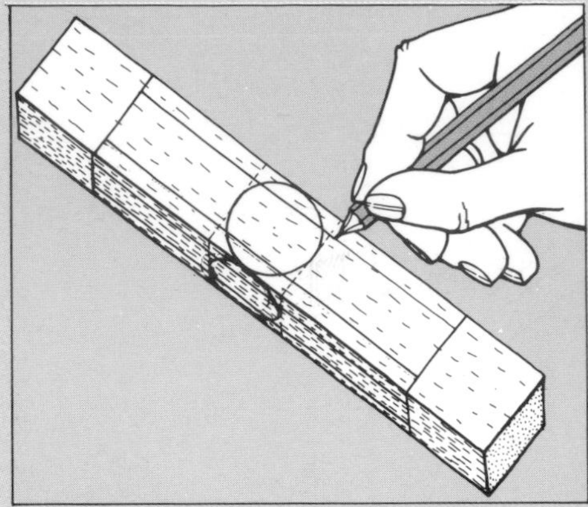

Considering the tools and materials, and setting out the design

Traditionally, whittling is a carving technique that spontaneously uses just about any found wood that comes to hand. However, you need to use a wood that is straight-grained, and free from knots, splits and bark. As an alternative to lime you can use holly or a well-chosen piece of white pine or bass wood, as long as the wood is easy to carve.

Check the wood over for possible flaws and leave it for a day or two so that it can adjust to the atmosphere of your workshop – the wood may dry out or take in water. Although whittlers traditionally tended to use just about any tools that took their fancy, this project is best managed with a small penknife and a fine-point scalpel.

Take a pencil, compass and metal rule, and set the wood out as illustrated. Mark off the 1in square ends with diagonals and 1in diameter circles. Set lines ¼in in from the edges of the side faces and mark out centre lines. Generally, set out the wood as shown in the working drawing. When you are marking out, bear in mind that the ball needs to be a little larger than about ¾in and the bars of the cage must be no more than ¾in apart.

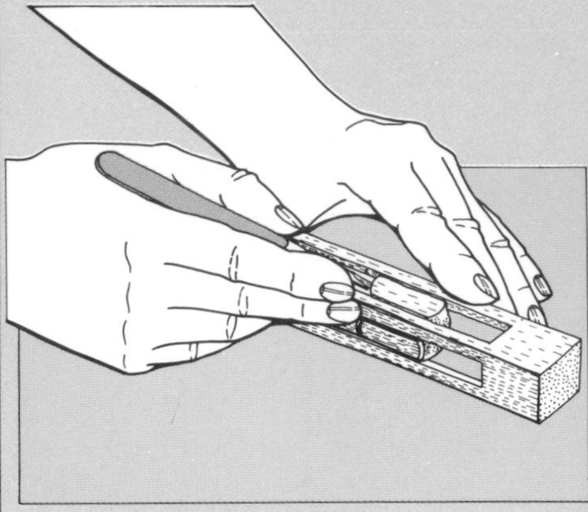

First cuts

When you have set out the wood as described, stop a moment and have a good long look at the photographs and the working model. Start by taking the penknife and cutting in all the stop-cuts – that is, score the drawn lines with the blade until the main cage grid is established. Having done this, cut in and outline the areas of waste wood between the ball and the top and bottom of the cage. Deepen the stop-cuts that go around the waste areas.

Now, make paring V-cuts at an angle to the stop-cuts, and gradually whittle deeper into the wood. Note that although to some extent you can take liberties with relatively easy-to-carve lime, you must not force the blade too deeply into the grain. Whittling is always, by its very nature, a gentle, little-by-little, slice-and-cut method of working.

Continue running the point of the knife down the sides of the cage bars, cutting in at the top and bottom of the ball, and gradually removing the waste. If you look at the various drawings you will see that there comes a time when the waste has more or less been cut out and the ball is almost free to move – it is at this stage that you must work with extra care and caution.

Use the scalpel to delicately pierce the last bit of waste. When you have cut through, above and below the ball, the carving begins to get a little easier. Shape and square the inside of the cage until the ball is free to move along the whole 4in length of the cage (see the working drawing).

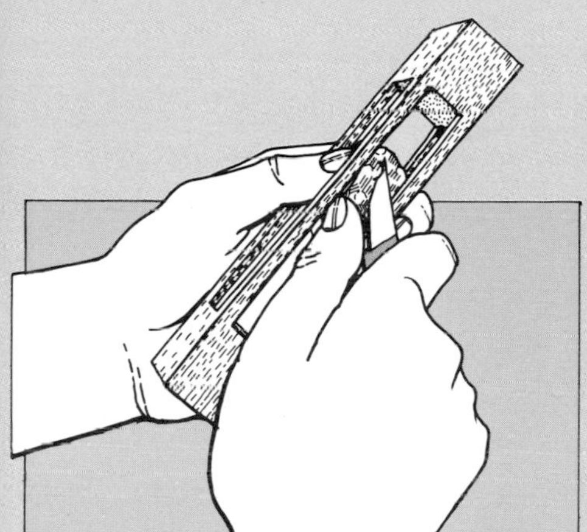

Finishing the ball

When the bars have been whittled and the squarish ball is free to slide along the full length of the cage, then comes the tricky business of shaping the ball.

Clear away all the waste wood and sharpen or replace the scalpel blade. Carve the top and bottom of the squarish ball until it begins to look more rounded. Work the grain from side-to-end, making sure that you never cut directly into the end-grain. As you work, hold the wood in one hand, the knife in the other, and pare away at the end of the ball that is nearest to you. Work with little slicing strokes.

Continue gently cutting and removing little chips and wedges from the sides, top and bottom of the ball. The exciting moment will come when you are able to turn the ball around in its cage; you will then be able to view and work the ball from all sides. Remember that the ball must always remain a little larger than the space between the cage bars. If you look at the end section as shown in the working drawing you will see that the relationship between the ball and the thickness of the bars is critical. Be careful to avoid splitting the wood of the bars, and make sure that you do not get so lost in your work that you make the ball too small.

Once the ball is finished, stand the whole length of wood on its end, hold the ball up out of the way, and then work the inside end-grain. Having done this, flip the wood over and work the other end in the same way.

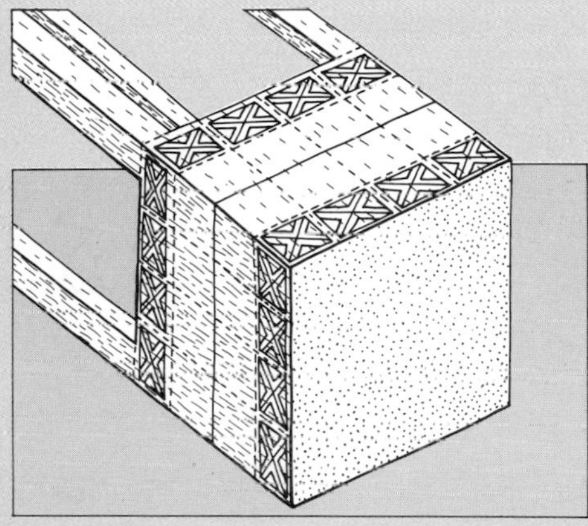

Considering and setting out the chip carved design

When you have achieved a nicely worked ball-in-a-cage, put it to one side and consider how you want the surface of the wood – the 1in square faces at the top and bottom of the cage – to be decorated. If you take a magnifying glass to the project photograph (see page 93), you will see that the knitting-stick sheath has been necked and narrowed at the handle and the surface is, more or less, divided up into squares. You will see that the squares, in turn, have been quartered with diagonals, incised and chip-carved. It is advisable at this stage to have a few trial cuts on the modelling wax, just to see how the design can be achieved. Look at the working drawing and see how this project has been modified so that the 6in long piece of wood is necked at both ends and chip-carved. Note how the chip carving is based on a ¼ × ¼in module.

Take a measure and pencil, and mark each of the 1in square faces so that they are divided up into sixteen ¼in squares. Mark out both ends and all four faces of the wood. Having done this, indicate the area that is to be necked and narrowed, and then set out the remaining squares with diagonals (see the working drawing). Finally, take a soft pencil and block in all the areas that are going to be worked and wasted – the necks, the little diamond-shaped chips and the incised lines.

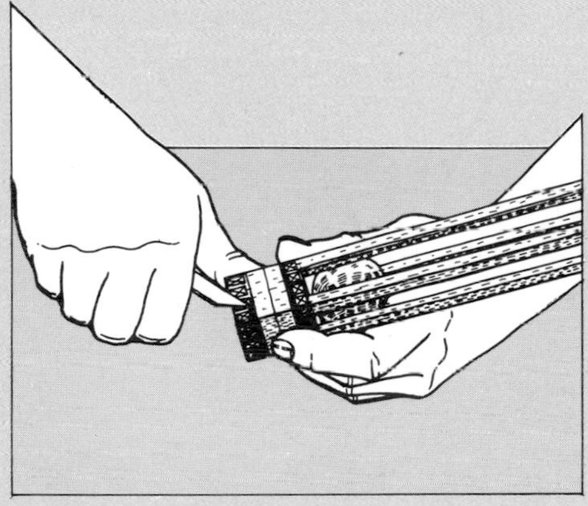

Incising lines, chip carving and finishing

Place the ball-in-a-cage on the work surface and, before you start work, refresh your eyes by looking at the various pieces of folk carving shown in the photographs. Now, take a scalpel and set-in all your drawn lines with delicate, incised cuts. Work V-section trenches that follow the lines of the design. Two cuts are made – one at an angle to the other – so that thin slivers of wood curl away. Work the square grid and the diagonals in this manner, making sure that you cut very fine V-trenches. It is a relatively straightforward process as long as you make sure that when you are cutting, the blade does not run into the grain and split the wood.

As you work, support and guide the knife with both thumbs – that is, brace one thumb on the wood and use the other to control the swing of the knife. When all the grid lines have been worked, you can start the chip-cuts. Make two stop-cuts that meet each other at right-angles, and then slide the blade at an angle into the stop-cuts and lift out the little triangle of wood.

The secret of success is a sharp blade and a well set-out design grid. Remember, as you draw the blade towards you and across the wood, always support, control and manoeuvre with a lever action of both thumbs. When the incised cuts and the chip-cuts have been worked, make stop-cuts around each end of the wood, and whittle and cut so as to achieve the necks (see the working drawing). Finally, wipe the wood over with a plain wax polish.

ABOVE LEFT *and* RIGHT *Hollow- and chip-carved nutcracker. Small carvings of this character were also often made with ball-in-a-cage features worked into the handle.*

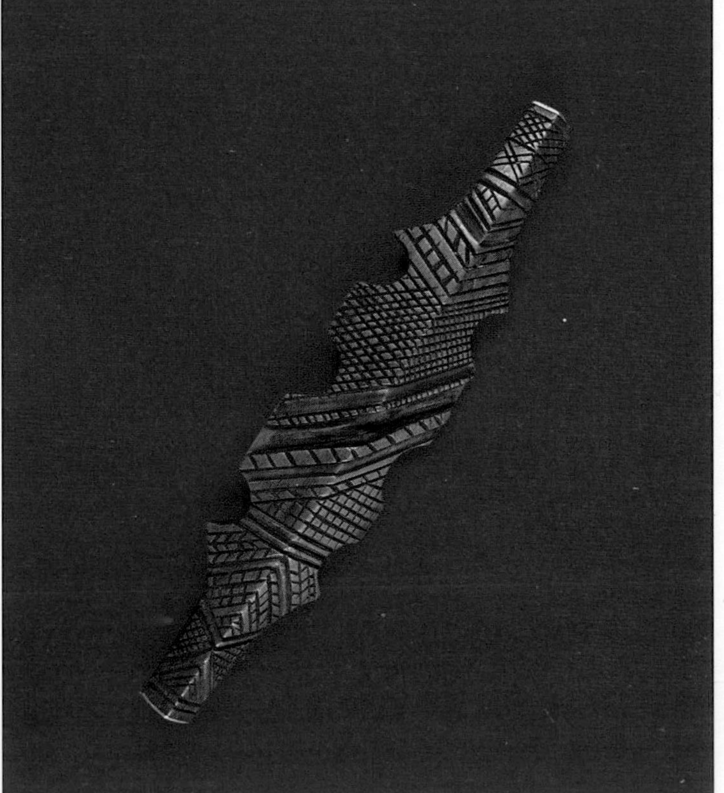

LEFT *Chip-carved and incised knitting-stick holder. The overall shape of the carving is probably significant and could have been inspired by a milkmaid's yoke.*

RIGHT PROJECT PHOTOGRAPH *Ball-in-a-cage knitting stick or sheath. Love tokens of this size and character were often made by young men and given to their sweethearts. Knitting sticks, when not in use, were hung from the belt in much the same way as a fob or a knife.*

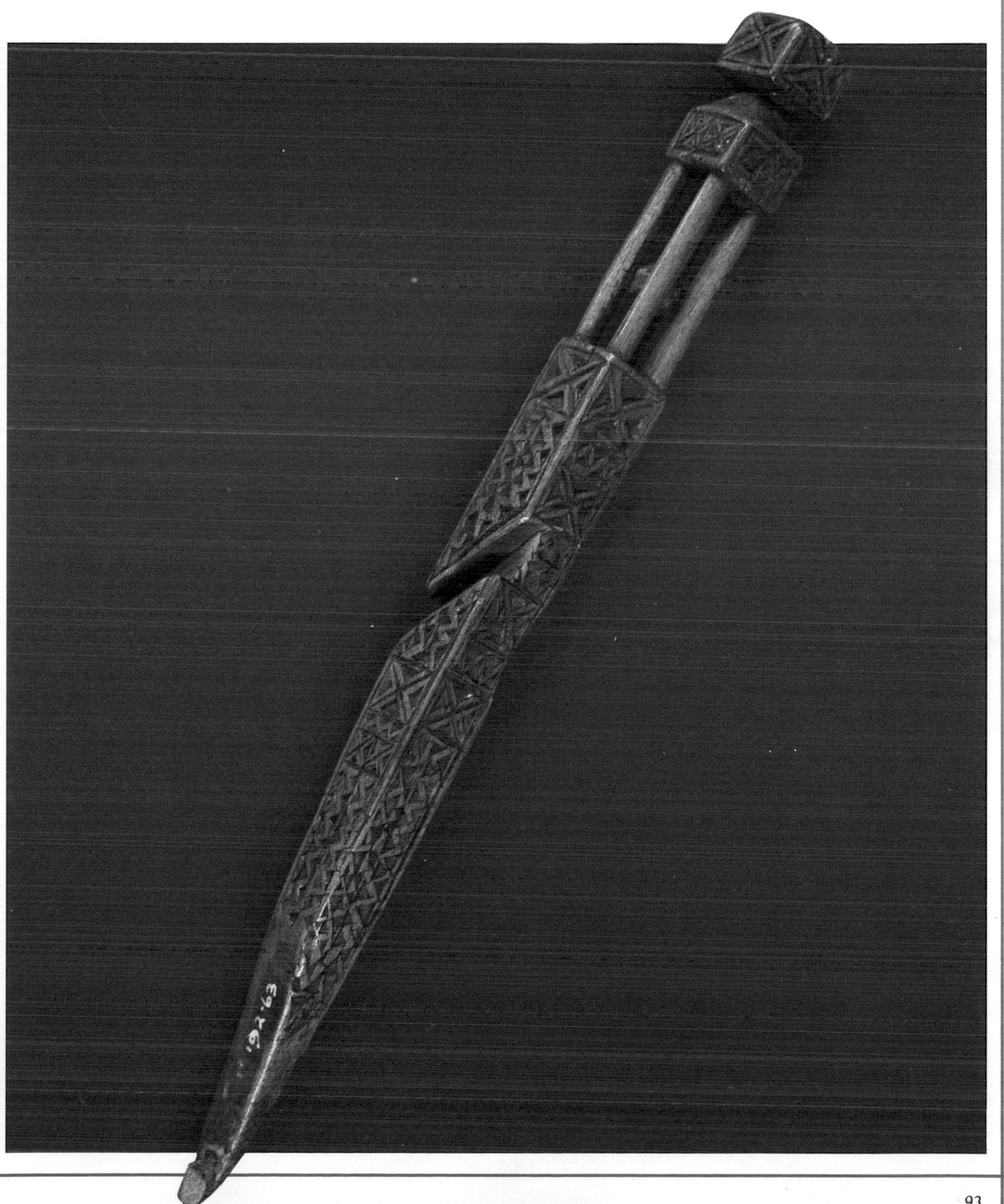
192·63

WORKING A SUNFLOWER PANEL

IN THE fourteenth and fifteenth centuries oak was used so heavily that by the sixteenth century it was in short supply. It was this shortage that led woodworkers of the sixteenth and seventeenth centuries to experiment with new forms of furniture construction. Gradually, over a period of 150 years, the heavy slab construction gave way to structures that were jointed and panelled – structures that were not only more economical in the use of timber but also lighter in weight. This use of much smaller timber sections resulted in a style of carving that was flatter; a style that could be worked within the thickness of relatively slender panels.

The most characteristic pieces of furniture made between the beginning of the sixteenth century and the end of the seventeenth are nearly always decorated with very shallow relief-carved motifs, with the ground wood in and around the design being cut away and lowered. The most commonly used motifs of this period are the sunflower and the tulip. These stylized blooms appear on just about everything – American bible boxes and dower chests, English chests and wall panels as well as cupboards and chests from Germany and Holland. In fact, so popular were these designs in the seventeenth century, that it was almost as if some sort of raging sunflower and tulip mania had swept across the whole of Europe and America. As regards the origins of these motifs, tulips were prolific in the seventeenth century. The whole of Europe was growing and collecting bulbs and, consequently, it is easy to see how the motif travelled across Europe and to America via Dutch or German Pennsylvanian immigrants. As to the sunflower – now often known as the 'Connecticut sunflower' – it could be related to the old English chip-carved rose or to the ancient German 'sun' symbol. Alternatively, it could be just a straight design inspired by the American sunflower.

TOOLS & EQUIPMENT

- Workbench
- Sketchbook
- Pencils
- Metal rule
- G-clamp or holdfast
- Small U-section adze
- Large shallow U-section gouge
- V-section tool
- Small straight chisel
- Mallet
- Spoon gouge
- Dog-leg chisel
- Oilstone and strop
- A flat-bent tool
- Punch
- Long-haired brush

MATERIALS

- A slab of quarter-sawn oak measuring 12 × 2 × 1in
- Grid cartridge paper
- Tracing paper
- Linseed oil
- Beeswax polish
- Turpentine

The scale is two squares to 1in. There are many variations on the Sunflower design. Have a close look at the photograph and see how that although the overall design is symmetrical, many of the details are pleasantly off-balance.

1 INCH

RIGHT PROJECT PHOTOGRAPH
Sunflower chest dated 1637. Stylized blooms appear on many pieces of sixteenth- and seventeenth-century furniture. In addition to the sunflower design, beautiful tulips and grapes appear in the border panel.

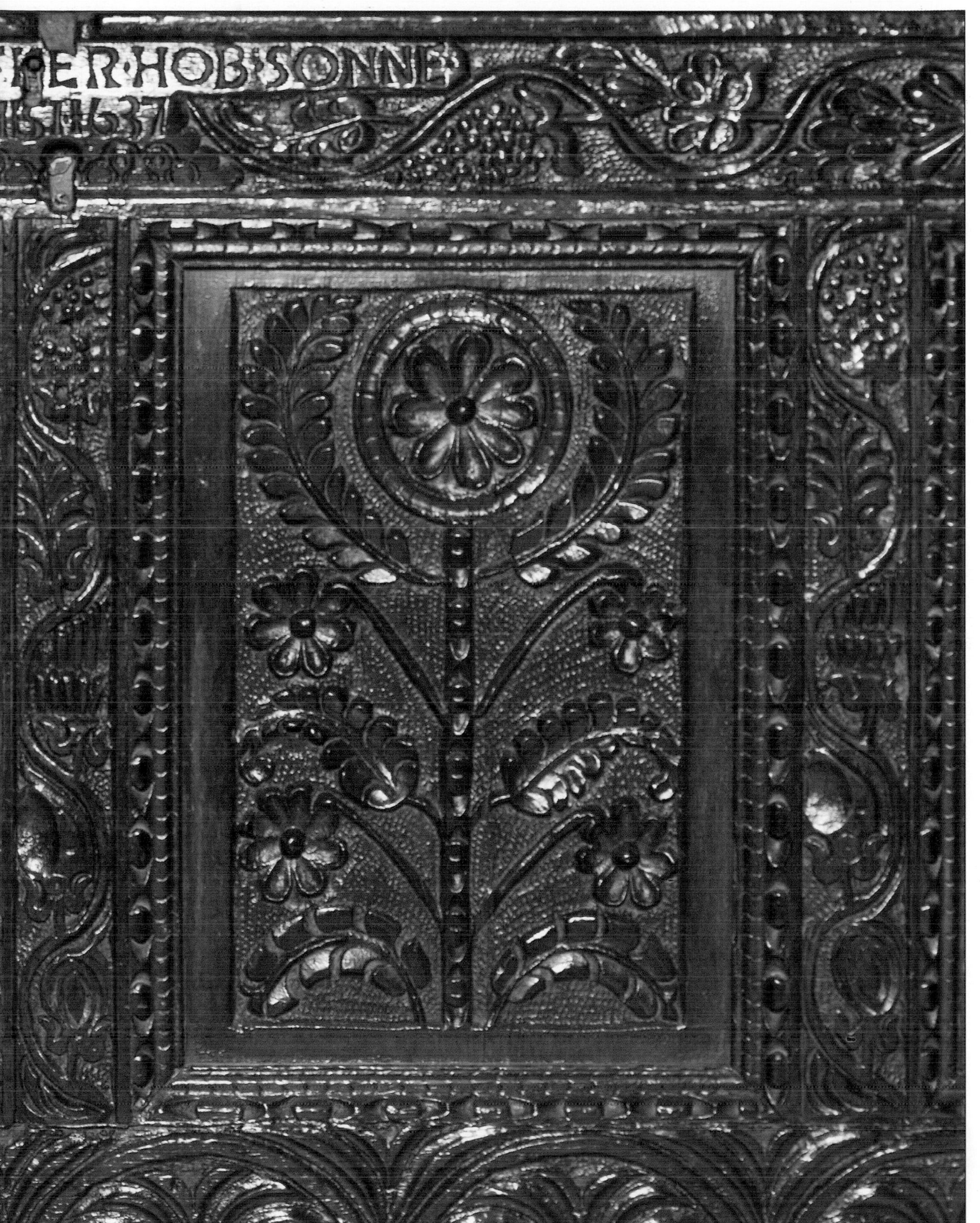
ER·HOB·SONNE

Considering the project and drawing out the master design

Start this project by considering the design in detail. Note how the two panels are more or less identical and that the traditional sunflower forms are symmetrical. Take the magnifying glass to the photograph of the panels (see page 97) and count the leaf segments and the sunflower petals. Generally familiarize yourself with the motif detailing and the character of the relief.

Have a look at the working drawing and see how this project concentrates on the use of oak and traditional woodcarving tools. Before you go any further, take a trip to a museum or a stately home, and try to see some English and American sunflower or tulip chests of the early seventeenth century. Study the motifs, note the beautifully worked forms and the simple, uncomplicated directness of the carving.

Take a sketchbook and make a series of design sketches. Focus on the scooped-cut leaves and petals, the balance between relief wood and lowered ground, and the gouge and chisel chops that go to make up the design. When you have done these necessary studies, take your research material back to the workshop and draw up a master design to scale. Using grid cartridge paper, tracing paper and a soft pencil, draw and trace a symmetrical half-design (see the illustration). Work from a centre line in order to achieve a motif that is squarely placed and balanced.

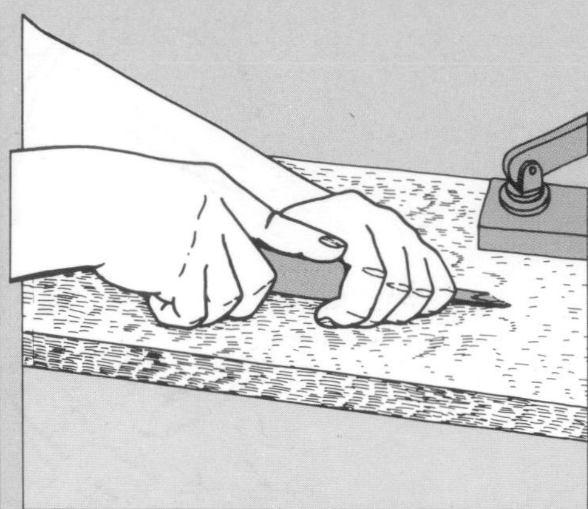

Considering the materials, preparing the wood and setting out the design

Set the slab of oak out on the workbench and spend time carefully checking it over – it needs to be straight-grained and quarter-sawn but, above all, it must be free from cracks, splits, dead and loose knots, warps and sappy edges. Before you start, stop for a moment and try to think yourself into the shoes of a seventeenth-century English woodworker, or perhaps a pioneer American carver. All you are seeking to do, to the best of your ability, is to carve and decorate a box panel.

When you have a clear picture in your mind of what you are trying to achieve in terms of quality and form, take your slab of oak and secure it to the bench with a G-clamp or holdfast. Now, with the adze or the large shallow gouge, bring the working face of the wood to a smooth, slightly rippled finish. Remember, you are not trying to work a slick and characterless machined finish, but rather a surface that is richly dappled with a soft, scalloped and tooled texture.

Having done this, clear away the waste wood and then draw with a pencil a centre line on the wood. Have another look at your design sketches. Although the design is more or less symmetrical, the leaves, stems and flowers are individually worked – all the details vary in size and form.

Finally, take the tracing of the design and transfer the traced lines through to the working face of the wood. Use the centre line as your reference point, and trace and reverse the design so that it is symmetrical.

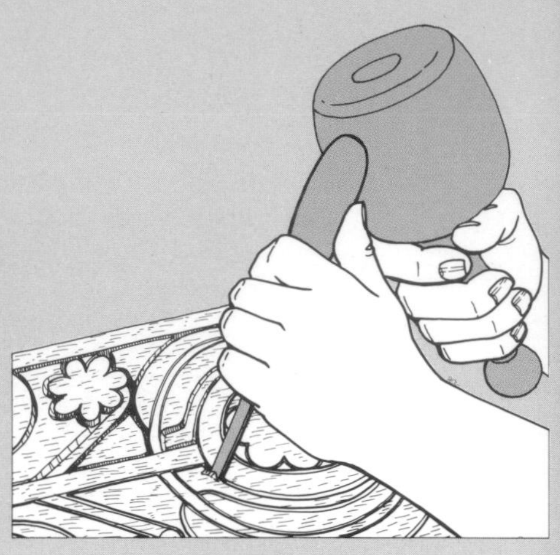

Setting in the design

Take the small V-tool and start to outline the drawn motifs. Cut a V-section trench around the whole design, working all the time on the waste or ground side and keeping about ⅛in away from the drawn lines. As you trench round the lines, bear in mind that you will be cutting both with and across the grain.

Always hold the tool firmly with both hands, one guiding and the other pushing and manoeuvring. Work with short, shallow and controlled strokes, and always be ready to stop if you feel the tool beginning to slip too deeply into the grain or run out of control across the surface of the wood. Work to a uniform depth of about ¼in and try to cut a smoothly worked trench. It is a relatively straightforward process but you do have to take extra care when you come to the short-grain areas – the delicate flowers, leaves and stems that spring out from the large central stalk.

Once you have completely trenched around the design, take a small straight chisel or a gouge with a shallow U-section, and start to set in. With the tool blade positioned on the drawn line and the handle held at a slight angle over the motif, work around the design with short, sharp taps of the mallet. As you chop, the narrow band of waste wood between the drawn lines and the V-trench should crumble away. Aim to keep the depth of cut constant, about ¼in deep. Be careful to avoid undercutting any portion of the motifs and try to keep the tight angles sharp-edged and crisp.

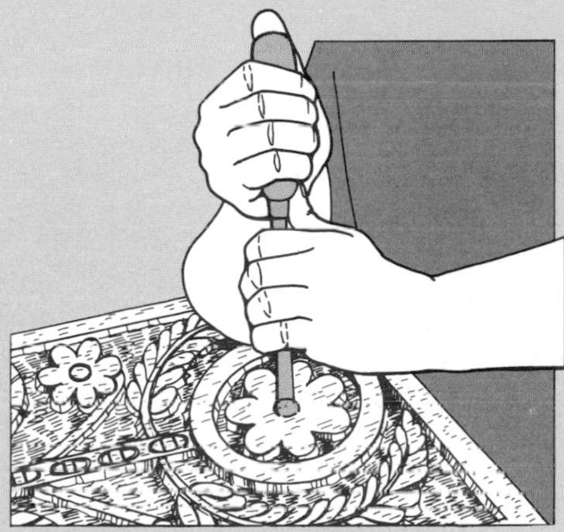

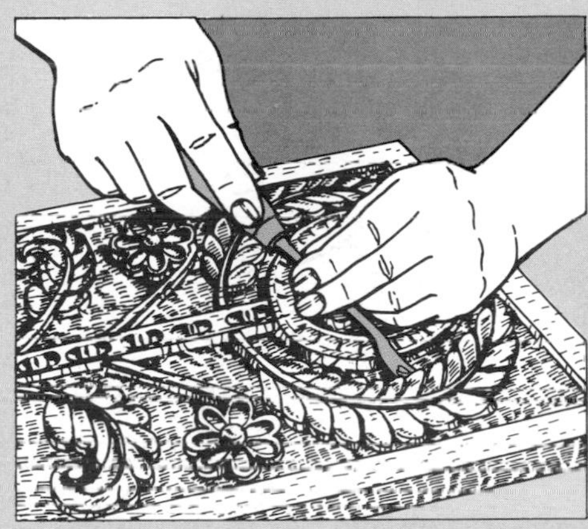

Clearing and wasting the ground

Once you have set in the design with a clean and well-established cut, you can begin to clear the waste ground. Take the shallow-curve gouge and cut a broad trench around the whole of the outline. Clear the wood to a depth of ¼in. Having done this, take a smaller tool, such as a spoon gouge, and lower the tight areas of waste ground wood that occur in and around the main flower motif and the larger leaves. As far as possible, cut across the grain, using the trench depth as a guide, and only remove easy crisp curls of wood. When you come to an area that joins a fragile cross-grain stem, work with extra caution and use a small dog-leg chisel to clear the ground.

In many ways, there are no definitive rules as to which tools to use – just choose the ones that you feel are best for the job in hand. Note: the chisels and gouges need to cut the wood very smoothly, especially in and around the short grain areas, so if you feel the tool crushing the wood rather than crisply slicing, then stop and bring the blade to a keen edge on an oilstone and strop.

Once you have established the depth of the lowered ground and have worked the smaller more difficult areas, you can take a larger tool and clear the whole waste area. Try to work the lowered ground so that it is smoothly and confidently cut, but do not overwork it so that you remove the tool marks.

Modelling the relief design

Refresh your memory by looking at the photographs and the various bits of collected inspirational material. Now, take a magnifying glass to the motifs and see how the forms have been achieved – for example, if you focus on the leaves and flowers, you will see that although overall the design comes across as being strongly worked, the individual details are rather stylized. In fact, there has been no real attempt to carve the forms in the sense of trying to achieve realistically modelled flowers – the motifs have been boldly carved with a series of swift chip-carved cuts and nicks. This means that the carver must have been working efficiently and at speed.

Now, take the curved and straight gouges, and work the flowers and leaves so that they are gently dished from side-to-centre. Note the depth and placing of the leaf veins, and the flower centres. Set these in with stop-cuts, and then continue to scoop out the wood from side-to-centre. As you are working, you will have to either keep moving around the wood or re-positioning the wood in the clamp.

Continue dishing out the main flower, scooping out the ring that goes round the main flower head and hollowing out supporting flowers and leaves. Note: be extra careful when you are carving the flowers and avoid running the gouge past the stop-cuts otherwise you may damage the short-grain veins and central buttons.

Finishing

Clear away the waste wood, and once again have a close look at the photographs. Concentrate your attention on the leaves at the bottom of the panel and note how the dished forms have been worked with a series of nicked and cut details. There is no fussy over-modelling or scratching about – the carver has simply taken a basic tool like a knife or straight gouge and rhythmically segmented the leaves along their length. The small leaves, the main stems and the small flowers have all been worked in a similar manner – half a dozen or so cuts and a little bit of fine modelling.

Start by sharpening all your tools, and then work all the details. When you have achieved what you consider to be a worked and modelled relief with all the motifs standing out boldly and confidently, then take a flat-bent tool and tidy up the angles between the low ground and the raised design. Make sure that all the angles are clean and free from rough wood, burrs and torn grain.

Ideally the marks left by the tools should create a natural, attractive finish. However if this is not the case, go over the whole ground area and texture it with a punch. Having done this, take a long-haired brush and clean out all the little nooks and crannies. Finally, rub down and darken the oak with linseed oil, leave it to dry and then polish with beeswax. Note: if you want the oil to dry quickly, add a little turpentine – 1 part turpentine to 3 parts oil.

WHITTLING AND CARVING A LOVE SPOON

LOVE TOKENS are labours of love that were traditionally carved by lovers and presented to their sweethearts. Lovelorn country lads would take up a piece of easily carved wood – usually close-grained varieties such as yew, lime or sycamore – and with a few basic tools would set to and whittle complicated, almost impossible to carve, tokens of love. Beautiful, linked love chains, busks, knitting-stick holders, spoons and all manner of small treen were worked with the most extravagant and intricate symbols of love. Free from the need to carve usable objects to a practical pattern, the lover tended to let his imagination and carving skills run wild. Consequently there are, for example, plump, wood-carved hearts covered with entwined initials, dates and coded messages; corset busks carved and incised with love hearts, dates, names and interlocking love rings; and knitting-needle sheaths with cleverly worked caged balls.

The project photograph (see page 105) shows a beautifully worked love spoon with all the characteristic design elements – initials, dates, love hearts, the ancient magic hex-circle and the bars of a 'lover's cage'. Traditionally, love spoons were, by their very nature, one-off whittlings without function, made by love-motivated amateurs. They required no special tools, woods or design skills – just a good sharp knife, a piece of wood and the romantic need of the lover to express his love.

TOOLS & EQUIPMENT

- Workbench
- Pencil
- Metal rule
- Vice
- Coping saw or fine-blade bow saw
- Straight-bladed knife
- Oilstone
- Slipstone
- Leather strop
- Compass
- A crooked or hooked knife
- Callipers
- Hand drill with an ⅛in bit
- Fret saw

MATERIALS

- A piece of straight-grained knot-free sycamore measuring 12 × 4 × 1in
- Workout paper
- Tracing paper
- Beeswax polish

The scale is three squares to 1in. With this project it is most important that you choose your wood with care. Choose a straight-grained material and make absolutely sure that it is free from knots and shakes.

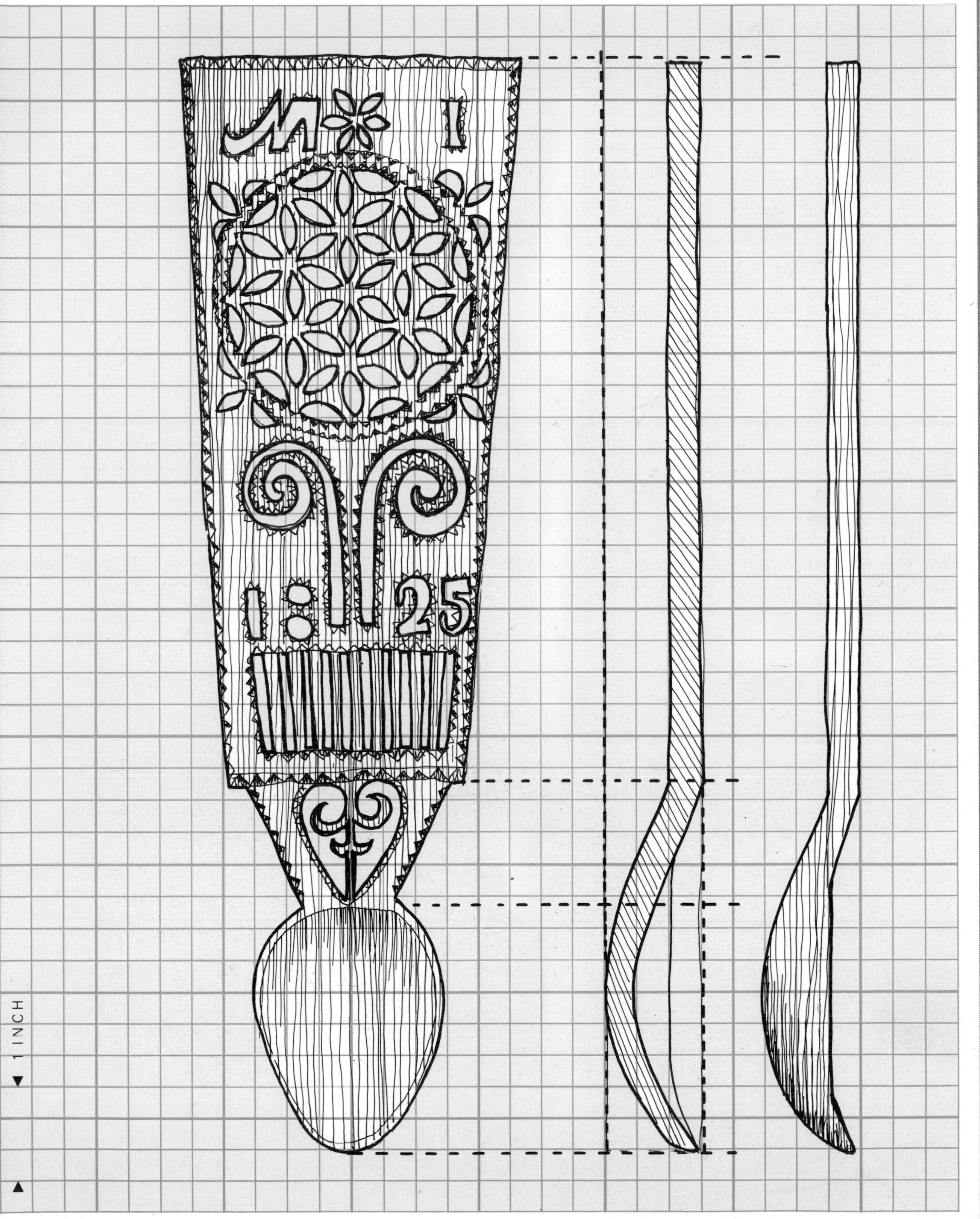
1 INCH

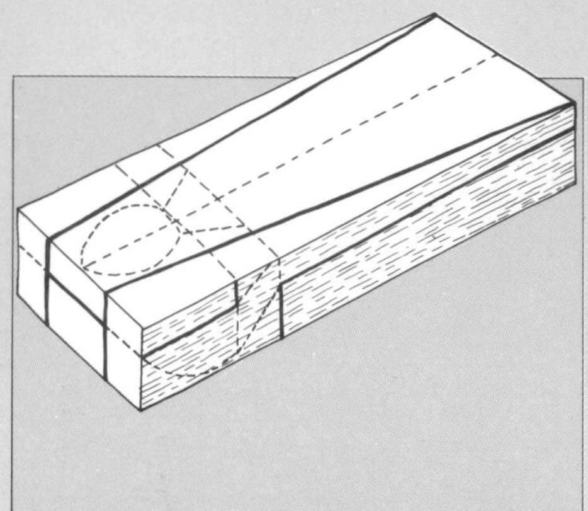

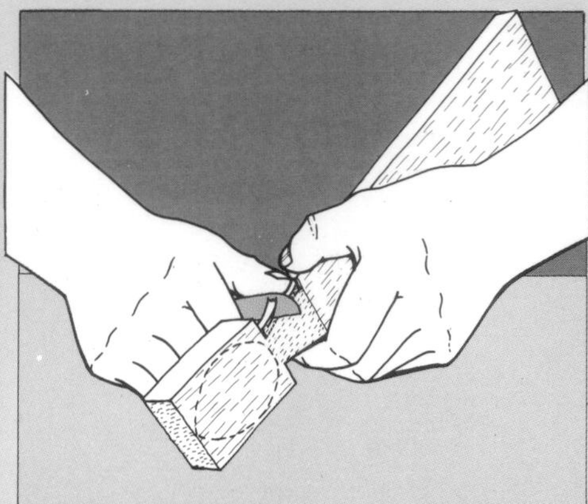

Considering the design and setting out the basic form

Have a look at the working drawing and the photograph, and see how the love spoon has been carved, whittled and pierced. Study the design in detail and note the hollow, rather delicate, concave dishing of the spoon bowl and the various motifs including the bars, date, initials, love heart and the large, pierced hex circle. See how the carver has concentrated his efforts not so much on three-dimensional sculptural form, but rather more on two-dimensional surface decoration.

When you have spent time considering the design and the related technical implications – such as, for example, the difficult to carve, short-grain areas within the hex – then take the workout paper, pencil and measure, and make a full-size working drawing. When you draw up the various elevations remember to modify the date and initials.

Take the piece of knot-free sycamore and check it over for quality. Make sure the wood is free from bad grain twists, stains, end splits and insect attack. When you have done this, take a tracing of the master design and transfer the lines of the traced profile onto the various faces of the wood. When you are setting out the design, make sure that the main body of the spoon is kept well clear of possible wood-grain problem areas. Finally, when the lines of the spoon have been transferred, blocked-in, and altogether clearly established, take a pencil and label the profiles 'top', 'side' and 'end'.

Cutting out the blank

Secure the wood in the vice, arrange the tools and have a look at the inspirational material. Now, take the large coping saw, or the fine-blade bow saw, cut out the profiles and clear away the waste wood. Work the top profile first. Try to keep the saw blade at right-angles to the working face of the wood, and take extra care when you come to short-grain areas.

When the waste wood has been removed, look at the spoon blank side-on and re-establish the lines of the side profile. Have another look at the working drawing and see how the main body of the spoon handle is level with the topmost surface of the piece of wood. Having done this, set the wood in the vice once again, and clear away the waste from below the handle with the saw. When all the waste has been removed or 'chopped out', the spoon form should be recognizable.

Take a pencil and go over the blank spoon setting out a few reference points – that is, the width and position of the spoon neck, the thickness of the bowl and the thickness of wood at the handle. Now, take the wood in one hand and the straight knife in the other, and carefully make stop-cuts around the spoon neck and at the point where the neck meets the face of the handle.

Hold the wood so that the handle end is nearest to you, then take the knife and whittle from one stop-cut to another. In this way, establish the broad general shape of the spoon neck and the bowl. Note: it is most important that after about five or ten minutes of whittling, you stop and re-sharpen the knife.

Setting out the handle design

When the overall spoon form has been roughed out, take the knife and with a firm thumb-pushing paring cut, go over the whole spoon bringing the surface of the wood to a dappled, tooled finish. Do not try to shape the underside and dishing of the bowl at this stage but just shape-up the profile of the handle.

With a pencil, measure and some workout paper, draw up the various motifs to size and shape. Work out the proportions of the love heart, decide how your dates and initials will fit in relationship to the rest of the design, and use a compass to draw out the pierced hex circle. Adjust and modify all the motifs and details until they fit into your design scheme.

Take a sheet of tracing paper and transfer the lines of the design onto the working face of the handle. Take a soft pencil and go over the transferred design thickening up lines, shading in areas that need to be cut away, and marking out the chip-carved borders and margins. When this has been done, stop for a moment and consider how the design will work in terms of the wood grain. For example, if you look at the photograph you will see that in certain instances the wood grain is very short and weak to the extent that parts of the design have broken off or are split.

Finally, go over the whole design and generally bring all the details to good order. Note: if you wish, there is no reason why you should not leave out part of the design and have, for example, an incised message, more piercing or more hearts.

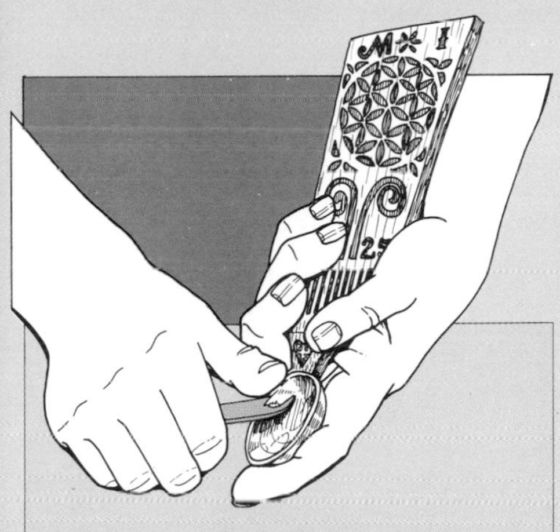

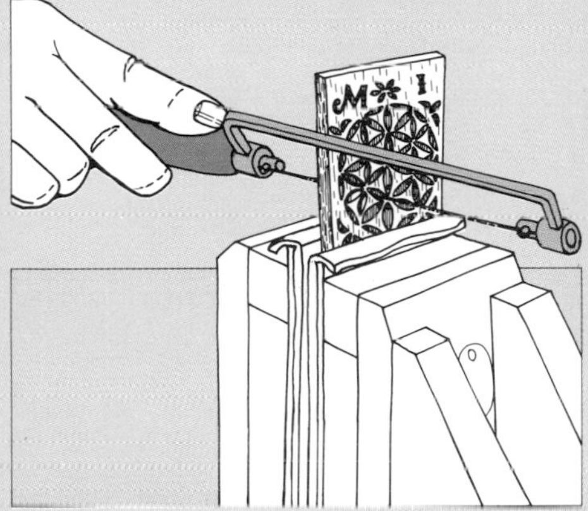

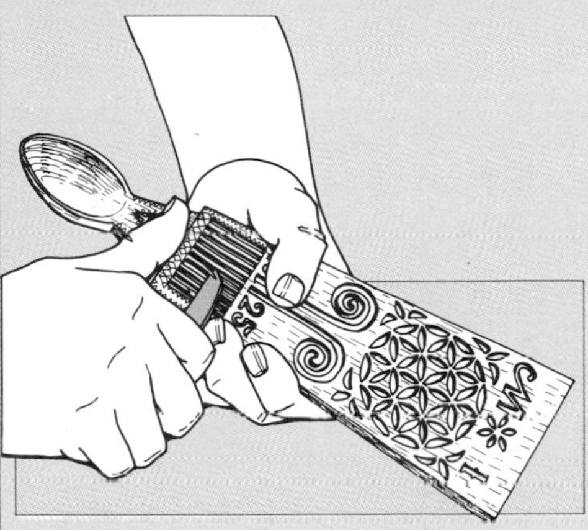

Carving the bowl of the spoon

Take the straight or curved knife and start to shape and whittle the underside of the bowl. Do not try to achieve a finished form at this stage but just trim off all the corners and edges, and establish the humped shape of the back of the spoon.

Having cut back and removed the main bulk of waste wood from the underside of the bowl, take the callipers and note the total thickness of wood between the top of the rim and the underside of the bowl. Take a pencil and clearly mark out the thickness of the bowl rim. Now take the crooked, or hooked, knife and cut away the waste wood. Work from bowl rim to centre, gently removing long scoops of wood. Always try to cut across or at an angle to the grain, and gradually manoeuvre, turn and gouge out the characteristic spoon-bowl hollow.

Throughout the working process, stop from time to time and assess the thickness of the bowl wall and base. If you have any doubts as to the amount of wood either removed or remaining, use the callipers to take a series of thickness readings. Aim for a wood thickness of about ¼in at the bowl base, and gradually feather up to a nicely rounded rim of about ⅛in thickness.

Bear in mind that with every paring cut you will be getting closer and closer to the spoon form that sits just below the surface of the wood. Work with great care, proceed slowly, and only remove the finest wisps of wood. Finally, cradle the spoon in your palm or lap and bring the surfaces of the bowl to a good, slightly rippled finish.

Piercing the handle motifs

Having whittled and worked the rather complex spoon bowl and having double-checked that all the drawn motifs work in relationship to each other and the grain of the wood, you can begin work on the handle. Set the wood in the cloth-muffled jaws of a vice (as illustrated above), take the hand drill fitted with the ⅛in bit and work pilot holes through all the motifs that are to be pierced and wasted.

Take the fret saw, unhitch the blade from its frame and pass it through a selected pilot hole. Fix the blade to its frame and then start to fret out the motif window. Work the saw with a steady, even stroke, trying all the time to keep the angle of cut at about 90° to the working face of the wood. When you come to the very delicate short-grain areas, be extra careful that you do not force the pace and twist or break the blade.

Continue, gently sawing and piercing one motif after another – that is, unhitching the blade, selecting the next area to be cut, refixing the blade, etc – until all the design windows have been worked. As you saw and fret out each of the windows, make sure that the cut is on the waste side of the drawn design: aim to keep the cut about ⅛in away from the drawn line. When you come to a tight angle or curve, do not stop sawing and try to wrench the blade round, but instead increase the speed of cut. As you work the various pierced motifs, you will have to continually manoeuvre the wood and the saw, so that the saw blade is always presented with the next line of cut.

Whittling, chip carving and finishing

Looking at the photograph, see how most of the designs have been brought to a crisp finish and then delicately edged with little triangular chip-cut nicks.

Bearing in mind how fragile some of the short-grained areas are, cradle the wood in the palm of your hand and, taking the straight knife, swiftly work all the raw, sawn edges. Pull the knife blade around the wood with a firm, thumb-supported paring action. Do not try to slice off great chunks of wood, but just remove little slivers until, little by little, you remove the bulk of waste.

As you work, so you will have to re-position the wood, change the angle of the knife, re-sharpen the blade, and generally work across the grain of the wood with short, crisp cuts. Never cut directly into the grain or try to hack off the wood with broad sweeping strokes. If you do this, the blade will almost certainly slip, run into the grain and split the wood. When you have whittled the bars of the 'lover's cage', brought all the sawn edges to a fine finish, and reduced the bridging wood within the hex to a minimum, put down the knife, stand back from your work and consider the total design.

When you feel that the love spoon is as refined as you want it, and you dare not cut away any more structural wood, take the straight knife and work the chip-cuts around the various edges and motifs. Finally, rub a little beeswax polish into the wood and consider the job finished. Note: if by accident you do split off an area of short-grain wood, improvise and change the design accordingly.

MD
18
56

LEFT PROJECT PHOTOGRAPH
Welsh love spoon. This example of a love spoon is rather special because it is more delicately carved that some of the earlier spoons. Love tokens of a similar nature were also made in Scotland and Sweden.

FAR LEFT *Nineteenth-century love spoons. All the usual motifs of love spoons can be seen here including rings for eternal love, hearts, initials and a date. Spoons of this particular type were made in Wales as gifts for betrothed maidens.*

CARVING AN ART NOUVEAU APPLIQUE RELIEF

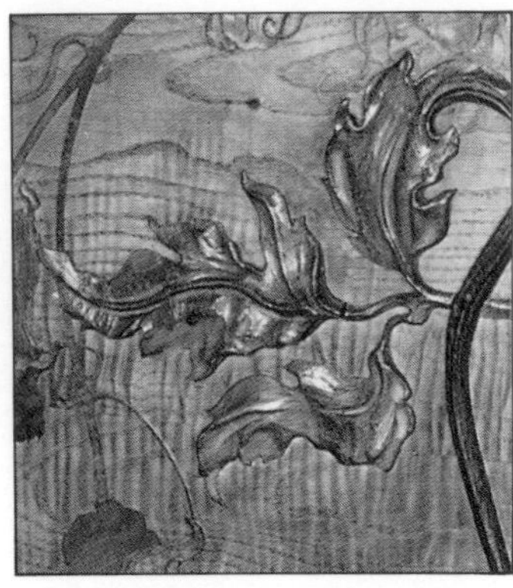

AN APPLIQUÉ or an applied relief carving is one where the motif that projects up from the flat ground is an applied addition. Of course, the term is a contradiction because in theory a relief carving means that the ground has to be cut away and lowered. However, with an applied relief, the motif is placed onto a ground that is already flat.

Many traditional carvers consider that the use of applied decoration is a poor, degraded alternative to using solid ground wood: they feel that the appliqué technique is in some way false. Having said this, if you look at many Art Nouveau woodcarvings – furniture, architectural details, etc – you will see that the applied reliefs are certainly not cover-ups in the sense that the carver has tried to use inferior materials or short-cuts in technique. In fact, it has been said that Art Nouveau carved appliqués are an explorative extension of the more traditional techniques. Carvers of the period experimented with all manner of exciting material and technique compositions.

Emile Gallé (1846–1904) was one such innovative artist/craftsman who designed and produced the most amazing pieces of sculptured furniture – tables with floriated carved appliqué additions, chairs with inlays and carved overlays, and screens with inlays, overlays, marquetry, veneers, carving and painting. Gallé experimented with a huge range of woodworking techniques. His philosophy was that if it worked, then it was valid. It is said of Gallé, 'he made wood suit his whims; he was always the master, never the servant.'

TOOLS & EQUIPMENT

- Workbench
- Pencil
- Coping saw
- Vice
- 2 clamping boards
- G-clamps
- Bench holdfast
- Small straight veiner
- Small straight gouge
- Shallow gouge
- Deep gouge
- Oilstone
- Shaped slipstones
- Leather strop
- Small straight chisel
- Carver's knife
- Soft-haired brush

MATERIALS

- A slab of ½in thick, straight-grained, knot-free lime (of size to suit)
- A slab of 1in thick ground wood (of type and size to suit)
- Grid paper
- Tracing paper
- PVA glue
- Wax polish

Adjust the scale to suit the project that you have in mind. See how the applied wood is ½in thick and the ground wood is 1in thick. If you decide to work this project on an existing piece of furniture, you will need to modify the wood thicknesses.

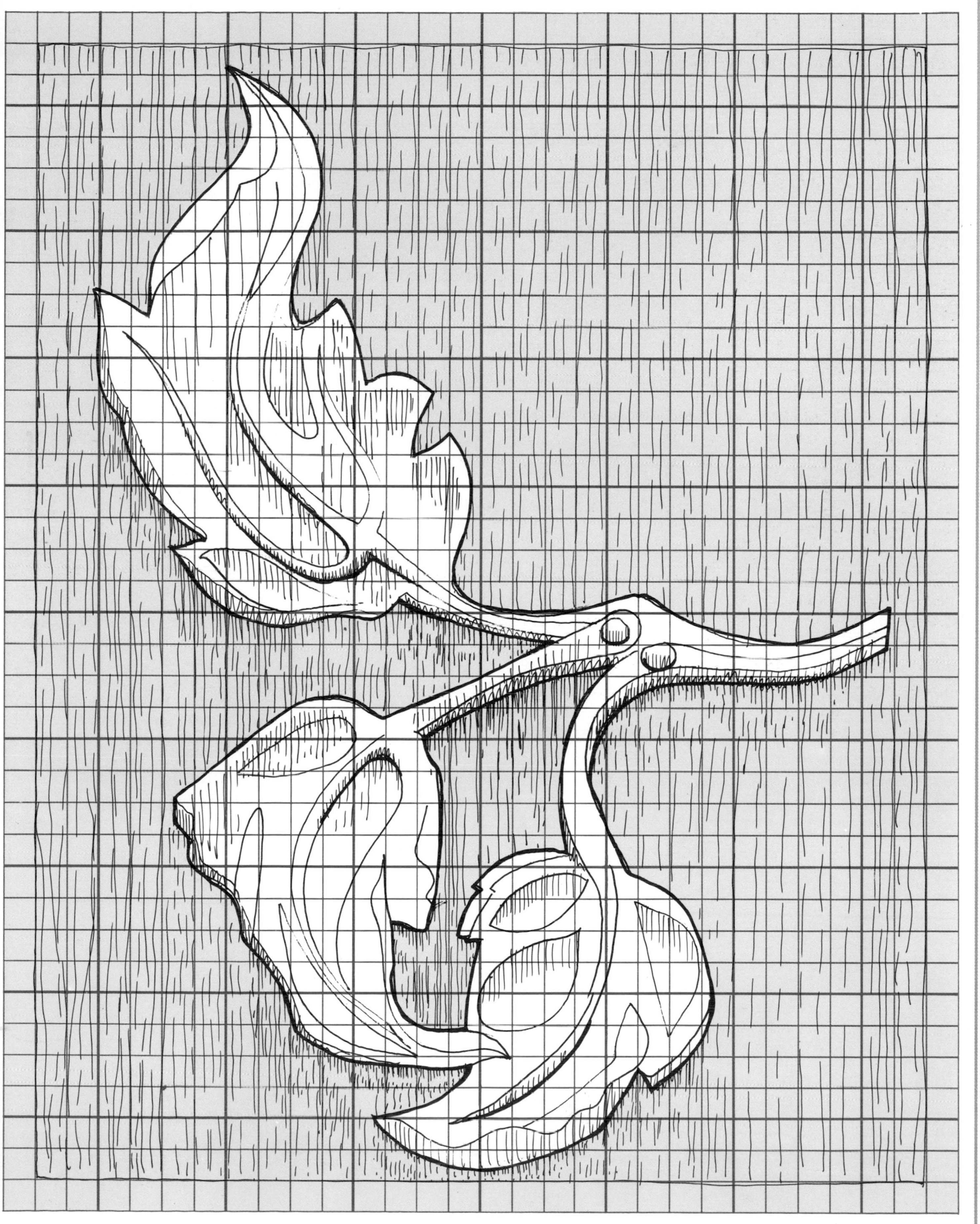

BELOW *Chair made in about 1900 by Louis Majorelle. The carved, applied and pierced motifs at the back of the chair are typically Art Nouveau. Notice how the sensuous forms run in a continuous smooth line from head to foot.*

ABOVE *Carved detail of an Art Nouveau* bonheur-du-jour *(writing desk). Take a magnifying glass to the carving and the enamel medallion, and see how the characteristic lily has been used as the main design feature. Note also how the delicate carving has been applied on top of a veneered base.*

RIGHT PROJECT PHOTOGRAPH *Screen made by Emile Gallé in about 1900. This screen is a complex piece using just about every woodworking technique including veneering, overlaying, appliqué work, piercing and painting. Characteristic of Gallé, the basically simple forms have then been loaded with stylized and applied motifs.*

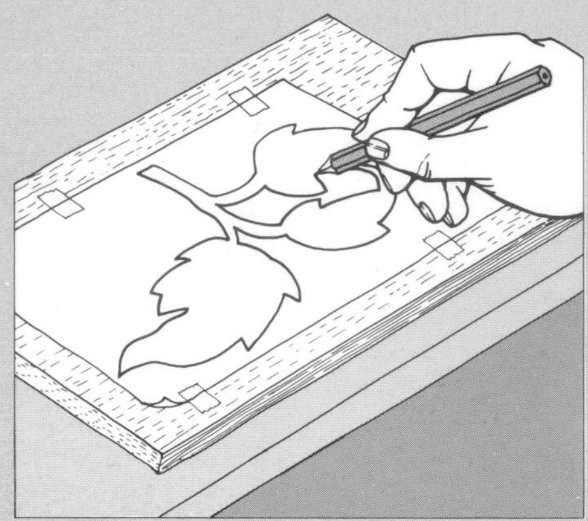

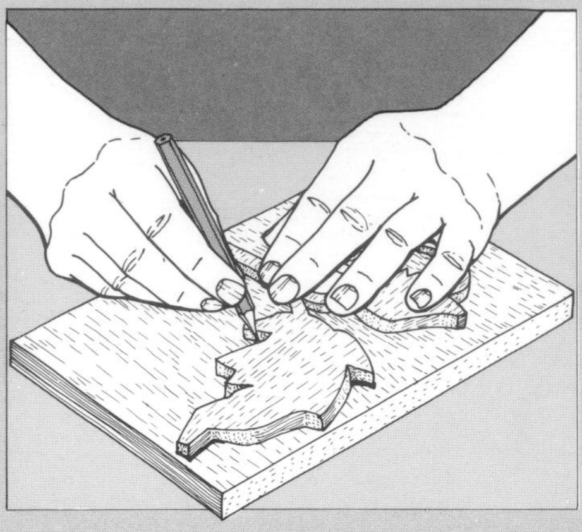

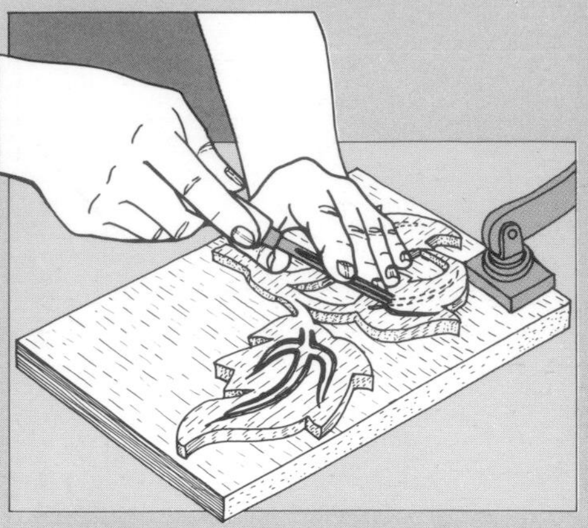

Considering the technique and master design

Before you put pencil to paper or tool to wood, have a long look at the working drawing and the photographs. Study the characteristic Art Nouveau furniture motifs – the tendrils, curling flowers and leaves. Notice how all the elements come together to give the impression of a living, growing organic whole.

Take a magnifying glass to the photograph of the Gallé screen (see page 109), and see how the piece has not been relief-carved from a single slab of wood, but instead is a beautiful composite of built-up veneers, overlays and applied carvings. Run your eyes down the main tendril and see how the grain of the wood is at variance to the grain of the light-coloured ground.

Move the magnifying glass slowly along the leaves and tendrils that go to make up the edge of the screen and the motifs, and note the breaks, the different grain runs, and the joins. When you have spent time analyzing the design, structure and form, have another look at the working drawing and see how this project concentrates on the three-leaf appliqué motifs of the larger whiplash vine.

Take your grid paper and a pencil, and draw up your own motif. Bear in mind all the associated problems of working with slender sections of wood and the difficulties of carving delicate, curling forms. Adjust and modify the project to suit your experience and skill level. Finally, notice how the appliqué carving has been worked as a panel.

Transferring the design, and fretting and mounting the blank

When you have made your master design and have considered the form and composition in terms of wood grain and technique, take a piece of tracing paper and make a fine copy. Having done this, place the slab of straight-grained lime on the workbench and transfer the lines of the traced design onto the working face of the wood.

Now, take the coping saw, put the wood in the vice or on a cutting table and fret out the overall form. Work with care, especially on the fragile short-grain areas, and cut the motif free from the waste ground wood. Having cleared the workbench of all clutter, take the cut-out blank and the thick slab of ground wood, and have a trial 'placing'. For example, the motif might be placed on a ground of lime, or it might become an extension of a carving like the Gallé screen. Alternatively it could be mounted so that its colour and grain contrasts with a darker ground wood.

Once you have achieved a well-considered placing and the choice of base or ground wood suits your design scheme, take a pencil and mark a few key layout, reference and registration points. Having done this, liberally smear both the fretted blank and the ground wood with PVA glue, and with great care bring the two together. Make sure the various registration points are aligned and put the glued wood between two clamping boards. Have another check to see that the alignment is as it should be and clamp the boards together with the G-clamps.

First cuts

After about 24 hours or when the glue is dry, take the work out of the clamping boards, set it on the workbench, and then arrange all your carving tools so that they are comfortably to hand. Start by having a brief look at the working drawing and inspirational material – see how the Art Nouveau forms curl, undulate, writhe and look altogether juicy and believable.

Now, take a soft pencil to the appliqué blank and mark out the ribbing of the tendrils, leaf veins, areas that need to be undercut, and the various lobes, swellings and stems that go to make up the plant form. Having done this, secure the wood with a bench holdfast. Taking a V-section tool such as the small straight veiner, go over the wood cutting in the lines of the design. Work the gouges with a controlled cut – that is, try to guide, hold and manoeuvre the tool with one hand, and push and thrust with the other.

When you have established the general undulations and ridges of the design, stop for a moment, sharpen the tools and consider the next cuts. Now take a small shallow gouge and, with great care, go around the motif profile stabbing down and slightly under, so that the blade slips through the applied wood and meets the ground. Do not stab too hard or use the tool as a lever; just mark out the motif with a series of well-placed cuts. When you have established the slightly undercut profile, take a small straight chisel or a knife, and hook and slice the undercuts, leaving a smooth, clean outline at the point where the applied wood meets the ground.

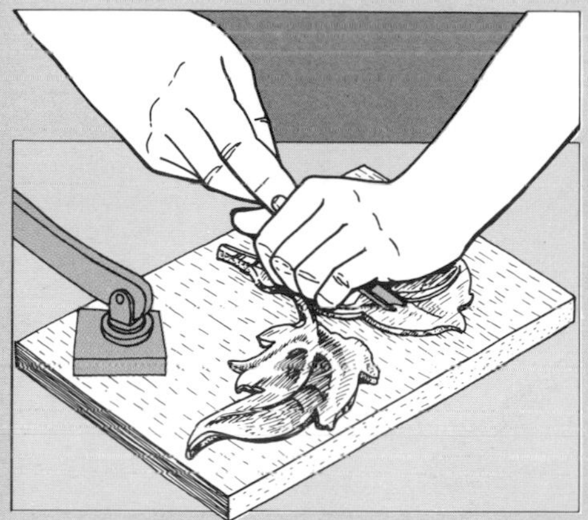

Bosting and roughing-in

Once the applied motif has been cut-in and undercut as described, it must be bosted and roughed-in. Work with a variety of shallow and deep gouges, and carve the wood so as to give the tendrils and leaves form. Leave the veins at a high level and make sure that the rippled leaf curls are left proud. Run the keen-bladed tools over the form, working with generous rhythmic sweeps of the gouge, and feel and follow the tools around and over the grain.

As you slice and sweep with the gouge, follow through with a slight rocking of the tool which will prevent the corners of the gouge from tearing the wood. In any one cut, the blade will shave away the crispest of curls and then come to a halt after juddering into an area of twisted grain. This is inevitable but when it happens you should stop, re-position the wood and then approach the cut from a different direction.

If, as you are roughing-in, the carving appears to be getting flat and formless then take a sketchbook, a soft pencil and a wedge of Plasticine, and spend time modelling and drawing from nature. For example, you might take a leaf or a plant stem and have a close look at its structure, study its leaf curls and notice how the stems are fluted or strengthened. Above all, see how one form flows, swells and grows into another. Berries, leaves, flower heads and stems all need to be looked at with a fresh, 'carver's eye'.

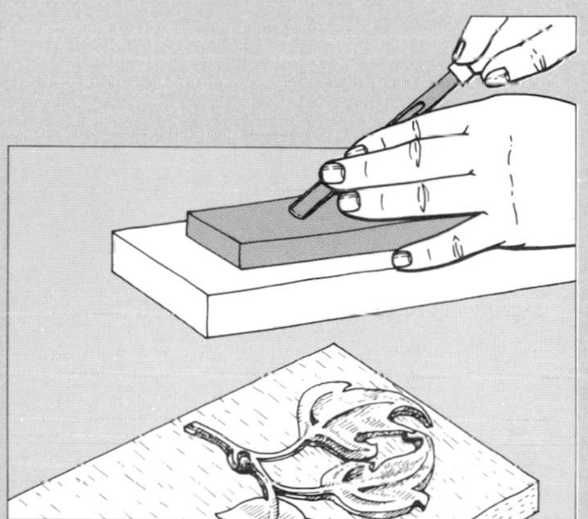

Modelling the form

With the working drawing and sketches fresh in your mind, it is now the time to begin modelling. You can cut in the fine details, consider tool texture and generally bring the work to a bold and vigorous finish. Before you start, however, it is most important that you sharpen all the tools with the oilstone, the shaped slipstones and the leather strop. Woodcarving tools need to be extremely sharp – that is, if the blade does not slice through the wood with the minimum of effort and leave the wood looking shiny, then it is dull-edged. Always start the final modelling by bringing the tools to a keen edge.

As you begin modelling, do not attempt for an overworked smooth texture, but allow the delicate dappled scoops to describe the flow of the form. Try to let the tool marks lead your eye over and around the form. Remove wisps of wood from leaf hollows, sharpen the vein creases with the knife, and give the leaves a generously rolled, but slightly angled, leading edge.

There will come a point when the carving begins to 'come alive' and it is then advisable to take a break and consider how best you might give the carving style, texture and character. For example, if you look at the Gallé screen, you will see that although the overall carving suggests lifelike forms such as snaking tendrils and leaves, the carver has nevertheless used, interpreted and exaggerated the forms. As you gain confidence, put away all the working drawings and let your own eye, the flow of the grain and the character of the wood determine the final modelling.

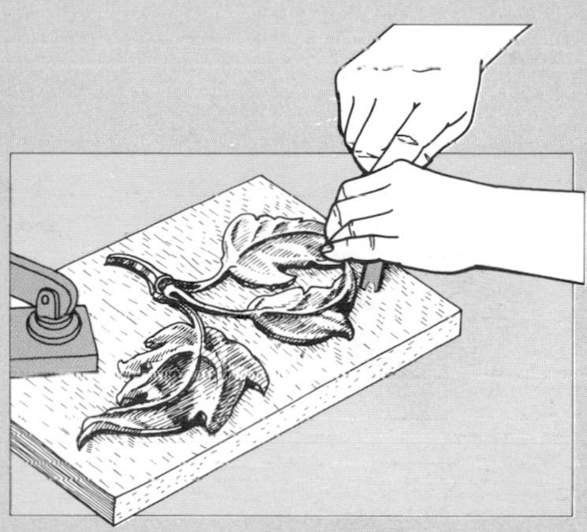

Final cuts and finishing

When you consider the carving nearly finished, take the shallow gouge and the knife, and start to clean up the carving. First, go over the wood, bringing the forms to a good order with the lightest of touches by trimming back coarse end grain, removing burrs and sharpening the undercuts. When this has been done, take the knife, strop it to a razor-sharp edge and go along the tendril undercuts making sure that the motif meets the ground with long, smoothly worked cuts.

Now, take the front-bent shallow gouge and clean up the rest of the ground work – try to finish with the ground, as this allows you to remove all the small marks left by the undercutting tools. When the carving is finished, take a soft-haired brush and go over the work, brushing out all the creases and hollows.

Stand back from the work and give it a critical looking over. Ask yourself whether the ground could be cut a little lower or should the fluting along the stems be a bit more positive. If necessary go over the work putting in a few last cuts. When you are sure that all is correct, put away the tools and clear the working area. Now, take a soft cotton cloth and some plain wax and give the whole carving a generous waxing.

Finally, take a stiff brush and, being careful not to damage fragile short-grain areas, bring the wood to a mellow, burnished finish. Note: after a week or so the wax will have sunk into the wood and it will be necessary to apply another coat.

CHAPTER 4

WOODCARVING IN THE ROUND

CARVING 'in the round' differs from flat and semi-flat relief carving only in that it has to be worked and seen from all sides. The term 'in the round' is therefore applicable to any free-standing, or almost free-standing, sculptural carving.

So why, you might ask, are the 'whittled treen' and 'love spoon' projects included in the chapter on relief work, and why is the Grinling Gibbons posy — which is after all part of a relief panel — placed in the 'carved in the round' section? Well, although the posy is indeed part of a panel, it has been worked and undercut so that for all intents and purposes it is three-dimensional and sculptural. And the same goes for the Chippendale chair lattice; certainly it is a deep relief carving that has the waste ground pierced, but it was designed to be seen from all sides. The misericord is another case in point. Technically it could be termed a deep relief, but it is so undercut and sculptural that in spirit it is 'in the round'.

If as a beginner this confuses you, bear in mind that there has always been an overlap and some slight disagreement as to what is relief work and what is carving in the round. That apart, carving in the round is more complicated than relief work, owing to the depth and bulk of the wood and the need of the carver to work forms that are three-dimensional.

The man in the street looks at a sculpture and expects to see a fully-rounded believable form, whether the piece is abstract or realistic. This desire for full-scale form — that is, a form that can be walked round and viewed from all angles — requires that well-considered drawings be made, and that the wood be built up. The parts of the carving that are to project — for example, an extended arm, or in the case of the horse, the head angling out from the neck — have, for ease of working and economical use of materials, to be built up from several pieces of wood.

Of course, it is possible to start with a tree-trunk and then 'discover' the form deep within the wood, but this method of working is fraught with problems, not the least being the initial weight of the material and the danger of the tree developing 'shakes' (cracks) down the length of the grain. This is not to say that building up a bulk of wood from small pieces is the easy option — it requires very careful planning and a knowledge of jointing. The component pieces can be pegged and glued, screwed, nailed or bolted — it does not matter as long as all the joints are firm, and the individual sections of wood relate in terms of grain and strength to the desired carving.

As for equipment — meaning a bench and a method of fixing the wood while it is being carved — it can be stood on the floor, fixed to the bench with a patent screw, holdfast or vice, or it can be hand-held. The rule of thumb is that the method should work for you. The same can be said of the tools; some carvers enjoy working with bandsaws and all manner of power tools, while others will only use slower, more direct and physical gouges, saws, chisels and rasps.

The projects themselves may suggest that you use a specific tool, material, technique or approach, but this is not to say that you must work in this way. In the first instance use the tools and materials that are to hand. Thus you might work on a stout kitchen table using an axe, knife and a piece of firewood, and then later, when you understand your needs, you can buy in additional tools and materials.

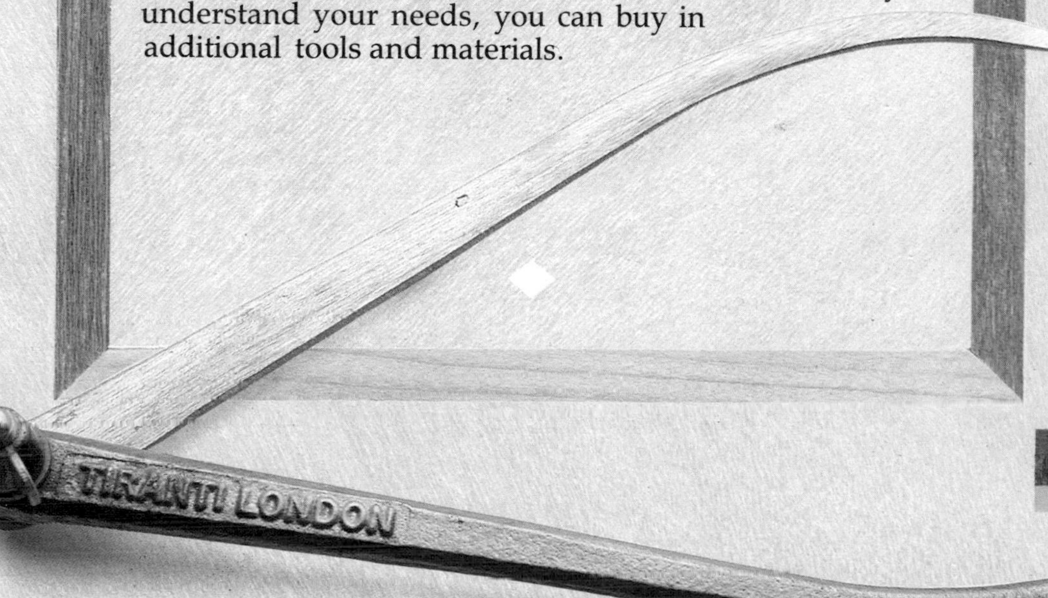

Carving an Oak Misericord in the English Medieval Tradition

MISERICORDS are carved seats that are found in many older English churches, cathedrals and minsters. In the past, monks and priests who had to attend very long services ingeniously devised slender shelves on the underside of the hinged choir stall seats. This meant that while appearing to be standing, the priests were actually resting and taking the weight off their feet in a semi-sitting position.

As these little shelves were hidden from view and designed for such a lowly purpose, the carvers were free to carve almost anything that struck their fancy. With this unique opportunity for self-expression, they worked everything from grotesquely lewd figures, through folk-tale groups and anti-establishment cartoons to ordinary everyday scenes. Unicorns, men and maids at play, mermaids, friars dressed up as pigs, rude tales, popular romances and strange fabulous creatures were all popular subject matter for the medieval woodcarvers.

From the carpenter's point of view, the misericord is no more than a narrow shelf which needs a bracket on its underside. This project concentrates on the carved bracketed support under the shelf. For reasons of design and structure, the misericord carving has to be small, compact and triangular with one side of the triangle forming the underside of the shelf or corbel. Also for structural reasons, the carvings are worked in very deep relief and, most important, are carved from the same slab of wood as the seat itself. All these specifications mean that the carvings need to be worked from massive slabs or balks of wood (usually oak).

TOOLS & EQUIPMENT

- Workbench
- Work board
- Callipers
- Pencils
- Carving knives
- Bench holdfast
- Small straight chisel
- Deep U-section gouge
- Mallet
- Flat spoon-bit gouge
- Front-bent shallow gouge
- Small gouges
- Oilstone
- Shaped slipstones
- Strop
- Soft brush

MATERIALS

- A well-seasoned balk of oak measuring 24in along the grain, 12in wide and 6in deep
- 15lb of Plasticine
- Workout paper
- Tracing paper
- Wax polish

The scale of the top working drawing is nine squares to 12in. When you come to setting out the design, do not try to work every last detail, but rather aim for the big broad shapes.

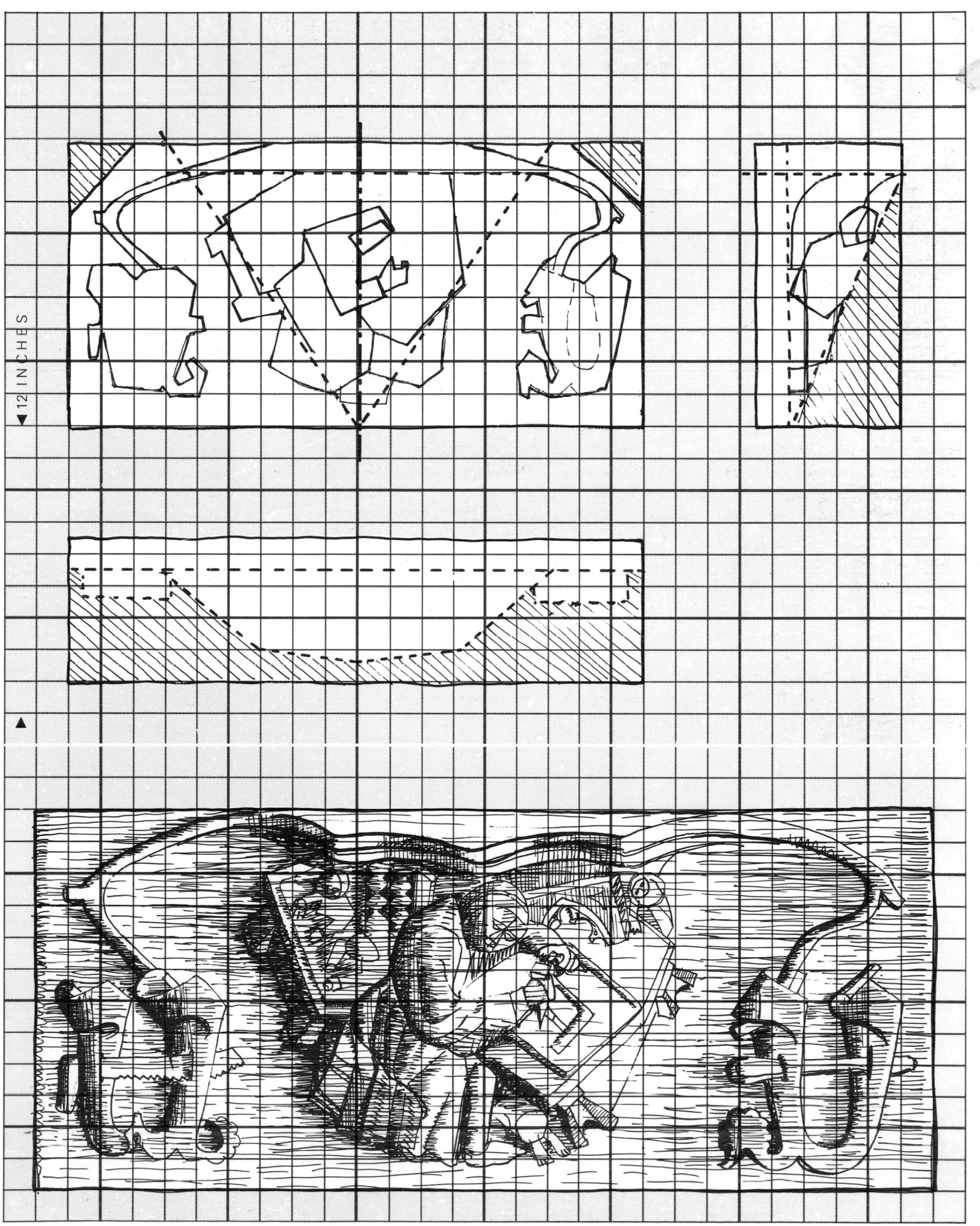
12 INCHES

PROJECT PHOTOGRAPH *Fifteenth-century misericord from St. Nicholas Chapel, King's Lynn, England. The scene depicted on this misericord shows a master carver working at his bench with a square and a pair of dividers. His two apprentices are to the left, and another is bringing him a jug. He has a dog at his feet, and in the background can be seen some carved tracery and two lengths of cresting.*

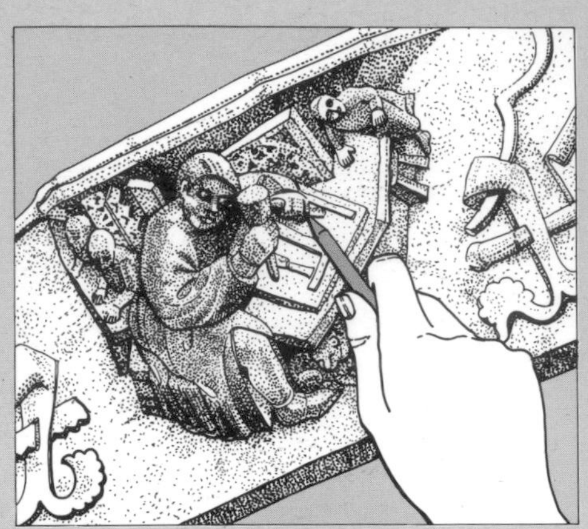

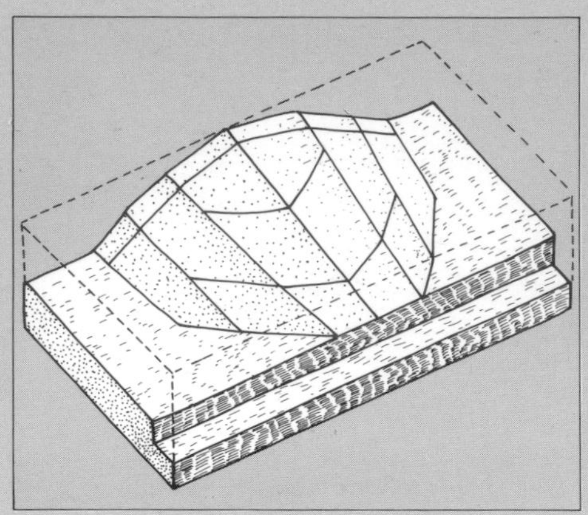

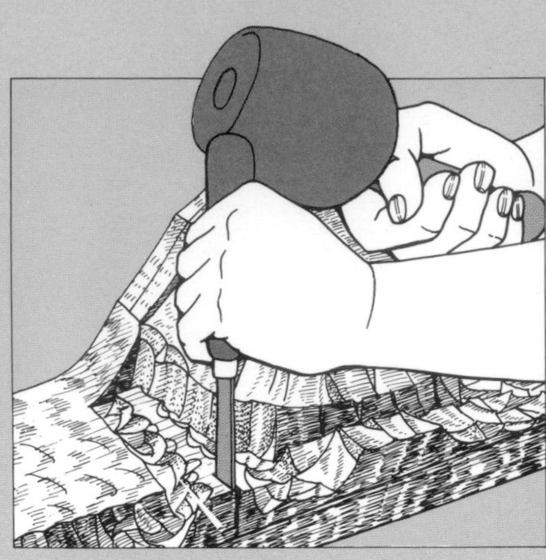

Considering the project and making a Plasticine maquette

If you can, visit a cathedral, church, minster or museum, and search out collections of pre-sixteenth century misericords. You could have a look at the carvings, and note the unusual depth and bulk of the wood as well as the overall strength and liveliness of the design themes. You might even run your hands over and under the carving, and let your mind dwell on how the medieval carvers were able to achieve such natural and uninhibited forms.

You would see how the carvers were restricted by structure – the total misericord consisted of a shelf or corbel that jutted out about 5–6in, a compact bracket, a smooth-curved corbel edge, decorative supports to terminate the leading edge of the corbel and a slab seat. The carvers would have been working with massive pieces of oak that were at least 6–7in thick.

Having considered all these points, you would do well to study the inspirational material, working drawing and anything else you may have, such as museum postcards.

Begin by taking the Plasticine and work board, and set about making a full-size model or maquette. Consider how the figures within the misericord relate to the corbel, see how the forms have been distorted to fit the wood, and then model the Plasticine accordingly. As you are modelling, bear in mind how you want your carving to be – the theme, type of figure, pose – and modify the maquette to fit.

Drawing the design and setting out the wood

When the maquette is finished, put it to one side and set out the paper, tracing paper, callipers and a pencil. Take a series of calliper readings from the maquette noting that this carving has great depth in relation to its size, and then draw out the main elevation profiles. Draw up a fully-worked front view that corresponds to the view in the photograph (see page 117), and then work several less-detailed secondary views.

Check over the balk of oak and make sure that it is free from dead knots, splits and bad grain twists. Having done this, set the slab of wood on the workbench so that the best 24 × 12in face is uppermost. Take a tracing of the master design and transfer the lines of the design onto the working face of the wood. Thicken up the main profile lines and clearly label the wood 'top', 'front', 'side' and 'waste'.

If you have any doubts at this stage as to how the figures are to come out of the wood or how the slab is to be worked, refresh your eye by looking at the inspirational material again. If you are not completely confident as to the working order, mould another scaled-down block of Plasticine and have a trial 'dry run' – take a knife or gouge to the Plasticine and chart out the first cuts. It is vital that you have a clear picture in your mind of just how the design is to emerge from the wood before you start to work.

First cuts

Secure the wood with a holdfast and arrange the tools so that they are comfortably to hand. Start by taking a straight chisel, a deep-scoop gouge and a mallet, and begin setting in the lines of the design. Working on the front face of the wood, go around the design keeping to the waste side of the drawn lines, and chop straight down into the wood. Do not try to work any of the smaller details; leave areas of wood that are big enough for the details to be carved at a later stage.

Take the deep U-section gouge around the waste side of the design and work a deep trench. Run the gouge around the trench in several stages until it is about ¾–1½in deep. Having done this, take the mallet and a small straight chisel and work carefully between the drawn lines and the trench. Try to chop straight down so that the wood on the waste side crumbles away.

Continue working until the various design areas look like islands or plateaux, each surrounded by a deep-cut trench. Of course, as the various parts of the carving need to rise up out of the ground at different angles and at different levels, you will have to modify the depth of the trenches. When you are satisfied with the work, take a soft pencil and clearly label the various parts of the wood so that you are in absolutely no doubt as to which bits have to be chopped out next.

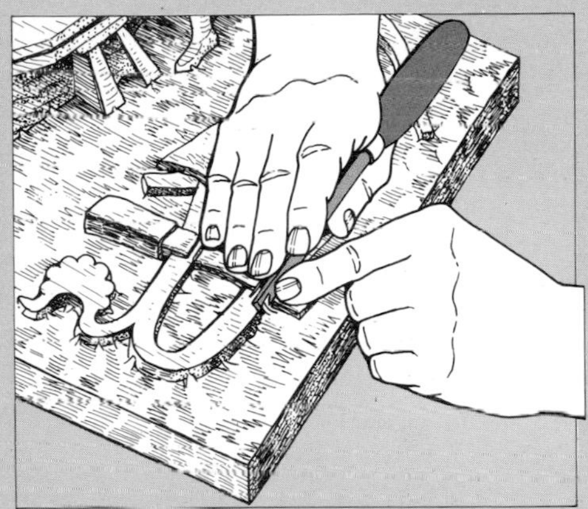

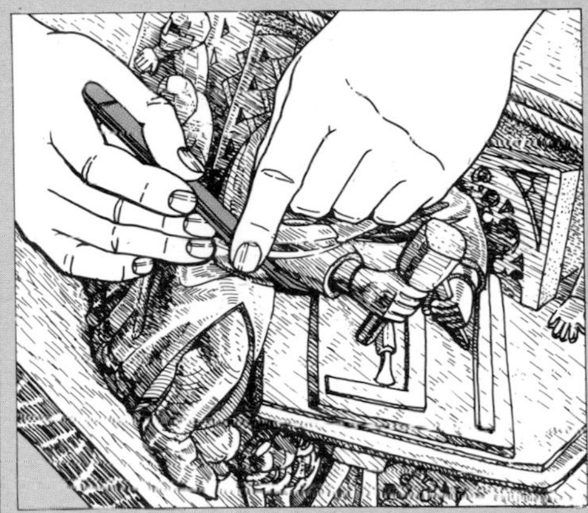

Wasting or bosting-in

Having had another look at the maquette, take the deep gouge and mallet, and start lowering all the waste wood that is outside the design. Clear the waste with generous, broad sweeps of the deep gouge until the whole ground has been lowered to the level of the next design feature, such as the top of the man's bench or the top of the two supporting motifs (see the project photograph).

Clean up the wasted surface, take a pencil and re-establish the motifs that occur at the lower level. Go around these secondary design features with the deep gouge, and again set in a trench, as already described. When this has been done, take the deep gouge, and once again waste away the ground wood until the level of the next motif has been reached. Continue setting in, wasting and drawing the next level of motifs until you finally reach the background or slab level.

Take the callipers to the maquette, read off and transfer a series of reference points to the roughed-out wood, and then start to make the more detailed cuts. Using a veiner, cut back the main blocks of wood so that they are nearer to the finished size.

Be careful that you do not chop too deeply and, as you work, keep re-establishing the design and setting out the area of next cut. In this way, the wood is gradually organized and lowered so that it begins to look like a many-stepped rock formation that is set on a flat ground. Clean up the faces and levels of the wood with a swift gouge, and then with a pencil, measure and callipers draw in the next set of reference points.

Grounding and modelling

Take one of the smaller tools such as the knife, flat spoon-bit gouge or the straight scoop gouge, and start the final modelling and undercutting. Do not be tempted to carve and finalize single isolated areas, but instead go over the whole design gradually working the wood and searching out the sum total of all the forms and shapes.

As you chop, cut, slice and pare, try to think of the various figures and details as being hidden away just below the surface of the wood. With this in mind, never rip off all the concealing layers in one great thrust but always gently pare the wood until the little forms are revealed.

Work with the whole range of tools, using the one you consider to be the best for the job in hand. Try all the while to cut across, or at an angle to, the grain, so that the end grain is left smooth and the waste wood falls away as crisp curls. When this final stage has been reached, discard the mallet and just hold and guide the tool firmly with one hand, and push and manoeuvre with the other. Continue working all the main forms including the man's head, the roundness of the man's shoulders, the table, the lines of the supporting motifs, the front of the corbel and the beautiful vine-like tendrils that link the supporters to the corbel. As the work progresses, carve with increasing caution, and aim to use smaller and sharper tools. Cut, chop, scoop, slice, slide and pare, all the time working in and around the little figures, removing curls of wood, and getting closer to the final forms.

Undercutting and finishing

When you feel that the carving is approaching completion, stand back, consider the whole work and then decide just how far you want the carving to be finished. For example, you can work a variety of textures such as smooth facial features contrasted with coarse clothes.

Re-sharpen the tools and set about the final modelling and undercutting. Cut and pare around the face, chop in the delicate undercuts where the man's arm rests on the table, clean up the wood where the legs of the table meet the ground and generally go over the work cutting in the details. There is no easy way of approaching this final modelling; just consider it as being a gentle, step-at-a-time process of swiftly running the razor-sharp tools over the wood until all the details look like part of a well-considered whole. As you work the final modelling, you must continually sharpen the tools, move around the wood and approach the grain from a different direction.

At this final stage, take the flat-bent shallow gouge and the knife, and work the whole ground area so that it cleanly meets the undercut figures and motifs. When you consider the carving finished, take a soft brush and a fine knife to the wood and remove dust, burrs and areas of rough end-grain.

Finally, bearing in mind that one of the greatest problems is knowing when to declare the work finished, leave the carving alone for a day or two and then give it another critical looking over. Bring the work to a good burnished finish with a plain wax.

CARVING A NAÏVE FAIRGROUND HORSE'S HEAD

IT IS an odd fact that, on the one hand, the steam engine was responsible for killing off the age of horse transport and, on the other hand, it made possible that wonder of the late nineteenth century – the beautifully carved and painted engine-driven horse carousel. Perhaps even more of a paradox is the fact that the carvers of ships' figureheads, who were put out of work by the introduction of iron-clad steamships, found work carving the leaping and galloping fairground horses. These uniquely gifted craftsmen who had once carved and decorated all manner of figureheads, including magnificent full-bosomed patriotic women in swirling robes, rampant lions, angels, eagles and unicorns, now put all their skills into carving equally lavish fairground horses.

Working in the same dockside workshops with the same tools and materials, these carvers built up blocks of wood, glued, pegged and carved these larger-than-life horses. Just as they had done with the ships' figureheads, they decorated the carvings with raw primary colours, swags, banners, scrolls and extravagant amounts of gold leaf. Wonderfully carved and exuberantly decorated, nineteenth-century fairground horses have been variously described as 'the climax of Victorian baroque', 'the European woodcarvers' last stand' and 'the brightest, brashest, most vital example of English folk carving to have survived.'

TOOLS & EQUIPMENT

- Workbench
- Pencils
- Callipers
- Measure
- Vice
- Cross-cut saw
- 2 sash clamps
- Bow saw
- Mallet
- Deep U-section straight gouge
- Shallow front-bent gouge
- Small straight gouge
- Small V-section tool
- Front-bent gouge
- Carver's knife
- Spoon-bit gouge

MATERIALS

- 3 blocks of straight-grained wood (quantity to suit) such as yellow pine, lime or jelutong
- Workout paper
- Block of Plasticine
- Packing strips and wedges of wood
- PVA glue
- Tracing paper
- Wax polish

There are two scales: the working drawing is one square to 1in and the 'grain' section detail is one square to 4in. Although this project works for a head that is about life-size, there is no reason why you should not adjust the project and change the scale.

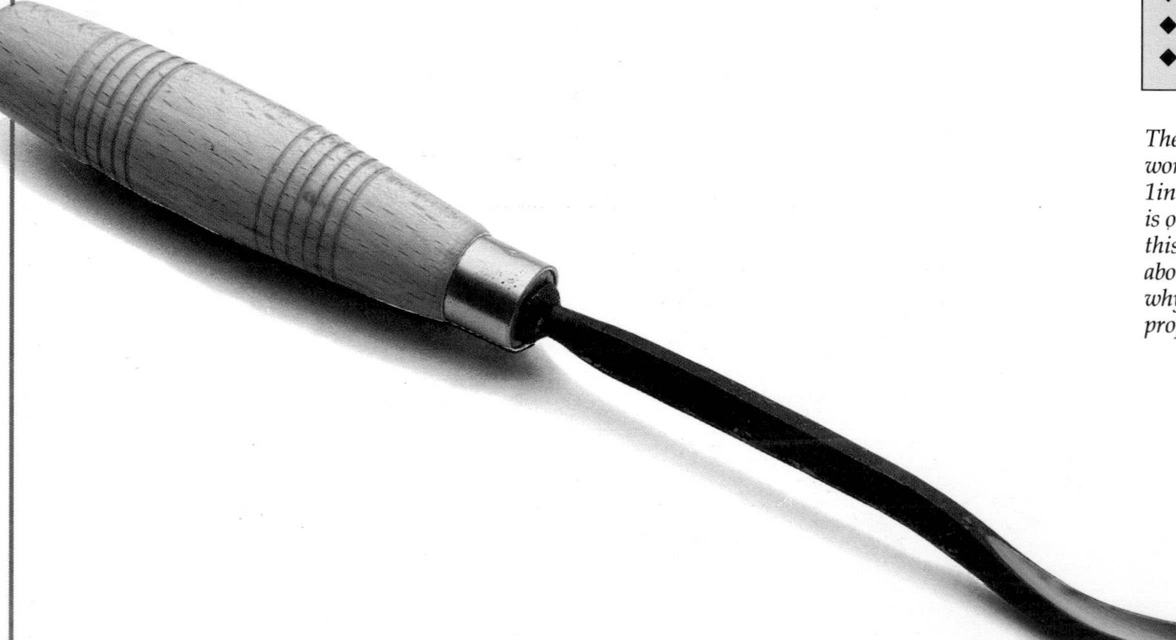

1 INCH
4 INCHES

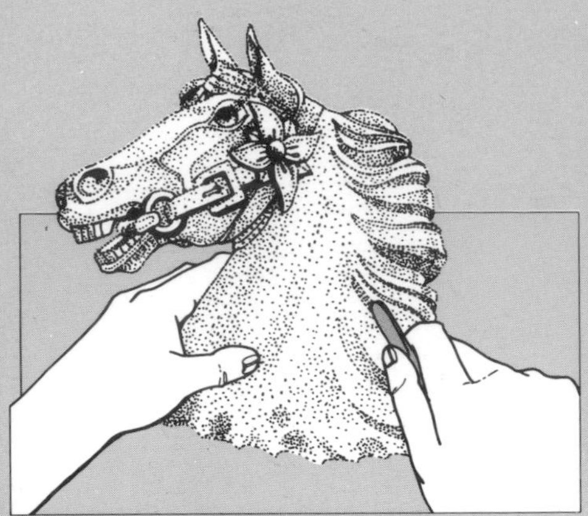

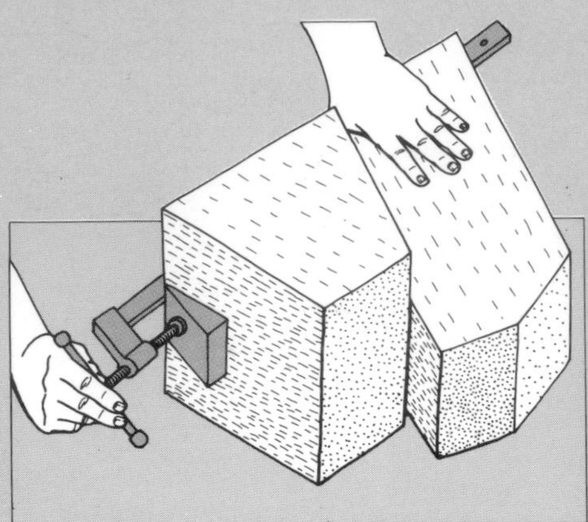

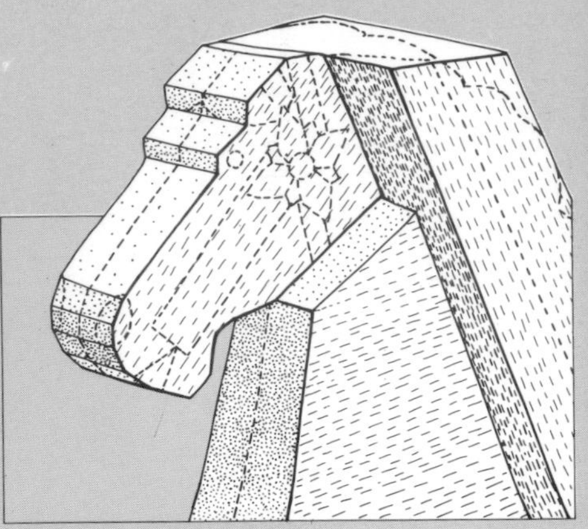

Considering the technique and making a maquette

Have a good look at the detailed drawing and the photographs, and then, if possible, go and see some fairground horses, perhaps in a museum or a restorer's workshop. When you get to see the horses 'in the flesh' note how all the carvings are magnificently larger than life in the sense that features such as the glinting eyes, the flared nostrils and the gnashing teeth are bold, exaggerated and thrusting.

Take a magnifying glass to the project photograph (see page 125) and focus on the run of the wood grain and the details of the blocked and pegged structure. See how the head is built up out of at least three blocks of wood – a block for the head, the chest and neck, and the mane.

Bearing in mind that you may want to add secondary blocks for the cheeks, neck muscles and ears, take your workout paper and a soft pencil and make a series of working drawings and sketches. Consider how the horse's head is to fit within the glued and pegged wood.

Take the Plasticine and make a scaled-down model or maquette of the head. Look at the form from all angles and consider how the built-up blocks are to be positioned so that the run of the grain is best presented. Now take your working drawings, callipers and measure, and go over the maquette taking off reference measurements. You may want to modify the design and, for example, make the carving half-size, or change the features, but the overall working methods are as described.

Building up, gluing and pegging

Set the blocks of wood out on the workbench and check them over for possible problems such as end splits. Reject any wood that is less than perfect.

Label the blocks 'face', 'neck' and 'mane', and place them in profile position. With a pencil, measure and callipers, mark out the main cuts: establish the overall head form and the angle of head to neck, and set out the position of the initial saw cuts. Mark out the wood so that the mane block can be notched and angled into the neck block, and then set the face block at an angle to the other two blocks (see the working drawing).

Once you have marked out the wood, set it in the vice, take the cross-cut saw and cut away the waste. Keep the larger pieces of waste wood to make into pegs. With the waste cleared, the three blocks of wood can be brought together for a trial fitting. The wood needs to come together so that the faces to be glued are a reasonably flush fit. Adjust and trim the wood, and when all is as described, take the sash clamps and have a dry clamping. Do not use any glue, but just fit the wood with packing strips and wedges (as illustrated) so that the built-up form feels stable and tight.

When you have had several fittings and have planned the assembling and the placing of the pegs, knock the structure apart and set the wood, glue, pegs and clamps out on the work surface. Having done this, glue, peg and clamp the face block to the neck block. Once the glue has dried, fix the mane block to the face and neck.

Pegging and sawing

Allow all the glue to dry before you start setting out the front and side profiles. Take a tracing of the master drawing and transfer the traced profiles onto the working faces of the wood. Having done this, emphasize the drawn lines with a thick soft pencil, and then cross-hatch the waste wood.

Secure the wood in the vice, take the bow saw and cut out the main side profile. Run the saw down over the face and nostrils, up under the chin and, finally, down and around the mane. Now, with great care, take the waste from around the nostrils and chin, and temporarily pin it back onto the main body of wood with a couple of oval nails. Still working with the bow saw, approach the head front on and remove the little bits of waste from between the cheeks and the mouth.

Set out the sawn blank, the Plasticine maquette and the inspirational material. Place the items side by side and make another revised series of study sketches. Work out the details of the harness, paying particular attention to the rather formal layout of the rosette. See how the mane rolls around the neck, and generally draw up and detail all the features.

When you feel that you have captured the stylized but lively lines, take a pencil to the rough-sawn wood and block in all the areas that need to be chopped out and wasted with a swift gouge. Mark out the dishing between the side of the neck and undercheek, and the beautiful strong ridge between the top of the nostrils and the eyes.

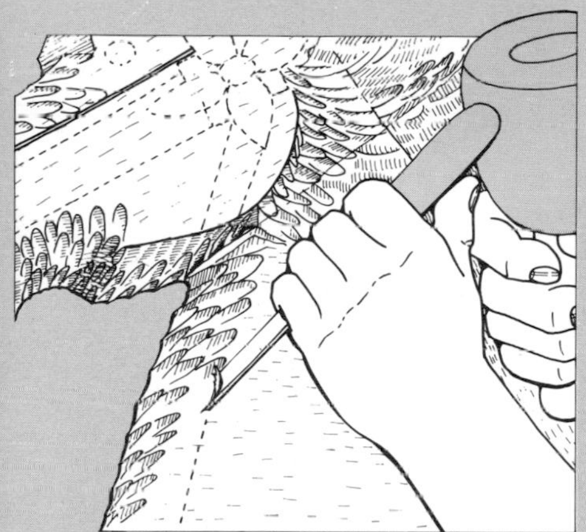

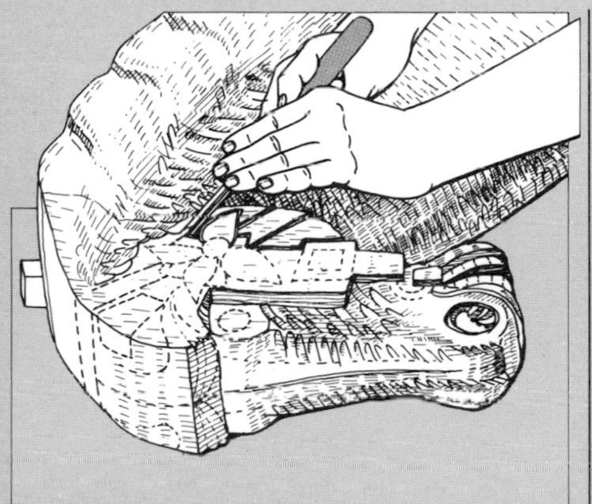

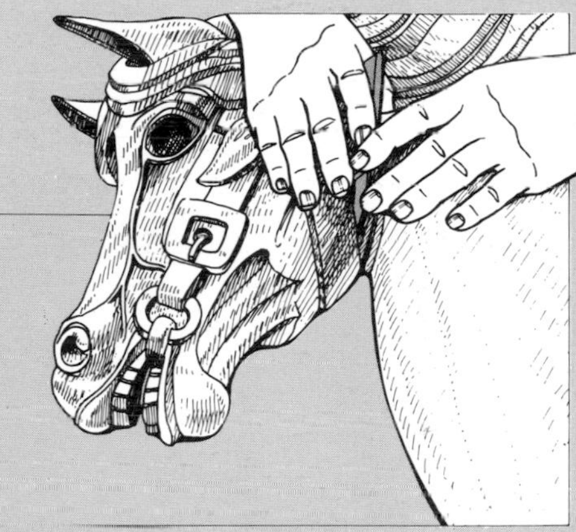

Roughing-out

Secure the marked-out blank in the vice, and set out the mallet, the deep U-section gouge and the shallow front-bent gouge. Check that all your tools are keen-edged. Have another quick look at the maquette and the photographs, and then set to work. With vigorous broad sweeps of the gouge, chop out the whole concave area between the undercheeks and the mane.

Work with care and, as wood is removed, keep changing the direction of cut so that you are working across, or at an angle to, the grain. Waste the wood from the shoulder, chin and mane, and scoop down into the neck in order to establish the powerful lines of the neck muscles. Having done this, change tack and work from the back of the neck, over the mane and into the neck hollow. Do not force the gouge blade deep into the wood or, at this stage, try to work any details, but concentrate on the main dips and hollows.

When you have dished the neck and have achieved the big primary forms, take the smaller gouge and start to get a little closer to the desired design. Remember, you are not trying to carve an anatomically correct horse's head, but are trying to carve and group a collection of stylized features. If you look at the photograph, you will see that although the head depicts the power and excitement of the horse, each individual feature including the nostrils, lips, veins, eyes, ears and mane, are really no more than rather basic, stylized forms.

Once the head has been roughed-out with the gouges, go over the wood with a soft pencil and draw out the fine details.

Modelling

Clear away the bench waste, and start to cut and set in the drawn details. With the mallet and V-section tool, set in and outline the rosette, the harness, the nostrils, the eye sockets and the mane.

Take a straight- and front-bent gouge, and lower the wood between the set-in details. Do not chop out much ground wood, or, at this stage, try to over-model any single feature. Instead go over the whole head cutting back the waste until the wood is slightly lowered and you are left with the primary features in relief.

Once all the main forms and motifs are raised relief wood, take the straight gouge, knife and spoon bit, and start to undercut and model the details. Hollow and scoop out the nostrils and eye sockets with the spoon bit, whereas the crisp furrows of the mane may be worked with a selection of gouges. The details of the harness can be cut with a knife and a shallow front-bent gouge. As you work, do not be tempted to rush headlong; always work slowly, so that each and every cut can be changed and angled to meet unexpected grain changes. You will soon get into a rhythm of work but always remember to keep your tools sharp and stand back from the work from time-to-time in order to view it critically.

Final cuts and finishing

Before you put in the final cuts, stop and consider just what it is you are trying to achieve. For example, do you want to leave the swirling grain patterns showing and finish with wax or varnish? Or do you want to go for a traditional fairground finish, complete with a white ground, golden harness and mane, a rosette picked out in primary colours, and the whole horse surface painted with flamboyant naïve art imagery? Note: these points have to be considered at this stage because if you decide to go for a painted finish, you can work to a swifter finish by covering the wood with filler and gesso.

Take a spoon-bit gouge, and go over the carving, cutting back the tool marks and leaving sharp, crisp edges. Work up and over the furrows of the mane, tool the upper lips, and gouge the sharp ridge just below the eyes. The nose veins and the rosette can be worked with a knife. Generally go over the whole work taking it to a smooth-lined flowing finish.

Watch out for brittle short-grain areas such as the high spots on the mane and the rim of the nostrils. As the work approaches completion, carve with increasing care and keep the tools sharp. Finally, when you consider the carving finished, brush it down and give it a plain wax polishing. Note: traditionally fairground horses have glass eyes which can be obtained from specialist suppliers.

ABOVE *Carved and painted fairground horse. It is not uncommon for fairground horses to bear the name of the fairground owner or, for example, that of his wife. With this particular horse, the emphasis is on painted decoration rather than on carving.*

RIGHT PROJECT PHOTOGRAPH *An unfinished horse's head made by the nineteenth-century British carver A. E. Anderson. The main features are all cleanly and crisply worked, particularly the harness and the nostrils. Interestingly, this craftsman was primarily a carver of ships' figure heads.*

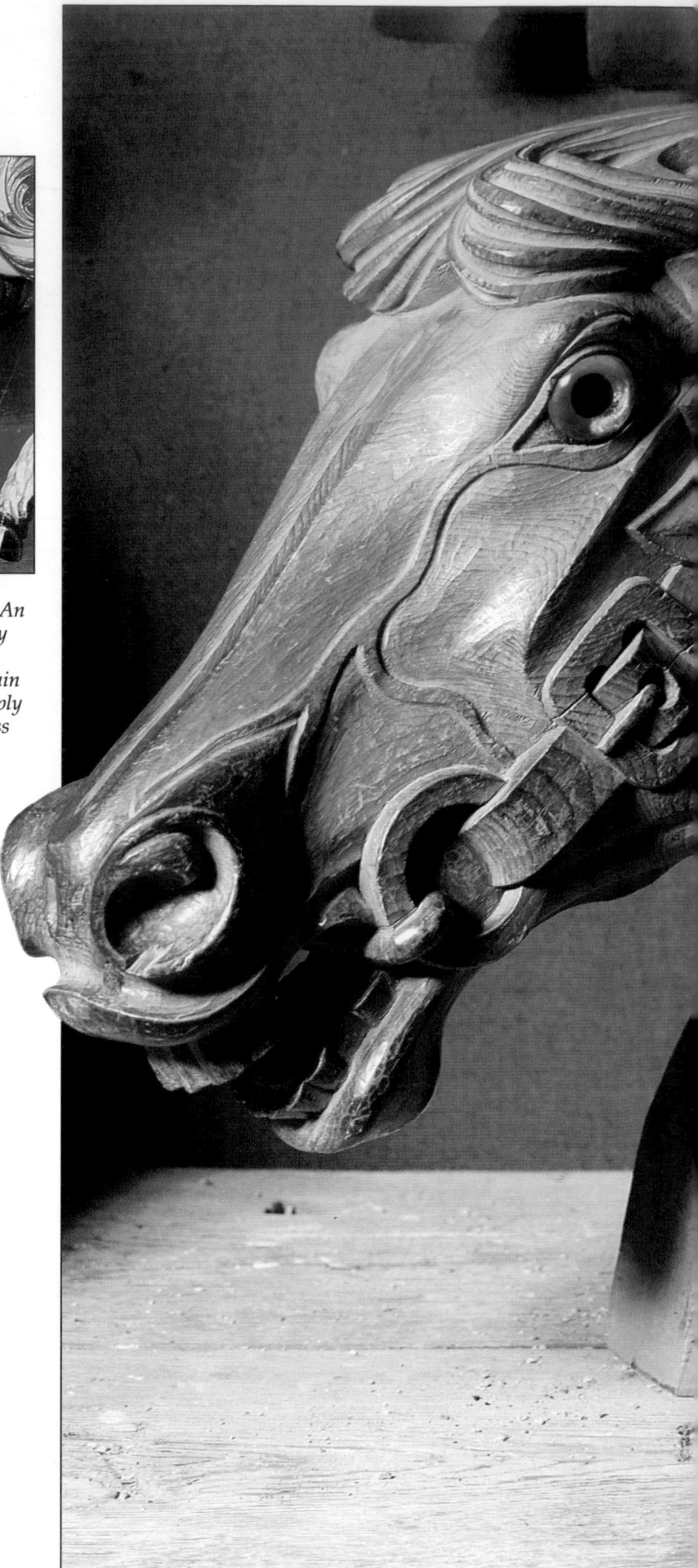

CARVING A POSY IN THE GRINLING GIBBONS TRADITION

GRINLING GIBBONS was born in 1648 in Holland, to an English father and a Dutch mother. When he was about 20 years old he was discovered working in England by the diarist John Evelyn. He was, said Evelyn, 'working in an obscure place . . . a poor solitary thatched cottage'. However, before the month was out, his work had been seen by the King, Wren and Pepys, and within the year, he had as many rich commissions as he could manage.

What is probably most admired about his work is its closeness to nature – birds, fruit, feathers, flowers and angels – carved with an almost overwhelming obsessive attention to detail. Grinling Gibbons worked as much in marble and bronze, but it is his delicate lime-wood carvings for which he is best known. Being of light colour, close-grained, relatively free from knots and easy to carve, lime was the perfect material for Gibbons. It has been said of him 'wood or stone, it makes no matter, the Grinling Gibbons style requires that the material be entirely dominated'.

During the Baroque period, a desire for realism and deep-relief carving led to the technique known as 'built-up' – the parts of the carving that project up and out from the main body of the wood are built up and glued additions. This method of working is not always successful or even desirable. However it does become valid if the 'span' of the subject is such that it cannot be worked from a single piece of wood. With many Gibbons designs it was often the case that a wing, flower or arm was so far out of relief that it needed to be carved and worked as a separate piece and then pinned on at a later stage. Examples of Grinling Gibbons carvings can be found in many English stately homes, and it is with these that you can best study his technique and style.

TOOLS & EQUIPMENT

- Workbench
- Pencils
- Sketchbook
- Workboard
- Modelling tools
- Bench screw
- Deep U-section gouge
- Mallet
- Compass
- Scissors
- V-tool
- Veiner
- Shallow curve gouge
- Small front-bent gouge
- Small spoon gouge
- Knife
- Fine-point hooked knife
- Small spoon bits
- Fine-blade scalpel
- Dog-leg chisel
- Soft brush

MATERIALS

- A slab of well-seasoned lime (of size to suit)
- A large block of Plasticine
- Tracing paper
- Stiff card

There are two scales: the posy is three squares to 1in and the flower detail is four squares to 1in. With this project it is most important that you choose your wood with care – go for seasoned lime.

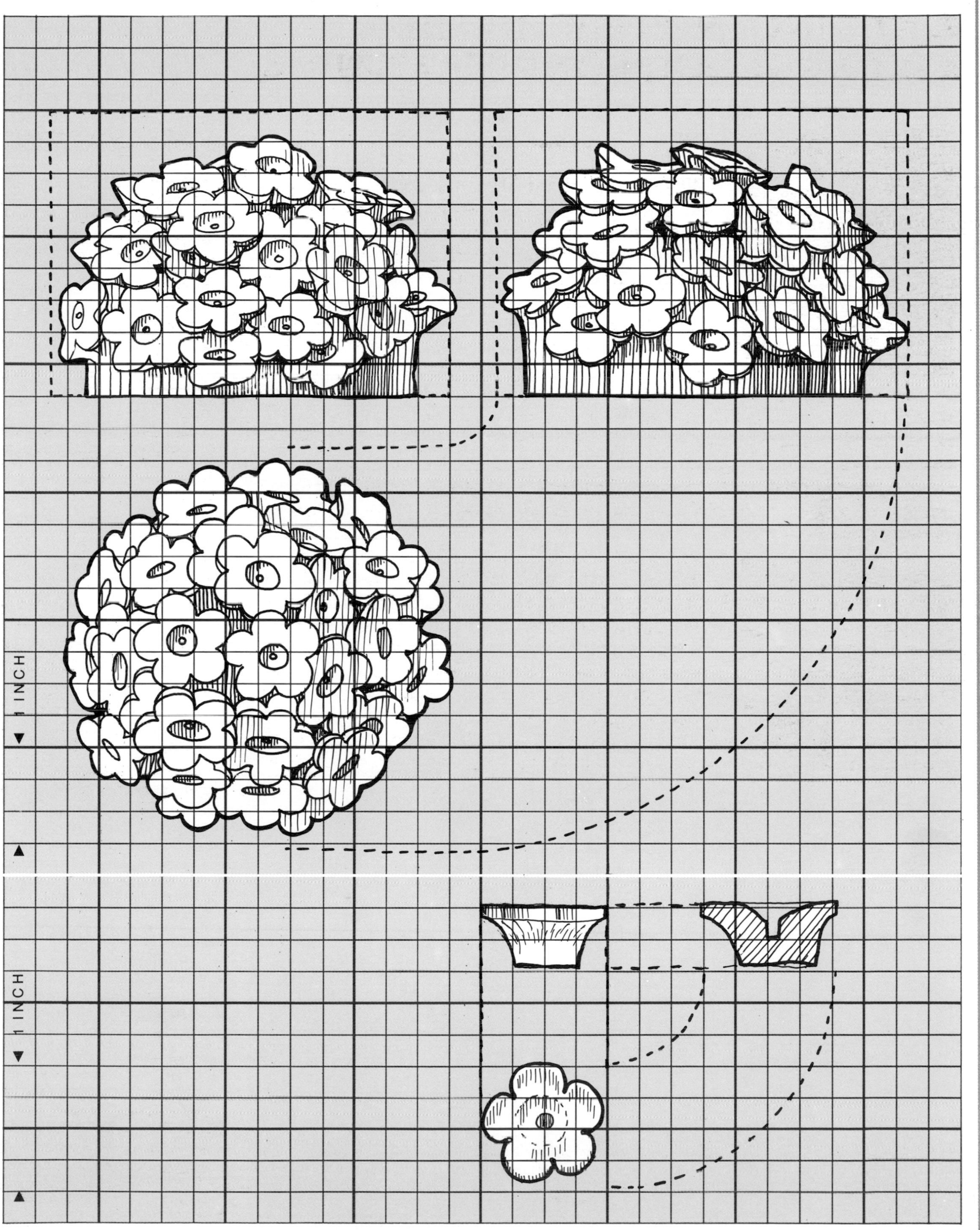
1 INCH
1 INCH

ABOVE *Sofa made in the reign of George II. This rather awe-inspiring piece of pine furniture is over 12ft long. It is an example of repetitious leaf and flower carving* **at its worst. Pity the carver who** *had to work this florid, over-embellished piece.*

LEFT *Lime-wood carving by Grinling Gibbons. Pieces of this size, type and style were often built up, with separate carvings being added to give bulk to the central cluster.*

RIGHT *Carving by Grinling Gibbons. This is a carving with all the most common details of this craftsman, including the musical instruments, flowers and lace. Perhaps not to modern taste in design, the quality of this carving is almost beyond belief. See how for the most part, the carving has been worked from one slab of wood.*

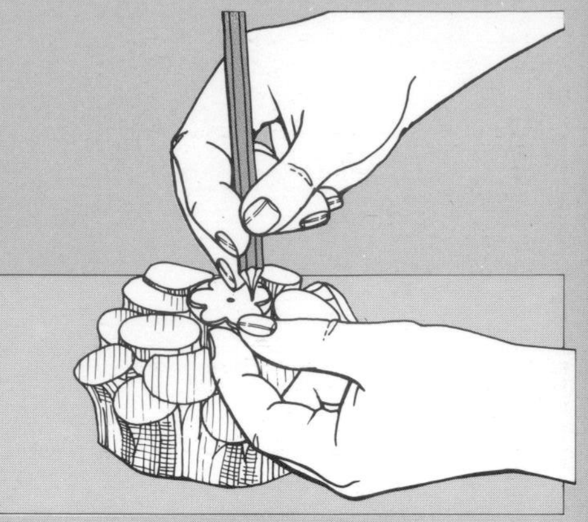

Considering the project and looking at details

Start by taking a magnifying glass to the photographs and look at the central posy of flowers. First study the whole design including the total shape and form of the posy in relation to the rest of the carving. Then, focus on the individual flower heads. See how, although they are very basic in design and form, the flowers look complex all together. For example, if you look at the central posy, and the flower heads around the medallion at the bottom of the photograph, you will see that they are very naïve and solid little shapes.

Concentrate your attention on a single flower head from the central posy, and with pencil and paper analyse its form and design. Note the five petals, the slightly dished face, the single central hole and the relationship of this one flower to the others in the bunch.

If possible, visit a museum or a stately home of the late seventeenth or early eighteenth centuries, and see examples of Grinling Gibbons's work. Ideally, search out some of his early flower, leaf and fruit festoons carved in lime. Looking over the photographs, run your eyes over and under the forms, and note how individual flower heads are not floating airily but are supported by a relatively large mass of ground wood and by neighbouring flowers. The illusion of fragility is achieved by having swift, angled undercuts.

Making a maquette and drawing up the design

When you have studied the working drawing and the photographs, arrange the inspirational material around your working area, and set out the workboard, the Plasticine and the various modelling tools. Start by knocking up a posy-sized block of Plasticine.

Refer back to the photograph and your studies and decide if you want to modify the design. For example, you may want to increase the size of individual flowers and have fewer heads or you may want to follow more or less the same design but increase the size. When you have considered all these points, then begin with the Plasticine and model what you consider to be a good, realistically workable design. Pay particular attention to the way individual flower heads angle out from the posy, and note how each flower conceals the sub-structure of neighbouring blooms.

Having achieved a nicely worked maquette, draw out a series of 'whole posy' profiles – that is, the posy as seen from the top, bottom and sides. Finally, make a tracing of the profiles, and block-in the design so that it can be seen in terms of flower-head circles and little areas of waste between circles.

Roughing-out and transferring the design

Take the slab of well-seasoned lime, set it out on the workbench and check it over for possible flaws. The wood needs to be tight and even in texture, and free from dead knots, splits and stains. Secure the wood with a bench screw, and then arrange all the tools so that they are comfortably to hand.

Take a deep U-section gouge and mallet, and with broad chopping strokes, rough-out the wood so that it relates to the Plasticine maquette. Waste and shape the wood so that each of the flower heads (as seen in your master design) has its own angled facet or plane, and lower the ground wood. When this stage has been reached, refresh your memory by having another look at the working drawing and the maquette, and then take a pencil and compass and go over the roughed-out block drawing in the position of the individual flower heads. Mark each facet with a central point and circle.

Now, with a piece of stiff card, pencil, compass and a pair of scissors, make a little five-petal flower head template (as illustrated). Having done this, go over the roughed-out wood and set out each of the flower heads using the template. Note: if you look at the photograph (see page 129) you will see that some of the flowers overlap, and it is important to build this feature into the design at this stage.

When all the flowers have been worked, take a soft pencil and block in the little areas of waste that occur between the flowers. Finally, draw in a few motifs such as a few flower heads to break and blur the edge of the posy.

Lowering the ground and setting in the flowers

When the wood has been roughed-out and the general position of all the flowers indicated, take a selection of tools including, for example, a V-tool, a veiner, a shallow-curve gouge and perhaps a small front-bent gouge, and continue to lower the ground wood so that the main posy is left in high relief. Work across the grain and slice, cut and pare until the ground around the posy is smoothly established.

Take a soft pencil and decide which of the flower heads are going to be proud, which are going to be partially covered by other flowers, and which are going to be almost hidden from view. Working with a fine V-tool and a knife, select the proud flower heads that are going to be in full view and set-in their outline. Bear in mind how the flowers overlap each other and cut each outline to a depth of about ⅛–¼in.

Using a small shallow-curve gouge, clear the wood from around the flowers so that they stand in relief. Now, with a knife and straight gouge, carve the blooms so that they are sharply undercut. When you have done this, take a pencil to the next level of flowers – the flowers that are to be partially covered or overshadowed – and draw in as much of the petals as possible. Then, take a fine-point hooked knife and work under the proud flowers.

Continue carving and cutting deeper and deeper into the wood until all the levels of flower heads have been set-in – those in full view, overlapped and almost completely hidden from view.

Modelling

When you have established the various levels of flowers, take a magnifying glass to the photograph (see page 129) and focus on the posy. Note how with some of the darker flowers at the top of the bunch, it is just possible to see the wood thickness at the petal edge. You can see that, in section, each flower is like an upside-down cone with the base of the cone being the face of the flower. It is the sharp petal edges and the undercutting that gives the illusion of thinness.

Take a small shallow gouge, a spoon-bent gouge and a small spoon bit, and set about undercutting and modelling. Start with the topmost flowers and gradually work deeper and lower into the bunch. Undercut each bloom until it is like an upside-down cone. Then, take a knife and cut in the five little nicks that mark out the petals. When this has been done, take a shallow-curve bent gouge and go over the whole carving giving each of the flower faces a slightly dished face. Do not slice too deeply but just aim to give each flower a delicate saucer-like hollow.

As you carve deeper into the posy, work with a probing, hooking action of the spoon bit, and be extra careful to avoid levering the shank of the tool against forms that have already been worked. When you eventually come to the flower heads at the base of the posy – the flowers that break up and blur the posy outline – work with increasing care, and lower and undercut the ground so that the flowers appear to be sitting just clear of the basewood. Note: although lime is very easy to carve and grain, it is still necessary to keep the tools razor-edged.

Finishing

When the carving is approaching completion, put down your tools, tidy the working area and then try to look at your carving with a clear, critical eye. Compare it to the maquette and the inspirational material, and then assess the total design – the quality of the modelling, the depth of the undercuts and the correctness of the details.

For the finishing stages you need a fine-blade scalpel, a front-bent shallow gouge, a small spoon bit and a dog-leg chisel. First, take a gouge and clean up all the dish-faced flowers – do not fuss the wood but just work each flower with a couple of crisp strokes. Take the smallest of the U-section spoon bits and scoop out the hole at the centre of each of the flowers. Now, take the scalpel and give each flower its characteristic five petals and carve the notches between the petals. With the knife and the shallow front-bent gouge pare away at the stalk of each flower – try to reduce the structural wood to a minimum.

Work with a delicate, paring and whittling action until you have achieved forms that are simple and well-textured with crisp tool marks. Once all the flower heads have been carved, take a dog-leg chisel to the ground and work it until it is level but dappled. Slide the cutting edge across the wood and skim off all the whiskers, end-grain burrs and rough spots. Finally, clear the carving with a soft brush and run the knife around the sharp edge of the ground board.

MAKING A DECOY DUCK IN THE AMERICAN TRADITION

DECOY DUCKS are no more than carved, moulded or slat-built imitations of real ducks. The word 'decoy' comes from the Dutch words *kooj* and *koye* meaning to lure, entice or snare. From an early date American Indians – and then later white American duck hunters – used carved wooden ducks as decoys. Along came a flock of wild duck and, attracted by the decoys, they settled on the water, providing easy targets for the hunters. Not a very sporting technique perhaps, but a beautifully simple and apparently very efficient way of hunting. Wilson's *American Ornithology* published in the first quarter of the nineteenth century describes the use of duck decoys: 'five or six wooden figures, cut and painted so as to represent ducks, and sunk by pieces of lead nailed onto their bottoms, so as to float at the usual depth on the surface, are anchored in a favourable position. The appearance of these usually attracts passing flocks, which alight and are shot down'.

Traditionally, hunters carved and whittled their own particular type of decoy. Some were hollow, carved and left unpainted, whereas others were realistically painted. More unusual were ones made of canvas. These decoy-makers had no illusions as to what they were making; for them the decoys were simply a means to an end. This direct approach to the craft is borne out by the fact that at the end of the duck-shooting season, the decoys were either just left in the water or dumped in the bottoms of the boats.

Decoy ducks are now considered to be prime examples of American folk art and, as such, are very collectable. The most interesting decoys from the collector's point of view, are those made in nineteenth-century New England and these tend to be of solid wood that has been worked with an axe, carved with a drawknife, whittled, painted and given glass eyes.

TOOLS & EQUIPMENT

- Workbench
- Sketchbook
- Pencil
- Measure
- Vice
- Hand saw
- Shaped rasps
- Drawknife or spokeshave
- Coping or bow saw
- Callipers
- Long-bladed whittler's knife
- Sandpaper
- Hand drill
- 2 drill bits, ⅜in and ¼in
- Small knife
- Long-haired pointed brushes
- Mixing containers
- Cloth
- Nail-and-slab turntable (see page 135)

MATERIALS

- A block of straight-grained and knot-free pine measuring 15 × 5 × 4in
- A length of ⅜in dowel
- A block of Plasticine
- Grid paper
- Tracing paper
- PVA glue
- Copper pins (optional)
- Modelmakers' gloss paints (black, blue, white and brown)
- White primer
- Undercoat
- Turpentine

The scale is three squares to 2in. If you want to use this duck to float on water then it will almost certainly need a small ballast weight. If this is the case, gouge out a base hole, plug it with a handful of lead washers and fix with a screw.

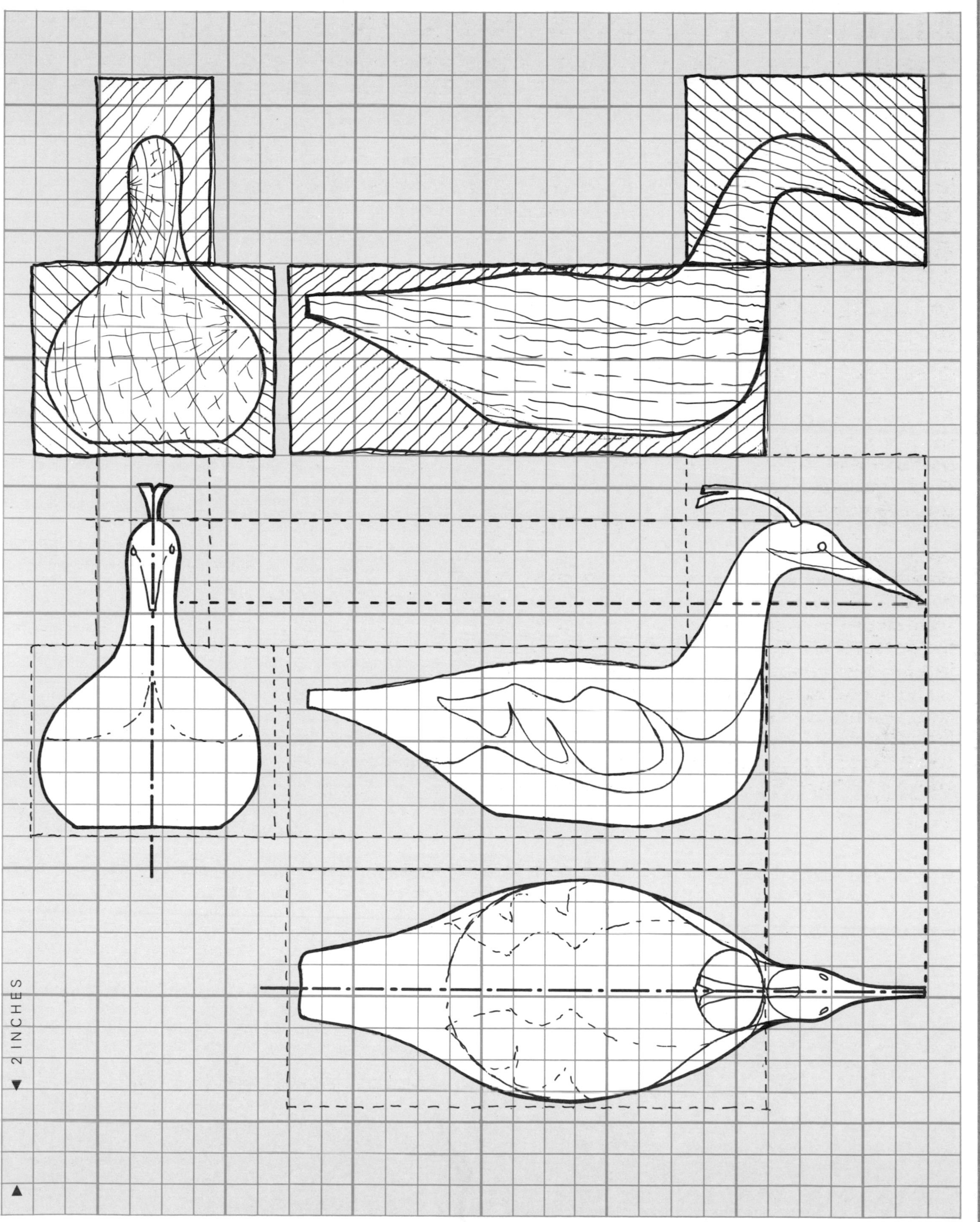
2 INCHES

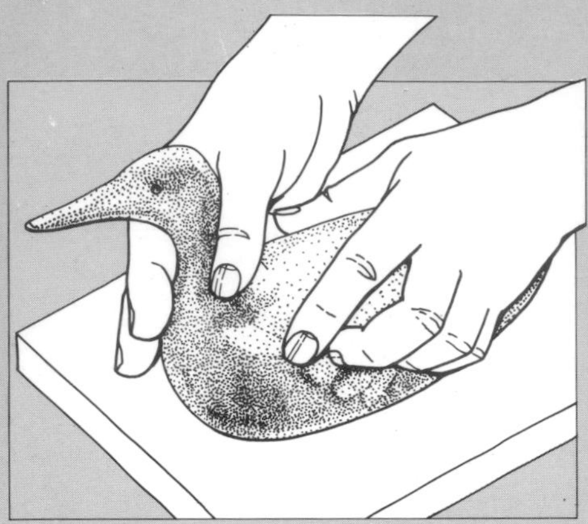

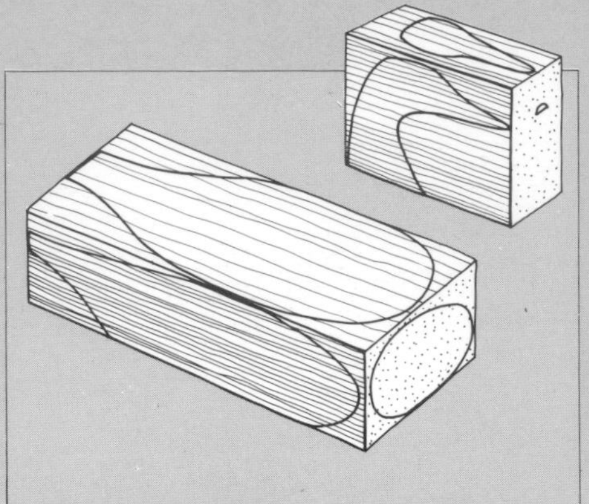

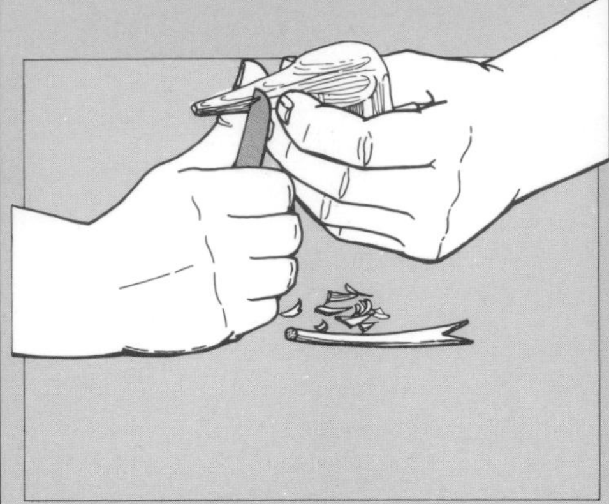

Considering the project and setting out the design

Study the project photograph (see page 137) and note the overall shape of the bird. See how in form, size and detailing it is, in fact, very much like a grebe or merganser. Take note of the rough, rasped texture, the join at the neck and the cresting.

Make a series of working sketches, drawing views of the top, sides and front. Now, take a wedge of Plasticine (or potter's clay) and make a full-size working model. As you work, modify and adjust the design to suit your own requirements. For example, you could turn the head over the back so that the duck is in the 'sleeping' position or, alternatively, you could model a more realistic bird with every feather and feature picked out in fine detail. This will not affect the project as long as your chosen design has smooth lines and an uncomplicated profile.

Once you have decided on a duck type and you have considered fully all the technique implications, take a sheet of grid paper and make a full-size working drawing. The drawing should include the position of the neck-line, details of the cresting and a painting guide of colours to be used.

Transferring the design and roughing-out the body

Take a tracing of the master design and transfer the traced lines onto the various working faces of your wood (see illustration above). Having done this, make sure that the run of the grain is as indicated, and then label the wood – top, side and waste

Now, take a pencil to the wood and make sure that all the profile lines are established. At this stage, study your inspirational material and put the working model out of harm's way but within view. Secure the wood in the vice and cut the head block from the body block using the hand saw. Then, set out the rasp and the drawknife or spokeshave. Put the body block in the vice, take the coping or bow saw and then quickly remove all corners of waste wood.

Re-position the boat-shaped piece of wood in the vice and set to work with the drawknife or spokeshave. Aim to swiftly reduce the waste until the wood more or less resembles the bird's body – it should have a flattish area at the front to receive the head and a sharp ridge at the back that sets out the line of the tail. Work the block from centre-to-end, so that it looks stream-lined like a duck, and so that it sits on a broad flat base.

View and work the wood from all angles and, if necessary, take calliper readings from your working drawing and the working model. At this stage, only rough-out the wood and stop when the form is slightly larger than finished size.

Whittling the head

When the body has been roughed-out, put it to one side and start work on the head. First, remove the large areas of waste wood with the bow or coping saw. Put the block in the vice, and set to work with either a small drawknife or a long-bladed whittling knife. Noting the run of the grain, work and shape the back of the head, around the face, the top of the beak, and the throat.

There are no set rules as to how you should work the head; it is more a case of sitting back with the wood in one hand and the knife in the other, and whittling and working little-by-little. Avoid carving the wood with slicing strokes, but whittle with small, well-considered paring cuts. Hold the wood in one hand, brace the thumb of the other hand on the wood and pull the knife towards you with a controlled cut.

From time-to-time place the duck's head on the body block as you are working and see how the two parts come together. Adjust the base of the neck or the body so that the angle at which the head meets the body is correct. Try to whittle the head so that when it is placed on the body the total form runs together as a considered whole.

When the head has been satisfactorily roughed-out, take a scrap of waste wood and whittle the little forked crest. Finally, have a trial fitting and adjust all three pieces of wood so that they come together to make up a convincing duck form.

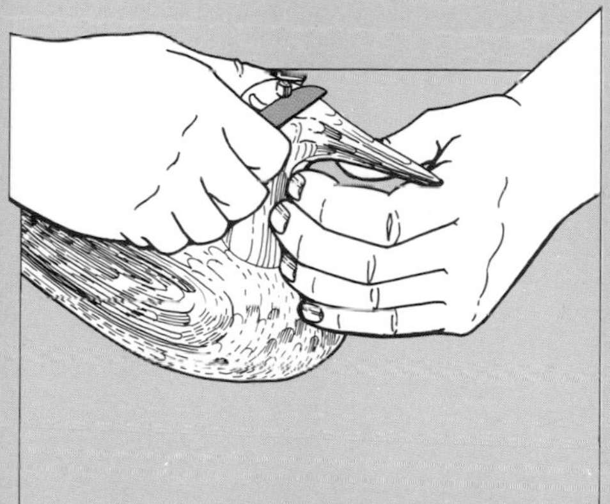

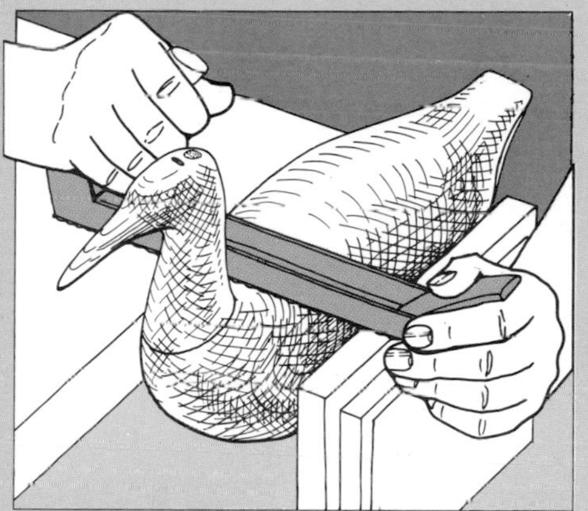

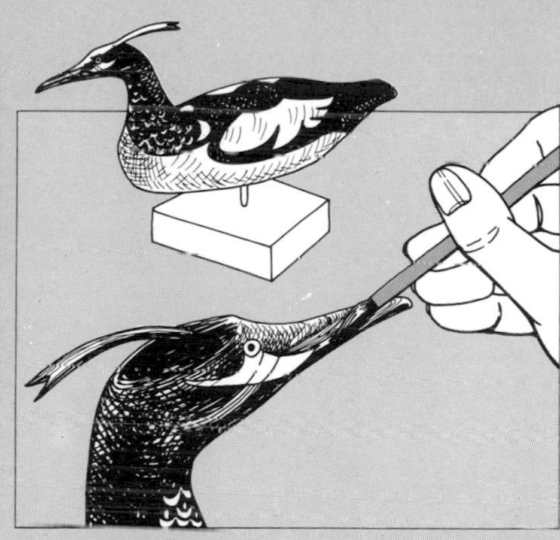

Putting together

With a sheet of coarse sandpaper, rub down the base of the neck and the flat of the body so that when the two are brought together they make an absolutely flush joint. Now, put the duck's body in the vice top side-up, and clear the bench of all waste wood. Set out all the tools and materials so that they are to hand – the length of dowel, the hand drill fitted with the ⅜in bit and a small quantity of PVA glue.

Position the head on the body, check for a good fit and then bore a ⅜in hole down through the duck's head and into the body. Note: this stage is best managed with the help of a friend so that the duck's head can be held while you operate the drill. Score the dowel with a piece of old hacksaw blade and then generously dribble PVA glue into the hole and over the joint. Fit the head and then gently bang the dowel home. Avoid banging too hard or you may split the wood. Gently tap the dowel into the hole until the head and body are a good close, flush fit.

After about 24 hours or when the glue is dry, take a knife and trim off the dowel so that it is slightly proud. Take the hand drill fitted with the ¼in bit and drill a crest hole at the back of the duck's head. Work the hole so that the crest can be correctly angled. Note: traditionally decoy heads were fitted together with nails and copper pins. If you intend having the decoy sitting outdoors, secure the head to the body with a couple of side-angled copper pins.

Modelling the form

Before you start the final modelling, sit your duck on the work surface and compare it to the project material – the photographs, drawings and working model. Take a soft pencil and mark on the wood the areas that need to be left or lowered. When you have done this, put the wood in the vice or hold it down on the workbench (whichever is easiest) and begin to remove waste wood with the shaped rasps. Work over the top of the head and cut back the end of the dowel. Hollow out the beautiful curve of the neck and taper the tail.

Take a small knife and finalize the subtle curve and taper of the beak, and work the slight hollows that will be the eyes. Put down all your tools and sit back with the duck in your hands. Run your hands and fingertips over its contours and try to feel any problems or irregularities. Once again mark the rough spots with a pencil and remove with the rasps. Continue working until the form is complete. Avoid overworking any one spot; it is much better to keep both the rasp and the wood moving in your hand, and aim to work the whole form. Finally, when you consider the duck finished, take the whittled crest, dip the stem in PVA glue and push it into the crest hole.

Painting and finishing

Clear the work surface of all clutter and set out the small pots of paint, primer, undercoat, paint brushes, mixing containers, turpentine and a cloth. Note: decoy painters use all manner of paints, including household gloss, modelmaker's paints, water-based acrylics, watercolours and artists' oils.

Start by spiking the duck on a simple nail-and-slab turntable (see illustration above). Paint the whole duck with white primer followed by an undercoat and a white gloss topcoat, allowing the paint to dry between coats. When the gloss top coat is dry, take a soft pencil and mark out the wing shapes, the breast line and the little flicks underneath the eyes. Mix a little black with the blue (thinning with the turpentine if necessary) and block in the top of the duck – the back, neck and head (see above).

Wait for the paint to almost dry, and mix a small amount of white with the brown to make the subtle throat plumage colour. Before you start this final stage, study the photograph (see page 137) and see how the actual brushstrokes are direct and uncomplicated although the throat gives the impression of being delicately worked. Make a series of little stylized V's that run up the throat and under the beak, and encourage the paints to bleed slightly into each other. Taking a fine brush, add a little white to the brown mixture, and detail the eyes and the motif that occurs just under the eyes. Finally, let the paint dry, and sign and date the base.

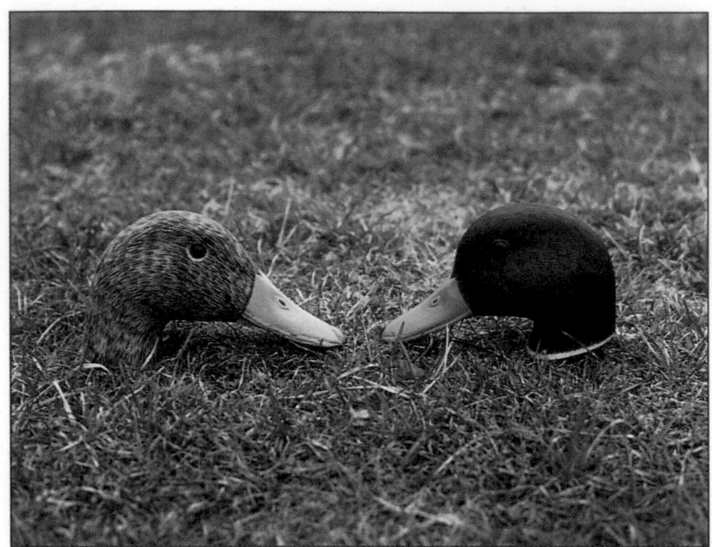

RIGHT PROJECT PHOTOGRAPH
American decoy duck. The surface of this duck has been left beautifully textured and, coupled with realistic painting, gives the bird a particularly lifelike quality.

ABOVE *Duck heads. Carved decoy ducks can be left unpainted and polished or, alternatively, they can be elaborately painted like the male and female ducks shown here.*

RIGHT *Unfinished decoy duck. Although this project concentrates on using two blocks of wood to make a decoy duck, they can be carved from just one block.*

LEFT *Decoy duck workshop. Decoy ducks carved in the traditional manner have become very popular as ornaments in recent years in both America and Europe.*

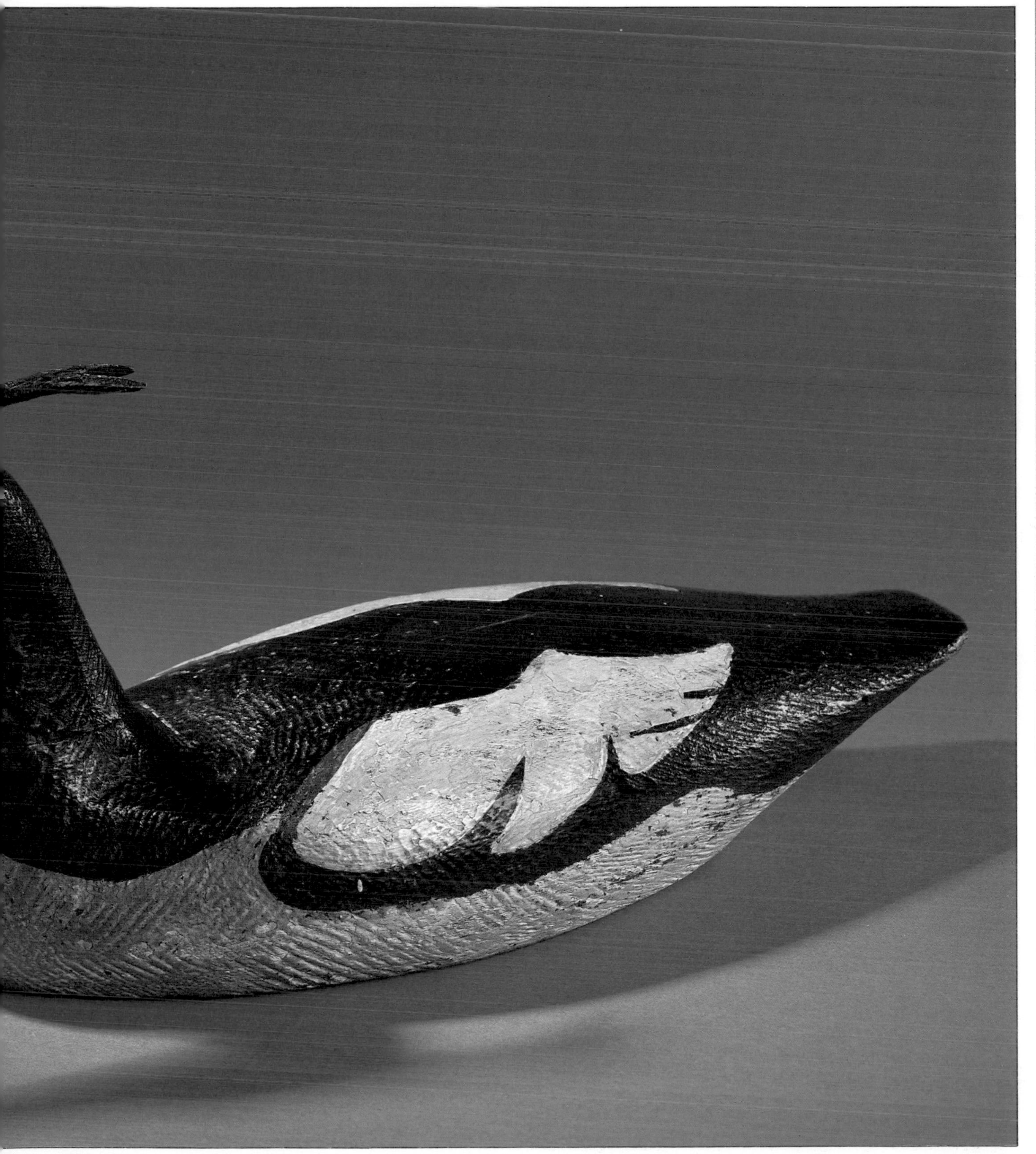

CARVING AN INTERLACED CHAIR-BACK IN THE CHIPPENDALE STYLE

IN THE eighteenth century there was a coming together of different woods, carving styles and fashionable designs. For the first time exotic woods such as satin from the West Indies, ebony from Africa and, most important of all, mahogany from South America, were readily available. These exciting new materials, together with easier travel and inexpensive book printing, influenced furniture and decorative design away from established domestic traditions. For the first time, furniture and interiors were related as designers became more concerned with the total 'feel' of a room.

Books and manuals which illustrated the work of carvers and designers began to be published. One published craftsman was Thomas Chippendale (1718–1779), the son of a Yorkshire carpenter. In 1754 his book *The Gentlemen And Cabinet Maker's Director* was published. It was intended for workshops and wealthy people who wanted fashionable furniture. The book contains illustrations, designs and instructions for almost every type of domestic furniture, but with the emphasis on rococo chairs made of mahogany. Within a very short time, the Chippendale style became widespread with the result that today it is difficult to identify a piece definitely made by Chippendale. In general, Chippendale chairs are characterized by having solid square frames, square-section legs and uprights, straight, plain or fretted stretchers, and pierced, carved and interlaced backs. It has been said of Chippendale that he was not so much a furniture-maker, but more a businessman who was able to predict and exploit current whims of fashion and stylistic trends. Chippendale was able to take, for example, the designs of the Chinese or French, then borrow and adapt the style in order to make it his own.

TOOLS & EQUIPMENT

- Workbench
- Sketchpad
- Pencils
- Penknife
- Measure
- Compass
- Fine-point scalpel
- Stencil brush
- Hand drill with an 1/8in drill bit
- Vice
- Coping saw with a pack of blades
- Straight-bladed knife
- 3/4in straight chisel
- Modelling tools
- Graded glasspapers
- Cotton cloth

MATERIALS

- A panel of prepared, straight-grained mahogany measuring 15 × 11 × 1/2in
- Block of Plasticine
- White cartridge paper
- Tracing paper
- Stencil card
- Masking tape
- Poster paint (colour to suit)
- Beeswax
- Methylated spirits

The scale is two squares to 1in. Note the direction of the grain, and see how the weak short-grain areas are kept to a minimum. When you are cutting out the initial fret, make sure that you keep all the corners and angles crisp and clean. This project will fail if you try to 'round-up' angles and forms.

1 INCH

ABOVE *George II mahogany dining chair. See how the pierced back has been carved, and note how the carver has related the run of the grain to the various piercings. On close inspection you will see that there are hardly any short-grain weaknesses.*

RIGHT PROJECT PHOTOGRAPH *Two of a set of eight stained beechwood Chippendale dining chairs. Again, the fretted backs have been designed so that the short grain has been kept to a minimum. Also note the Chinese-style back-frets and the leg brackets.*

ABOVE *Mahogany ribband-backed chair made in about 1760 by Thomas Chippendale. See how the back has been designed so that the emphasis is on the strong vertical wood grain. Also note that where there is cross grain at the centre of the back, the wood is thickened to compensate.*

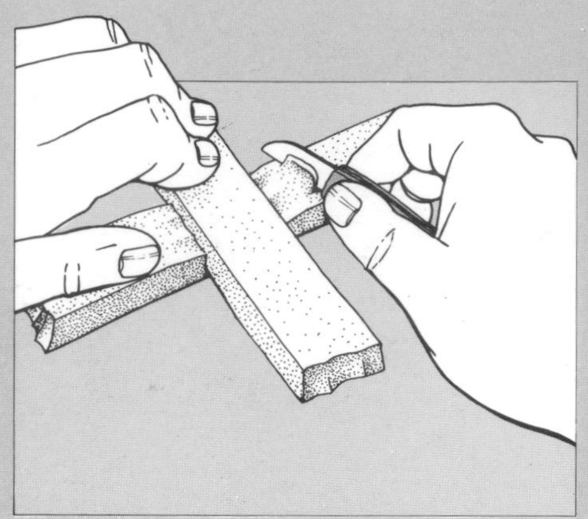

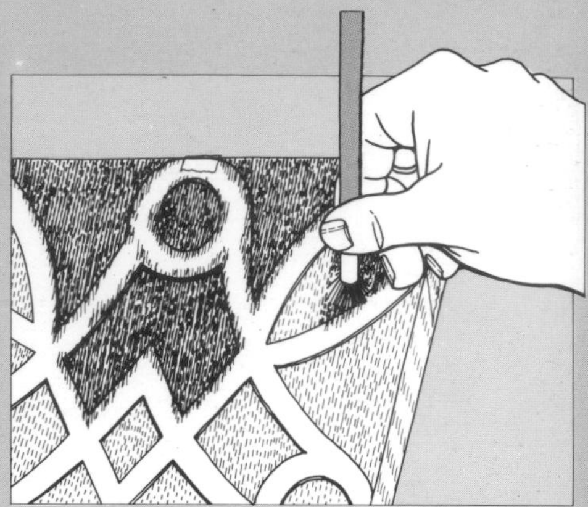

Considering the design and making a working model

Have a look at the photographs of Chippendale chairs and, if possible, visit a museum and have a close-up look at chairs. Notice how they are latticed — pierced and 'ribbon' carved — and fretted in the Chinese style. Make a series of design drawings, structural notes and detailed sketches, and work out how the chair has been put together.

Study the project photograph and focus your attention on the rather formal, pierced and carved back. See how the back has been worked and carved so as to give the impression of interlaced bands of wood. Take a magnifying glass and study a single 'under-and-over' interlaced detail. Note how the wood thickness has been reduced each side of the cross-over in order to achieve a flowing line and a feeling of depth.

Take a piece of Plasticine, roll it out to a thickness of about ½in, and then cut yourself a simple ¾in cross-over ribbon band. Using a penknife, cut away the Plasticine (as illustrated) so that the crossed bands look gently curved and interlaced. Note: if you start off with a thickness of about ½in and then lower the wood each side of the cross-over, the ½in thickness will be reduced to about ⅜in (see the working drawing).

Drawing out the lattice and making a stencil plate

When you have made a series of design sketches and have understood how the interlaced back has been worked, you need to draw out a full-size master design. First, have a look at the working drawing and then, with cartridge paper, pencil and compass, set about copying (or modifying) the Chippendale design. Quarter your paper, and then draw up a quarter of the total design.

Once you have achieved what you consider to be a good drawing and the balance between fretted areas and wood looks right, trace and transfer the drawing so that the initial quarter is mirror-imaged and repeated to make up the whole design (as illustrated). Keep making adjustments to the lattice until the design is suitable in terms of balance, structure and workability. Note: see how the central diamond lozenge just touches the two side circles. This is a structural necessity if you are to avoid short-grained fragile wood.

Make a tracing of the whole design and transfer the traced lines onto a sheet of stencil card. When the lines have been transferred, fix the stencil card to the cutting board with a few tabs of masking tape. Using the fine-point scalpel, start to cut away the waste windows of the design. Continue until you have removed all the waste. You should have the whole interlaced pattern cut out of the stencil card and should now be able to see how the final design will look.

Stencilling the pattern

Clear your working area and set out the panel of prepared mahogany, stencil plate, stencil brush, poster colour and the masking tape. First, position the stencil plate on the wood making sure that the registration points match, and then tape it down with tabs of masking tape.

Take the brush and the thick paint, and work the windows of the stencil with a steady, up-and-down stabbing action. Work with care until all the wood that you can see through the windows of the stencil has been blotted out. Once the paint is dry, remove the masking tape and peel off the stencil plate. If you have worked as described, the lattice design should be well-established and clean-edged.

Turn the wood over so that it is paint-side-down on the work surface. Wait for the paint on the stencil plate to dry and place it paint-side-down on the wood. Match up the registration points and, having checked that all is correct, fix the plate with masking tape and work the windows of the stencil. Wait for the paint to dry and remove the stencil plate.

Finally, take the hand drill and the ⅛in drill bit, and work a couple of test holes through one of the stencil-painted windows of the panel. If all is correct and the stencil plate was correctly positioned, the test holes should confirm that the design (as printed on both sides of the wood) is perfectly aligned.

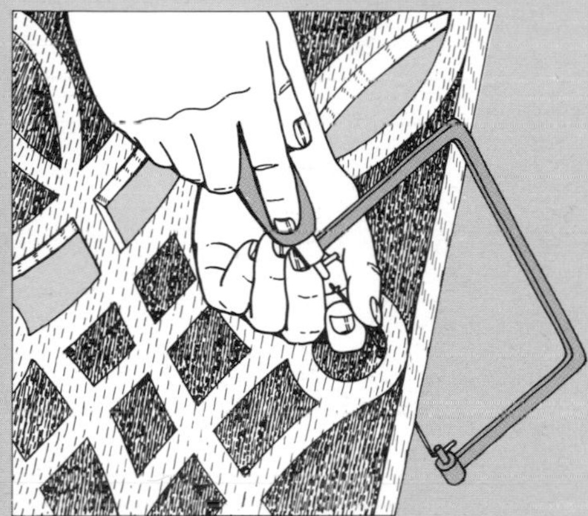

Sawing the lattice

You can now start to pierce the lattice properly. Place the wood in the vice (as illustrated) and set out your tools — the hand drill and bit, and the coping saw. First, drill pilot holes through each of the stencilled windows at all angles and turning points. When you are working the holes, hold the drill square with the wood thereby ensuring that the holes enter and exit correctly.

Have a look at the saw and notice how the blade can be easily removed and refitted by unscrewing the handle. Select one of the pilot holes, pass the blade through the wood and fit it in the coping saw frame. Work the saw with an even, steady action. Cut along the edges of the stencilled pattern and try to keep the saw blade at 90° to the working face of the wood. Have a look at the other side of the wood from time-to-time and check that the line of cut is correctly placed.

Keep the coping saw moving as you slowly alter the position of the wood in the vice, and generally make sure that the saw blade is always presented with the line of the next cut. When you come to a corner or a tight curve, keep the blade moving and manoeuvre both the wood and the saw. Note: it is possible that you may break some blades so make sure that you have a couple of spare packs at the start of the project.

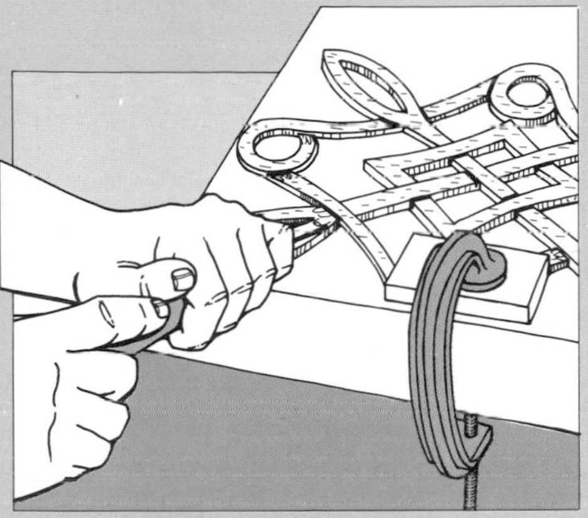

Carving the interlacing

Once all the stencil-painted windows of waste have been sawn, clear away the clutter and clamp the panel (best-side-up) on the bench. Set out the knife and straight chisel. Now, have another look at the working drawing, the photographs and the working model, and see how the lattice bands are cut and lowered each side of the cross-over in order to give an over-and-under bridge effect.

Take a soft pencil to the fretted wood and mark the position of the various interlaced elements and cross-overs. Hold the knife at right-angles to the working surface of the wood, and make stop-cuts either side of all the bridges. Do not twist the knife or try to cut any deeper than about ⅛in, and be extra careful when the blade is pushed into the wood along a grain line.

Noting the direction of the grain, hold the shank of the chisel almost flat to the wood and slide the blade at a slight angle into the stop-cut. Work and lower the wood little by little until the bands appear to be curving, dipping and rising under each other. If you keep the chisel razor-edged and slide the blade at an angle to the grain, the wood should come away in beautiful, crisp curls.

Carve and lower the whole lattice until all the bands appear to be interlaced — they should look as if they are going over and under each other. Note: if you wish, you can turn the wood over and work the other side. Reduce the wood at the cross-over to about ⅜in.

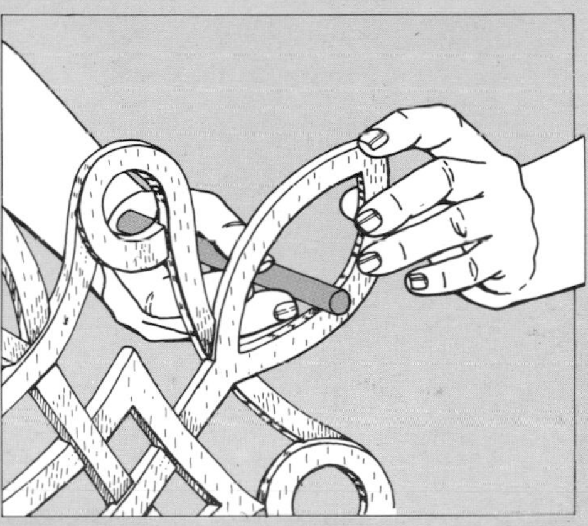

Finishing

When you have worked and carved all the cross-overs of the lattice and you feel that the wood has been reduced to a minimum, clear away the waste and set out a pack of graded glasspapers, several modelling tools and beeswax polish. Starting with a medium coarse paper, clean up the sawn edges and tidy up the curves so that they run smoothly around the whole design. Bearing in mind that, in this instance, you want to remove all tool marks, work through all the grades of paper and rub down the whole work. Do not let the paper run off the corners or edges — keep them tight and crisp.

Once you have rubbed down the wood to a good finish, take a modelling tool and a fine-grade paper, and concentrate on the subtle curves of the central diamond lozenge. Work the little central motif until it looks a single unit. The end result of rubbing down and adjusting should be a design that has a smoothness of line — lines that run and flow around the whole motif. There should be no disjointed breaks, weak curves or necks in the bands.

Wipe the wood over with methylated spirits and clear away all the tools and bench waste. Finally, take a soft cotton cloth and the beeswax polish, and burnish the wood to a smooth finish.

CHAPTER 5

FINISHING

WOODWORK can either be 'finished' — that is to say it can be variously tooled and then waxed, oiled and burnished — or as, with the projects in this chapter, the wood can be given a surface treatment that is termed a 'decorative finish', meaning an applied finish. For example, a marquetry table or a piece of inlay can be french polished; a functional or sculptural piece of woodwork can be stencilled and painted; a carving can be gilded; and pieces of furniture can be decorated with metal powders and lacquers, as in the Hitchcock stencil project.

Although the fashion, generally speaking, is now for woodwork that is waxed and left natural, there was a time when woodwork and the use of brilliant strong colours went hand-in-hand. Church interiors were once painted in primary colours; furniture was painted and stencil-decorated; carvings were gilded and painted; and walls, floors and ceilings were often painted with raw colours. The use of colour has always been subject to fashion trends but in general the earlier the environment in which the woodwork was made and the more basic, the greater the chance that it would have been brightly coloured and patterned. In the first instance, styles were almost certainly initiated by sophisticated woodworkers, their pieces being inlaid, gilded and decorated with all manner of precious metals and exotic woods. Country craftsmen, seeing these pieces but lacking the skills to work the inlays and other decorative embellishments, tended to use stencils and freehand painting to achieve what they thought were similar results.

While this chapter deals with gilding and polishing, its emphasis is on naïve, country and folk methods of achieving a painterly finish. Free from the need to slavishly follow fashion, folk colourists and decorators worked patterns and designs that we now consider works of art. American and European folk art techniques of decorating woodware are going through a revival worldwide, with designers and artists drawing their inspiration from traditional works. The techniques described in this chapter are now being used to decorate furniture and interiors. We are in the peculiar situation of having trendy artists and designers decorating all manner of woodworked items with gilding, stencils, hand-painting and all the rest, and yet describing their styles and techniques as 'new' and 'modern'.

American painted furniture inspired by early European folk painting; furniture painted with exuberantly coloured, uninhibitedly sensuous designs; Hitchcock stencil techniques that draw their inspiration from Oriental lacquer work; designs and patterns so full of life that one wonders at our own rather bland non-art woodwork — this chapter shows you how to create it, guiding you gently through all the techniques.

PAINTING A DESIGN IN THE AMERICAN DOWER CHEST TRADITION

JUST AS early American settlers employed itinerant decorators to stencil and paint designs and motifs on the walls and floors of their homes, they also had the same decorators embellish and enliven their rather basic country-made furniture. Huge German-American *schrank* wardrobes painted with 'cat's paw' patterns survive and there are tables, desks, chairs, beds, cupboards and boxes painted to look as though they are decorated with expensive veneers and inlays. Of all these painted items, perhaps the most beautiful are the exuberant dower chests. Many New Americans — the Pennsylvanian 'Dutch' (Germans) and immigrants from Holland, Sweden and Switzerland — had folk customs of presenting their newly-married daughters with painted dowry chests in which they could store special bed linens, embroidered Christening gowns and other treasured items. These dowry or dower chests were nearly always named, dated and painted with motifs that related to much earlier Old World traditions. The range of these symbols is really quite amazing, encompassing pagan motifs connected with magic ritual and fertility, Christian emblems, such as unicorns symbolizing virginal purity, magic hex with stars, love hearts, the tree-of-life — the chests are literally covered in boldly painted naïve folk designs.

Although these chests are now variously described as having their roots in particular traditions — German *fractur* writing, Dutch pottery, Swedish rosemarling and so on — it is now thought that really they are not the product of any single Old World craft or folk art but represent a coming together of all of them. Taken collectively, painted furniture of this type has come to characterize and represent a form of American folk art that is now described variously as naïve, primitive, pioneer or 'kitchen hearth'. It is a folk art that represents the independent spirit of the country.

TOOLS & EQUIPMENT

- Workbench
- Sketch book
- Selection of brushes
- Drawing board
- Pencils
- Pair of compasses
- Ruler
- Measure
- Glasspaper/sandpaper
- Paint-mixing dishes and tubs
- Cloths

MATERIALS

- Panel or a piece of furniture to be decorated
- Poster paints
- White cartridge paper
- Tracing paper
- Masking tape
- Acrylic wood paints
- Wax-based varnish

The scale is two squares to 1in. Note the symmetrical layout, and see how the compass is centred on a point that is at about chest height. When you are drawing out the design, try not to be too dogmatic, but adjust and modify the design to suit. When you are selecting colours, choose strong, bold primary colours.

1 INCH

TOP *Naïve American dower chest. This chest has characteristic arched panels, tulips and hearts. The motifs relate to much earlier European inlay designs.*

ABOVE *Dower chest. Decorated with hex symbols on the lid and two 'flower and pot' panels, once again the artist has used the very popular tulip motif.*

RIGHT PROJECT PHOTOGRAPH
Pennsylvanian dower chest made in 1790 in Berkshire County. This chest is particularly beautiful, having been painted with flowers, unicorns, hex stars, love hearts, doves and just about every folk motif of the period. Note how the main lines of the design are characteristically high-lighted with dots and dashes.

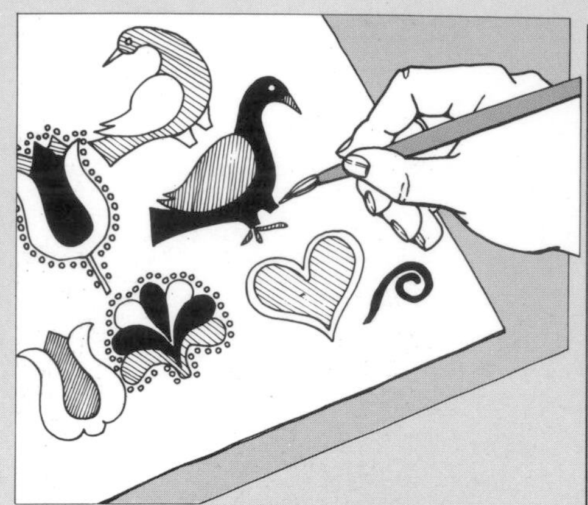

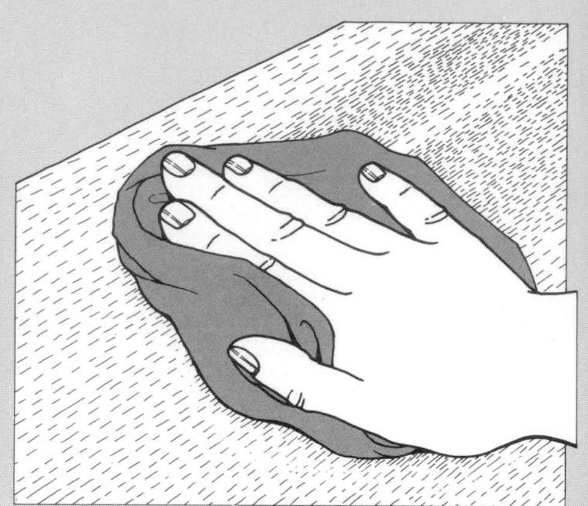

Considering the project and making a series of brush-worked design sketches

Start by taking a magnifying glass to the project. Look at the beautifully naïve patterning around the three painted panels, and notice how the uncomplicated spot-and-dot designs are set out symmetrically. Take note of all the classic and characteristic symbols and motifs — the unicorns, love hearts, doves that symbolize married bliss, and the flowers, scrolls and buds. Observe how the whole design has been balanced. If possible, visit an American folk museum and see dower chests that are dated about 1780 to 1810. Pay special attention to the range of motif forms and the traditional fractur lettering and date numerals, and of course note the use of brilliant bold primary colours.

When you have done all this, take a sketch pad, colours and fine brushes and make a series of design studies. Try to imagine yourself in the shoes of an American itinerant painter. Imagine that you have been asked to paint a dower chest, let yourself go and put all your remembered and gathered folk motifs into the work.

You might also, at this stage, consider what item — a panel or a piece of furniture — you are going to paint and whether you are going to modify the design. Obviously you will need to change dates, initials and names. Maybe you could also include in the design a short motto or line of text in the German-American tradition. This done, take note of the rather soft milky textures and the vibrant primary colours, and work out your own colours to suit.

Working up the master design

When you have completed a series of brush-worked sketches, go back to the drawing board and, using white cartridge paper and a soft pencil, work out your own full-size design. Grid both your paper and the sketches, then bring the design to size. This project relates to the 'Unicorn' panel, the whole design being symmetrically based on a centre-line that runs up through the middle of the tulip motif. Therefore, you need draw only a half-design to size.

This done, take a pair of compasses, centre it on the tulip at a point just about level with the chest of the unicorn (see the working drawing) then strike off an arc that sets out the top of the panel. Now reduce the radius of the compass, and strike off the other arcs that set out the various curved borders and zigzags.

When you have achieved a well-balanced top arch take the pencil and ruler, establish the side limits of the panel, then drop down lines for the borders, triangles and zigzags. Now comes the difficult task of drawing the unicorns and working them so that they not only fit the panel but also look lively and skittish. Do not try for anatomical correctness (who has ever seen a unicorn anyway?), but aim for forms that are bold and heraldic.

Finally, when all the main motifs have been worked, fill in and balance the design with stylized scrolls, curls, flowerheads and flourishes.

Preparing the ground

Once you have worked up a full-size gridded master design, put it to one side and arrange, close to hand, the article that you want to decorate. You might choose to paint a wooden panel that can be hung on the wall like a picture, or to decorate a small chest or box. This project concentrates on a panel, but whatever you have chosen to paint, it must be well-prepared.

To this end, take your chosen piece, remove dust, dirt and loose paint from it, then rub it down with a series of graded glasspapers. Work the wood in the direction of the grain, and aim to achieve a finish that is smooth and sound. This done, wipe down the work surface with a damp cloth, then set out your chosen colours, a selection of long-haired brushes and various cloths and paint tubs. As to the paint, you could use household gloss paints, inks, flat water paints, matt paints under varnish, dry powders mixed with beer and milk in the American tradition. This project uses a range of acrylic wood paints. These special paints are semi-flat acrylics that can be mixed with water — the wood grain can be seen through the paint.

When you have prepared the article to be painted, lay on a single well-brushed base coat; try to relate this to traditional colours.

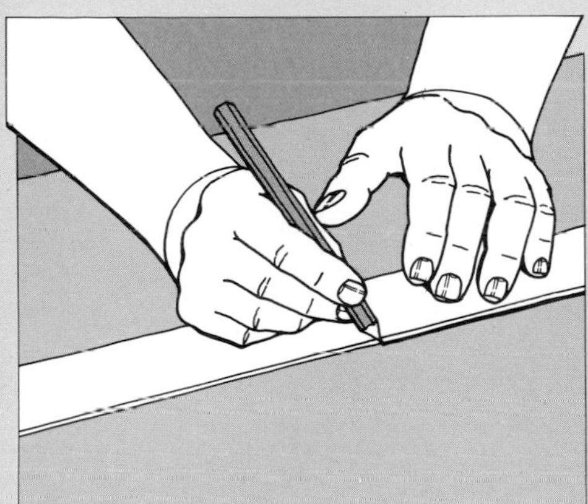

Transferring the design

Allow the base coat to dry, rub it down with the finest of flour papers, and set out the master design, the tracing paper, the masking tape and the pencils. First, take a tracing of the master design (the half-design). When this has been done, draw out a centre-line on the surface to be decorated and then, using tabs of masking tape, fix the half-design into position. Now, transfer the traced lines through to the working surface. When all the lines have been transferred, very carefully turn the tracing paper over, making sure it relates to both the centre-line and the transferred half-design; fix it with masking tape.

Having checked that all is correct, take a hard pencil and transfer the other half of the design through to the painted ground. Make sure that you have gone over all the lines, then peel away both the tape and paper so that the design is revealed. If you have worked as described, you will have a symmetrical design that is mirrored about the centre-line.

If all is well, take a soft pencil and go over all the transferred lines, making sure they are well-established and nicely set out. At this stage stand back from the work, consider the design as a whole and, if necessary, adjust and modify the design so that it fits into your scheme of things.

Finally study the colour guide and perhaps label or colour code the various design windows. If you have chosen to work dates and initials these will, of course, have to be worked not as half-designs but direct.

Blocking in the main areas of colour

Clear the work surface of all clutter — paper, dust, scraps and so on. Pin the inspirational material up around the working area, then arrange all your tools and materials, the brushes, the colours and dishes, so that they are close to hand. Refresh your eye by looking at the master design and the photographs, then start by establishing the main blocks of colour. You might start with the blue-black of the unicorn, or the red-orange of the zigzags and flower petals.

Mix the paints to a good consistency. This project uses acrylics, so they can be mixed with water, but your chosen paints may need to be thinned down with spirit. Before you put paint to wood, have a try-out on a piece of scrap wood. Work through your range of brushes and try to achieve a loose-wristed fluidity of line. The lines should not be so loose that they are weak, nor so tight as to look to be restrained — try for the middle way.

When you have mixed the paints and had several trial runs set to work on the transferred motifs. And so you continue, blocking in the various windows of the design so that they relate to the master design. Paint the unicorns, the triangular zigzag infills, the lines in the border and so on. Acrylics dry very fast — so fast that they can touch each other without fear of bleeding or colour runs.

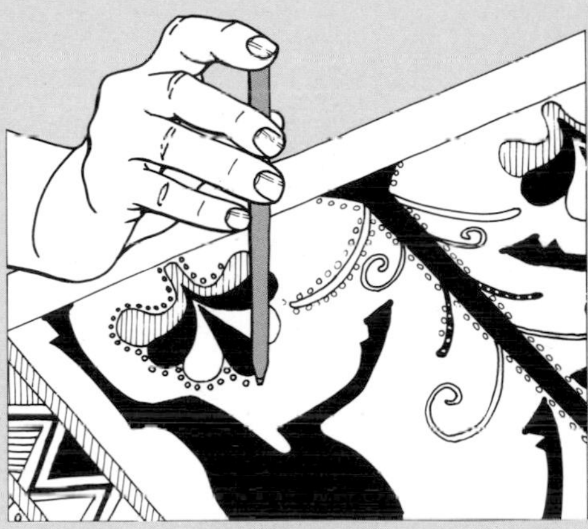

Picking out the design and finishing

When all the main areas of colour have been blocked in wash the brushes and leave the work to dry. While the paints are drying, sit back and study the project photographs and any other collected material — books, catalogues, museum handouts and such like. Use a magnifying glass to see how nearly all the Pennsylvanian dower chests painted between 1790 and 1820 have designs and motifs that are picked out with dots and dashes. The main forms are embellished with little brush or stick-pressed dots that give the forms a lively, bouncy character. Now, bearing in mind that the design needs to be free, take a matchstick or the end of a brush, dip it into the paint and then dab in the design. Work the dabber much as you would if you were printing with press sticks or doodling on scrap paper.

When you feel that the design is finished and the various dates, names and initials have been painted in, clean all the brushes and clear the work surface. Finally, when the paint has had time to dry — say three to four hours — take a suitable varnish (for acrylics use a wax-based varnish) and brush a thin coat over the whole work. If you are painting a piece of furniture then break the colours on edges and corners with a scrap of fine glasspaper before applying the varnish — it gives a very pleasant worn effect.

FRENCH POLISHING

FRENCH POLISH is no more than a thin, clear or coloured varnish that is used to achieve a high-gloss finish. Think of a traditional piece of furniture such as a large bureau or a grand table, a piece that has a high-shine mirror finish, and almost certainly it will have been french polished.

There are, of course, many traditional 'best' recipes — for example, a white polish can be made up from 6oz of bleached shellac in 1pt of methylated spirits, and brown polish can be made up from 5oz of orange shellac in 1pt of methylated spirits — then there are additives and improvers such as gum sandarac, gum benzoin and so on. However, while there are many mixtures and formulas, the polish base always includes a solution of resin or gum in alcohol or wood naphtha.

Various 'easy-to-use' kits are now on the market, and certainly these go some way to removing the hit-or-miss elements of the craft. Nevertheless, the success or failure of a french-polished finish still depends on the wood being well prepared and the polish being built up in many thin coats. The technique is as follows: the surface to be polished is rubbed down and filled. A rubber — a cotton wool pad covered with soft cloth — is filled with polish and worked systematically over the wood. The work is left for a day or so, then the polish is worked over with a rubber dampened with methylated spirit until all the oil has been 'spirited off'. By working in a succession of oil-lubricated coats and then removing the oil, a deep and even high-gloss polish can be achieved. French polish gives a uniquely beautiful finish that is hard-wearing, long-lasting and easy to keep clean; a finish that emphasizes the beauty of the wood grain and figure.

TOOLS & EQUIPMENT

- Workbench
- Pack of graded glasspapers
- Rubbers made from cotton wool covered in well-washed cotton or gauze
- Clean cotton rags
- Full-headed polish mop
- Various dishes, tubs and throwaway containers

MATERIALS

- The wood to be polished
- A suitable filler
- Prepared french polish (colour to suit)
- Spirit stains (colours to suit)
- Linseed oil
- Methylated spirits

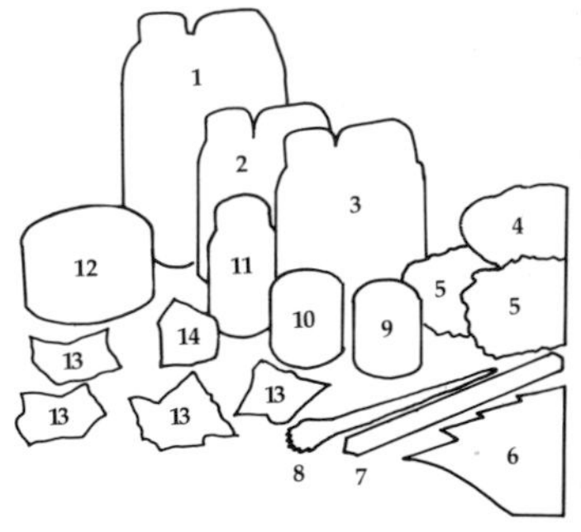

A selection of tools and materials for French polishing. **1** *shellac,* **2** *linseed oil,* **3** *methylated spirits,* **4** *rubber,* **5** *wire wool,* **6** *sandpapers,* **7** *shellac stick for filling,* **8** *polish mop,* **9** *light oak stain,* **10** *yew oil stain,* **11** *white oil (linseed oil substitute),* **12** *beeswax,* **13** *earth pigments,* **14** *wax filling.*

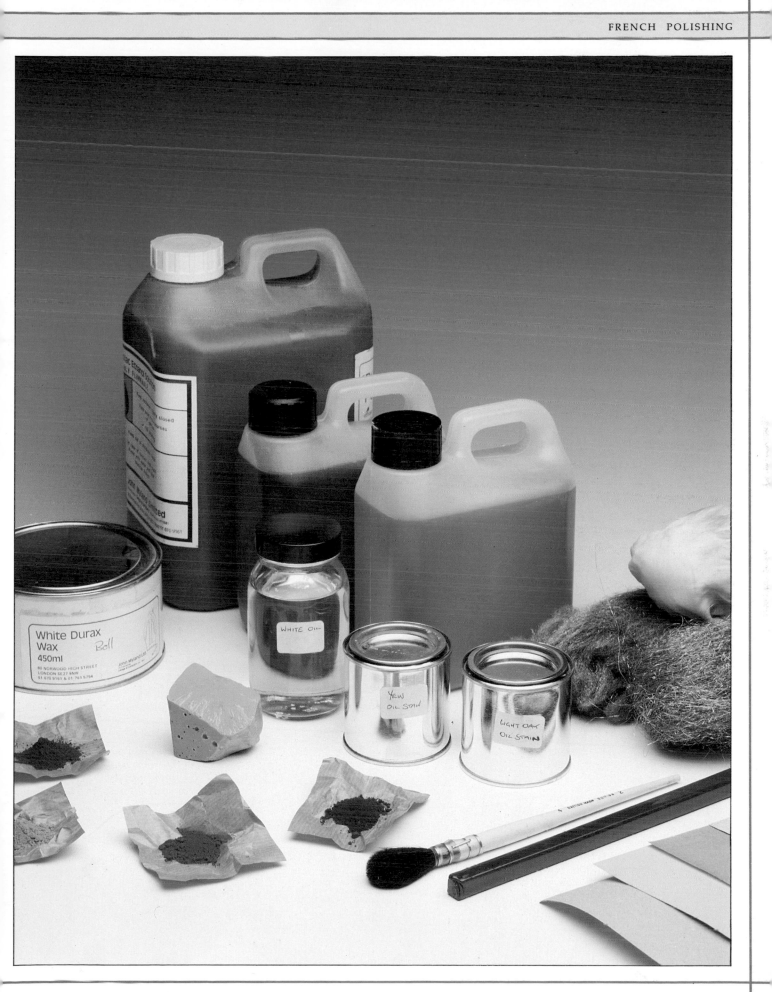

White Durax
Wax
450ml
WHITE OIL
YEW
OIL STAIN
LIGHT OAK
OIL STAIN

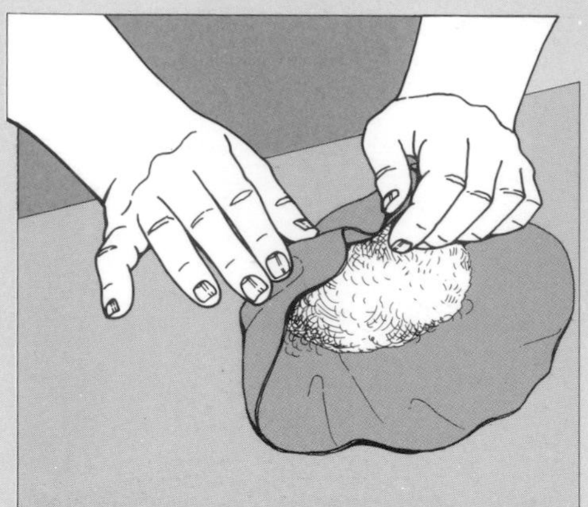

Considering the project and making the rubber

Before you set out on this project, note that some woods and some items of furniture are more suited to being polished than others. For example, oak with its bold open grain might be better waxed, and although french polish is hard-wearing and long-lasting, it has little resistance to heat and damp. It is not a good idea, therefore, to french polish items such as coffee tables and bathroom mirror surrounds. If you are a beginner, seek out an uncomplicated piece of furniture such as a small table, preferably one that has a close grain and an interesting figure. Perhaps you could french polish an article made in another project — for example, the games board (see page 62).

Having decided which item you want to polish, you need to obtain or make the few basic tools. Apart from the polish mop (brush) and the fine glasspapers, the only other tool you need is a rubber. This can be as basic as a pad of cotton wool covered with a piece of soft cotton cloth (as illustrated) or it can be a little more complicated and made of rag strips rolled up and covered with fine cotton or some similar material. It is worth noting at this point that french polishers all have their own formulas for making the 'traditional' rubber. It might be as well at this stage to visit a french polisher's workshop.

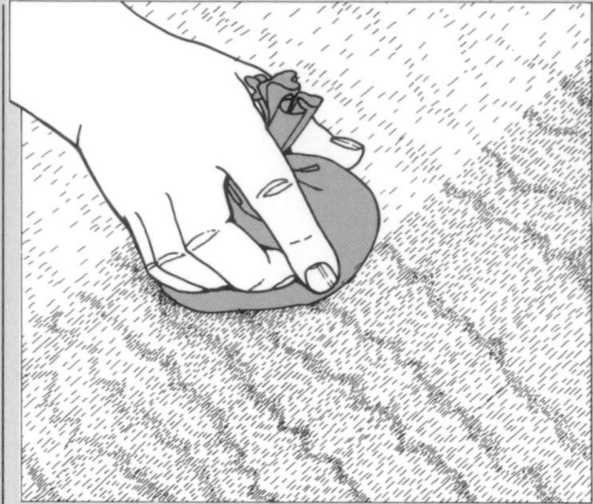

Wood preparation

Make sure the article to be polished is well prepared. Start by rubbing it down with graded glasspapers, then set it out on the work surface and arrange all the tools and materials so that they are close to hand.

Take a close look at the wood to be polished. If it has a large open grain it needs to be filled. You might buy and use a ready-mixed filler, make one up using a special filler powder and a little turpentine, or use fine plaster of Paris and water. Whichever recipe you use, make sure your chosen filler is colour-matched to the article you want to polish.

Take the filler paste, smear a little on the wood and, with a piece of clean cloth, rub it well into the grain pores. This done, make sure all the corners and mouldings are free from pockets of hard filler, then take the glasspaper and rub off the excess in the direction of the grain.

While waiting for the filler to dry, make sure the working area is clean and well organized. Wipe down the work surface with a damp cloth and check that the workshop is at a correct working temperature — it must not be overwarm or dry and dusty.

First steps

When the filler is dry and all the workshop conditions are just right, the work can be given its first coat of polish. Take the mop (the full-headed brush) and apply an even coat to the face of the work. Take care not to puddle the polish or let it run down an edge, lip or side-face. This first brushed coat will bring the wood to more or less its finished colour — subsequent coats of polish will improve the quality of the finish rather than change the colour. If you do not like the colour, now is the time to change it. There are several ways to adjust the colour; for example, if the wood looks too raw or highly coloured add a small amount of black spirit stain to a small quantity of polish and tone down the wood accordingly — all manner of spirit stains and colours can be bought from specialist suppliers.

When you feel that the wood is well matched and of a good colour, let the brushed-on stain dry, then take the fine glasspaper and rub down the piece with steady, even strokes. Wipe the wood and the working surface over so that they are free from dust and get ready for the rest of the many coats.

Take the wad of cotton wool, work it into a hand-size lump, dip it into the polish and slip it inside the soft cotton or gauze cover. Make sure the polish-soaked rubber lets the polish flow in a controlled bleed, and then set to work. If the whole pad drips and splodges, it is either too full of polish or the cover material is too open.

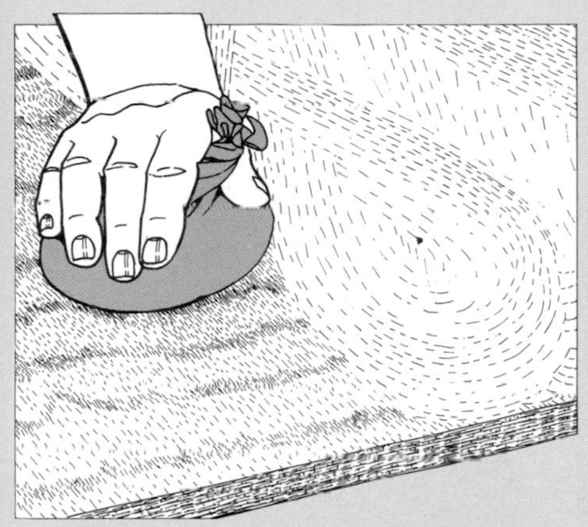

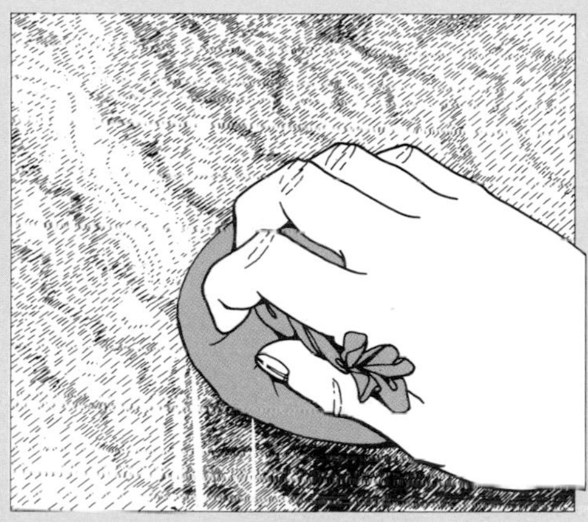

Building up layers

Take the soaked and covered rubber, dribble a few drops of oil onto the cover and start polishing. Work the rubber from left to right and then right to left in a continuous figure-of-eight, backwards and forwards movement. Do not stop in the middle of the work — avoid leaving puddles of polish — and do not lose concentration and overwork any single area. Gradually move down and across the face of the wood.

When the rubber runs dry, add more polish and a few drops of linseed oil and continue as before. Do not overdo the oil — it has to be removed at a later stage; add just enough to enable the rubber to move freely without pulling off patches of polish.

When you have worked a number of coats and achieved a good, even film of polish, let the work stand so that the polish can sink in, harden and dry. If you have overloaded the wood with polish and it looks like a sticky mess, let it dry out and then cut the polish back with glasspaper and repolish as described. Finally, rub down in the direction of the grain. You might at this point — or indeed at any stage — change the rubber cover or make a new rubber. Always choose a soft, well-washed natural material and make sure the cover is fluff-free and unwrinkled.

Polishing

Arrange a couple of dishes on the work surface, one for the polish and one for the methylated spirits. Continue rubbing, as before, but now at the end of each run 'dip-up' the rubber with a greater proportion of methylated spirits to polish, and hardly any oil. Aim to gradually change the rubbing composition until you are working with nothing but the spirit. Never change the mix mid-way, and try to maintain an even pressure. In this way you can ensure that the quality of the polish remains constant and the rubber never sticks. If the rubber does stick there is a chance that it will pull the polish off in a great lump.

If, as you are working, the polished wood takes on a slightly blue tinge, increase the room temperature, wait until the 'bloom' disappears and continue as before. Again, if the surface of the work looks less than perfect let it dry off, then cut back the polish with glasspaper. At this stage it is difficult to judge how much oil-to-spirit to use; do not use so much oil that you smear or blur the shine, and avoid using so much spirit that the polish threatens to lift.

When you reach this stage change the movement of the rubber and work the surface with a continuous side-to-side action. Take special care with edges, corners and mouldings — do not leave runs or drips. Finally, let the work dry off, change the rubber, wipe up the mess and clear away the bench clutter.

Finishing

Once you have achieved a bright, hard finish, stop applying the polish and oil and use just the rubber and a little methylated spirits. Rub backwards and forwards across the face of the work, gradually removing all traces of oil. This 'spiriting off' can be quite difficult, especially if you used too much oil in the early stages. If this is the case change the rubber cover after every few rubbings, as often as necessary. Take your time and be patient. Continue working, using less and less spirit and working off the oil. After rubbing and cover-changing, if the surface of the work is free from oily smears you can start finishing.

Wipe down the polish with a clean duster and prepare a clean rubber. Put the very smallest amount of spirit on the rubber and work the wood in the direction of the grain. This time, however, work with quicker, broader, longer sweeps, and decrease the pressure until you are working with a feather-light touch.

There is no easy fast way to achieve a perfect finish. Certainly there are improved products such as finishing spirits, but these are not 'cure-alls'. The secrets of success are to keep moving, maintaining an even pressure throughout the early stages, working the rubber dry before re-charging, and using as little oil as possible. The more you practise the better. If you have doubts do not start with the antique table, but try out your technique on a scrap piece or on an inexpensive sale item.

ABOVE *English table of about 1830. Although a lengthy process, French polishing is well worth the effort. It produces a high-shine finish that is long-lasting and easy to keep clean.*

RIGHT PROJECT PHOTOGRAPH *Pembroke table of the late eighteenth century. Decorated with intricate marquetry designs, this table has been French polished in order to protect the delicate woodwork.*

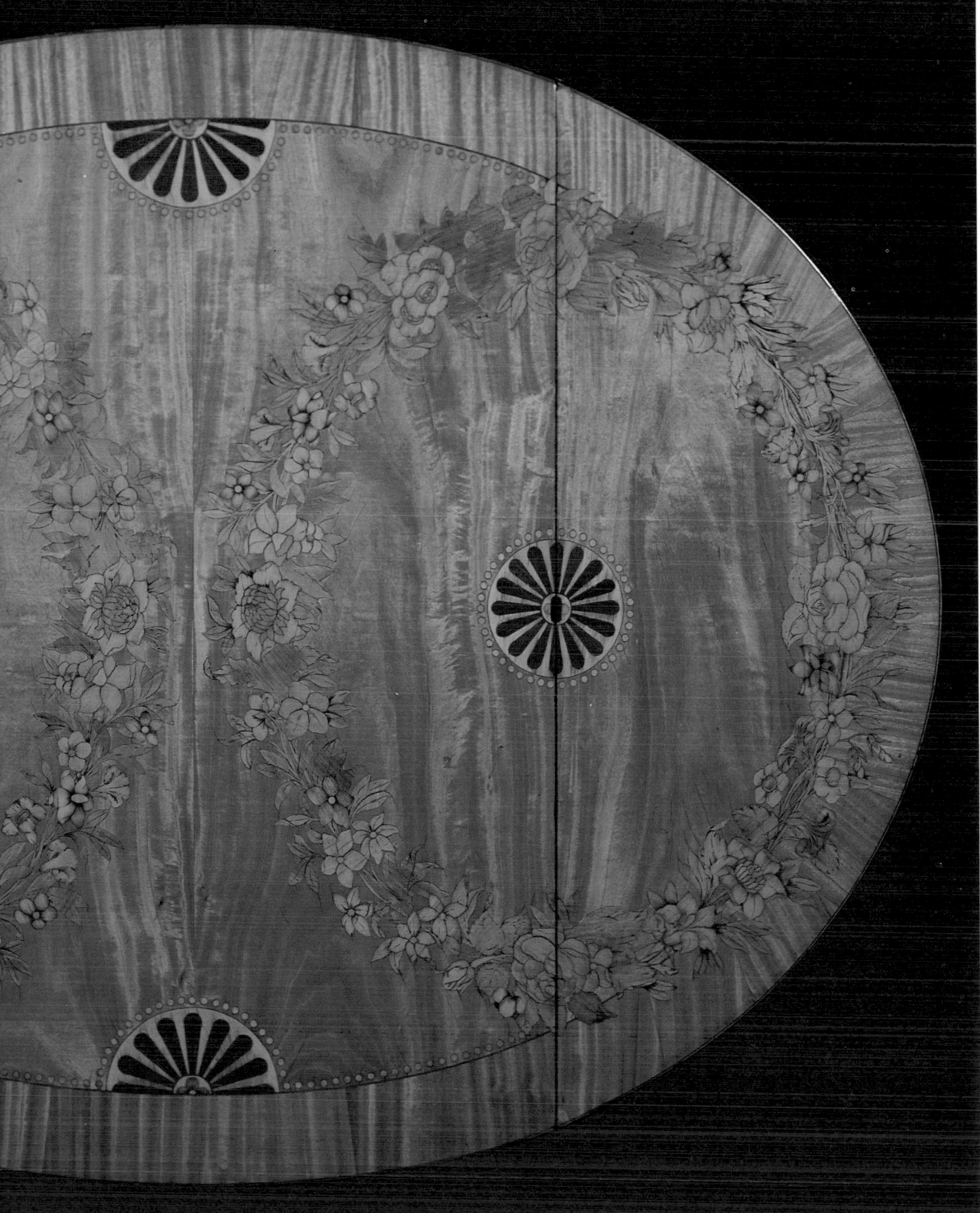

STENCILLING AND PAINTING IN THE AMERICAN FOLK TRADITION

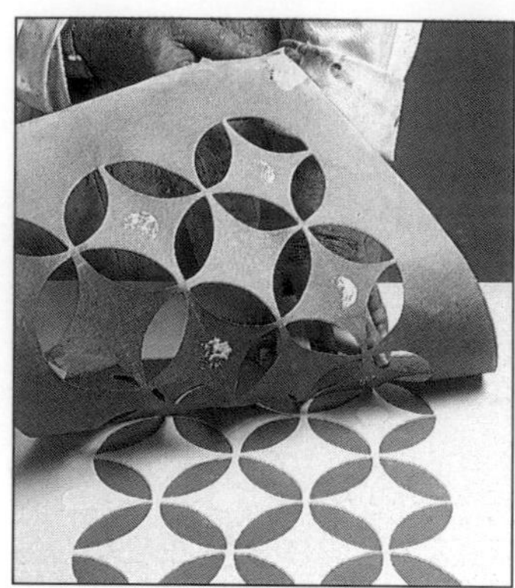

THE EARLY American settlers lived first in log cabins and later, when larger communities were established, in timber-framed and boarded houses. Quite naturally, it was not long before the new Americans wanted to have decorations and furnishings that reminded them of their 'old country'. As they could not afford the luxury of imported goods, they had to improvise. With roots in Sweden, Norway, Germany and many other countries, the arts and crafts of the various communities tended to be naïve home-spun echoes of their native lands. Of course, the settlers are known for their carved wood and woven cloth but the 'kitchen hearth' style is perhaps best characterized by the craft of stencilling and painting.

Itinerant 'stencilmen' used to travel around the countryside calling on farms and homesteads. The stencilman would arrive with his brushes, a stock of designs, a few earth colours and some leather or tin stencil plates. For a small fee and a meal or two he could decorate the whole house from top to bottom – walls, floors, furniture, and sometimes he would even paint a family portrait for good measure. Within a few days the whole house would be glowing with painted stencils – flowers, petals, leaves, buds, fruit and swags. Designs were frequently suggested, borrowed, and exchanged. It is difficult to pinpoint any particular European traditions as being the sole inspiration behind traditional American stencilling. It is widely acknowledged that it comes from a great many Old World art and craft styles including German fractur drawing, Norwegian rosemarling, English panel-stencilling, Romanian furniture painting and Polish oven painting among others.

TOOLS & EQUIPMENT

- Plate-glass cutting board
- Pencils
- Sketchbook
- Measure
- Fine-point scalpel
- Oilstone and strop
- Felt-tip pen
- Fine glasspaper
- Stencil brushes
- Paint dishes
- Paint brushes

MATERIALS

- The item of furniture to be decorated
- White cartridge paper
- Tracing paper
- Sheets of stencil card
- Rough paper
- Acrylic paints
- Paint thinner
- Varnish/glaze compatible with the paints

The scale is two squares to 1in. With a stencil of this character it is important that the forms are simple. See how the brush strokes are used to broaden the design. When you are selecting your paints, choose quick-drying acrylics.

1 INCH

RIGHT PROJECT PHOTOGRAPH *Chair stencilled in the American Colonial tradition. A simple chair has been enlivened by decorative stencilling using strong primary colours.*
BELOW *American rocking chair. A subtle combination of stencilling and painting has produced this beautifully simple decoration.*

TOP *Stencilled wardrobe by Fiona Skrine. Plain functional furniture can be enlivened by simple stencilling. Teak, deal or pine make ideal surfaces for paint finishes.*
ABOVE *Nineteenth-century stencilling. If you look at the photograph closely, you will see that the stencilling has been used to cover up knots in the wood.*

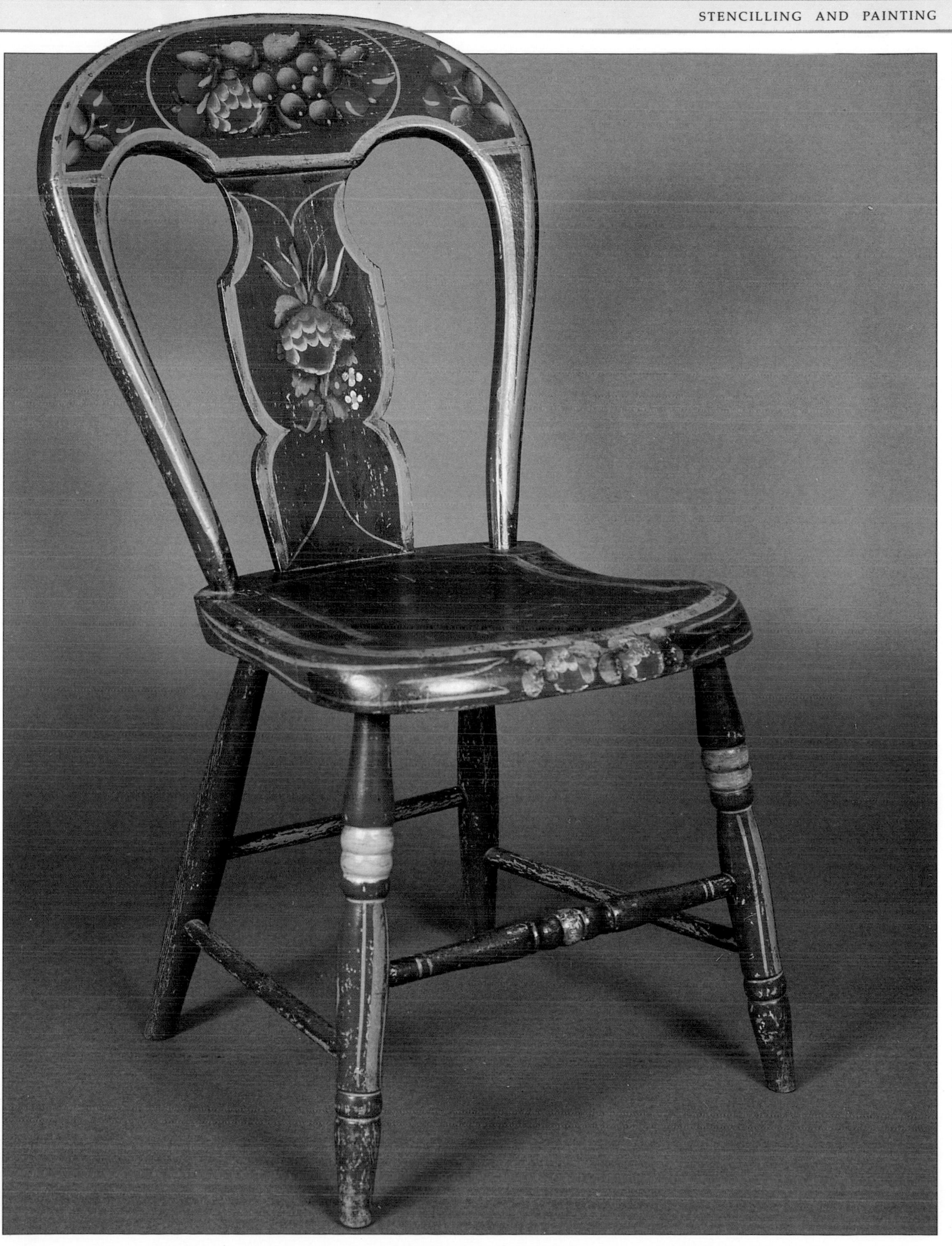

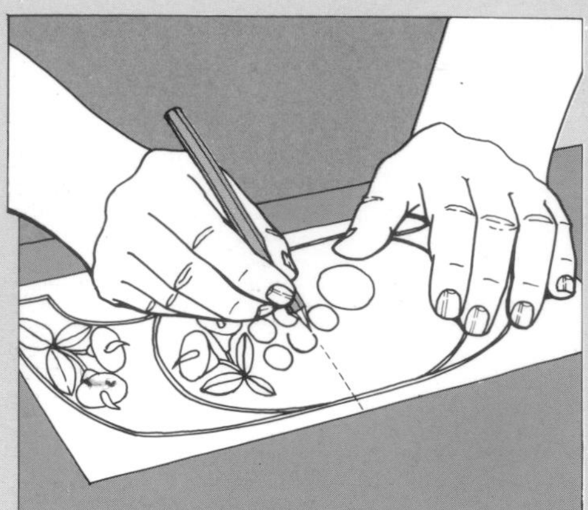

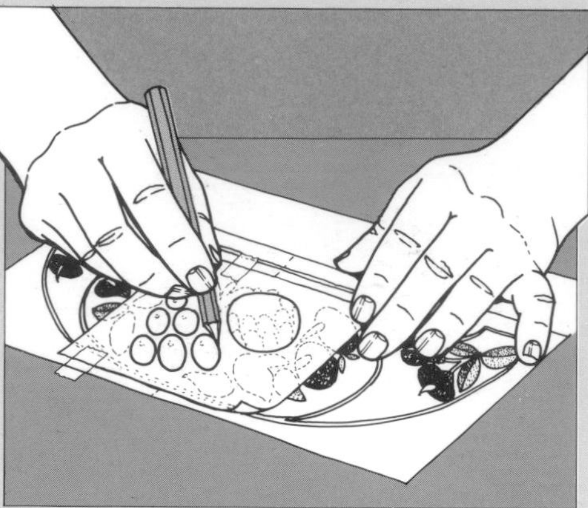

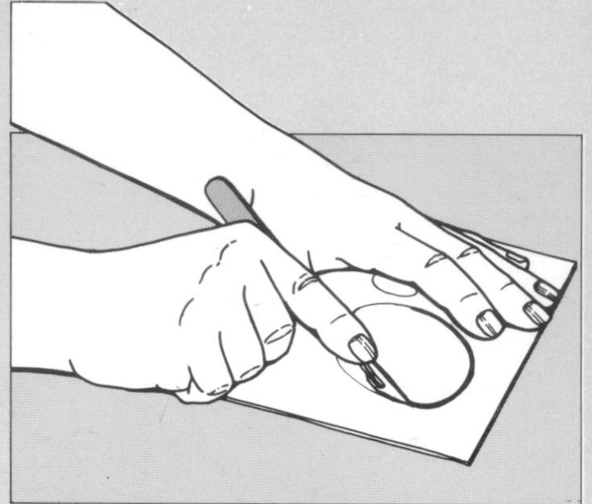

Considering the technique and drawing out the master design

Take the project photograph and have a look at the design – the central motifs, the supports and the cluster of blooms on the central splat. See how the big hard-edged shapes within each of the motifs have been worked with a stencil. Also note how the smaller details, including the leaves, the flower centres and the shading, have been worked with simple, direct brush-strokes. As you run your eyes over the design, consider how the details are painted with 'quick' brush-strokes. It might be helpful to visit a museum or crafts centre to see examples of more modern European craft painting.

Take a pencil and sketch pad, and analyse the various pattern compositions and layouts. When you have made a series of design sketches, have a look at the working drawing and the inspirational photographs, and decide whether you want to modify the design. For example, you could use an alternative colour scheme, or you could alter the type and number of shapes.

Finally, take the white cartridge paper and the coloured pencils, and draw up a master design to scale (as illustrated).

Transferring the design

If you now have a look at the project photograph (see page 161), you will see that the chair-back design contains about half a dozen different stencil prints – a green three-leaf motif, a red two-flower form, a large red rose, a group of purple plums or grapes, three green pears and a group of leaves on the central splat.

Look at your master design, and break it down into its individual stencil plates – that is, chop up the design so that each colour grouping can be considered as a separate stencil.

Take a tracing of each group and carefully organize the windows of the design so that the bridges between them are at least ⅛in wide. Allocate a piece of stencil card to each of the tracings and then transfer the traced lines so that they are well placed on the card.

At this stage, stop for a moment and consider the stencil techniques in a little more detail. It is possible to use your design layout and the stencil plates to build alternative patterns and motifs. For example, traditionally stencils were used to repeat large numbers of the same design. Assuming that you do not want to stencil hundreds of chairs, you might consider adapting and modifying the stencils so that they can be used in a larger context – decorating walls or floors. Consider all aspects of the design and explore the possibility of working linked repeats in the American wall-stencilling tradition.

Cutting the stencil plate and the registration marks

When you have set out the stencil card with the lines of the design, it is time to cut and pierce the stencil plates. It is essential that the edges of the stencil plate are clean and without burrs, and for this reason it is best if the actual cutting is done on a thick sheet of plate-glass.

Clear the work surface and arrange the plate-glass cutting board and the fine-point scalpel. The stencil card needs to be cut through in a single stroke – the knife should be drawn towards you with one hand while the stencil card is held and manipulated with the other. When cutting curves, the knife can be drawn slowly forward, and the card gently turned and manoeuvred so that the line of next cut is immediately in front of the moving blade. Note: as it is necessary to cut on a sheet of glass, the knife blade will need to be re-sharpened frequently so have an oilstone and strop at hand.

Continue cutting until windows in all the stencil cards have been cut. Bearing in mind that the total design is made of several independent stencil printings, it is necessary that each plate is linked to the total design with registration windows or keys. These registration windows will not be printed but, in use, are aligned with part of the previous print. Working in this way, it is possible to ensure that all the individual printings come together to make a perfectly related design.

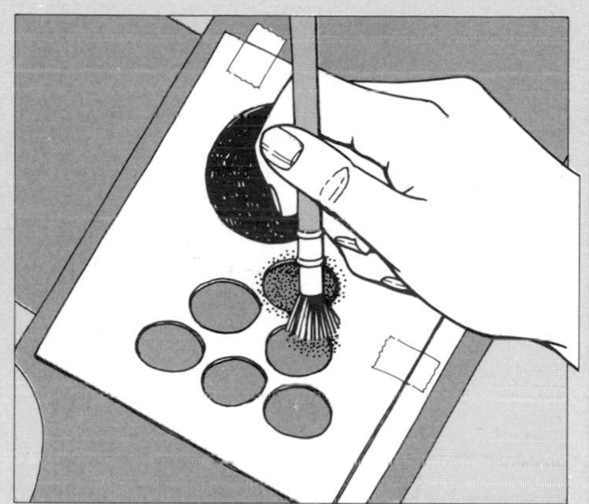

Preparing the ground and stencil printing

Before you start printing, take the stencil plates in sequence and, with a felt-tip pen and a scrap of paper, have a quick trial 'printing'. If necessary, adjust the registration windows so that the design is better placed. When you have done this, have a good look at the item to be decorated and decide on the colour arrangement. For example, you might copy the project and have exactly the same matt colours under a thin glaze or you could use inks. Alternatively, you could experiment with traditional American paint mixtures such as 'earth colors mixed with equal parts of stale beer and fresh milk'. This project uses modern flat-colour acrylics and a suitable glaze varnish.

First rub down the piece of furniture with fine glasspaper and then lay on a thin coat of base paint with a long-haired flat brush. Avoid building up too much paint, but keep it thin so that the grain of the wood is clearly visible.

Once the paint has dried, select the first stencil plate and, working with an almost dry stencil brush, blot out all the windows of the design. Wait a short while for the paint to dry and peel off the stencil plate. In a similar fashion, work the next and subsequent printings. In the course of printing, take a sheet of paper and print several rough proofs.

Note: you can secure the stencil plates with masking tape when you are printing.

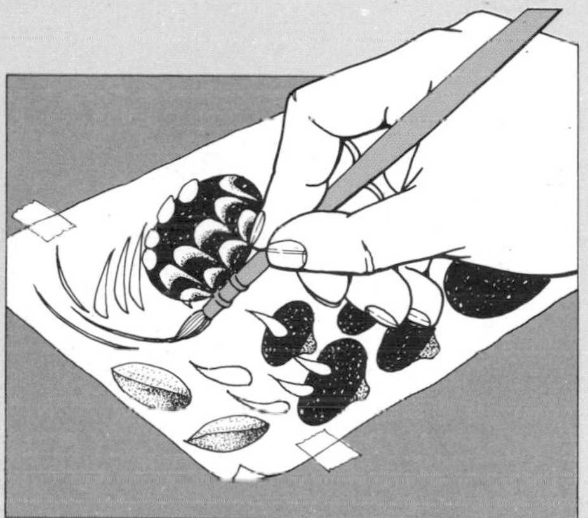

Painting and picking out the design

Having worked all the stencil plates in sequence, set out your selection of long-haired brushes and your chosen paints. Start by experimenting with all the brush types and seeing if you can achieve a variety of effects and textures. Work with thin fluid colours and the fine brushes for a long, smooth calligraphic line. Use short-haired, flat brushes and dryish paints to make marks that vary in density. Experiment with thinning the paints and laying on shadow effects.

Take the sheet of rough proofs and have a trial painting. Work with a loose wrist and a series of swift strokes, and see if you can achieve an uninhibited naïveness as seen in the project photograph (see page 161).

When you feel that you have loosened your wrist and worked out a suitable sequence of colours and brushes, take the stencilled item and swiftly go over the stencil picking out the various flower centres, dashes, petals, shadings and shadows. Work with swift but controlled haste.

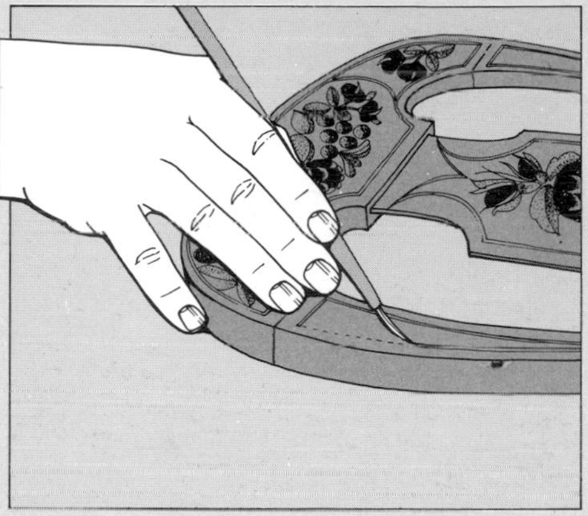

Striping and finishing

While you are waiting for the painted motifs to dry, take another look at the inspirational material, and see how the various panels of the design have been picked out and emphasized with striped lines. Notice how the banding contains the design in a direct way – there has been no attempt to over-work the lines in the manner of the late Victorian chair-painters.

Bearing in mind that these lines need to be worked swiftly and confidently, spend time practising lines on a piece of rough paper. Using a fine brush, gauge and set the distance from the edge of the wood to the line with your fingertips. As if you were using a carpenter's marking gauge, run the line around the design. Do not overload the brush with runny paint, but try to work the lines from start to finish so that they are smooth and unbroken. Once the whole design has been painted, leave the project for a day or two so that the paint can dry.

Finally, take a clear varnish and a soft brush, and lay on a coat as thinly as possible. If necessary, thin the varnish. When the varnish dries it should have a slightly dull, soft finish – you should easily be able to see the thickness of the paint and the texture of the wood grain. Note: you can also experiment with water-based colours under a wax polish.

WATER GILDING

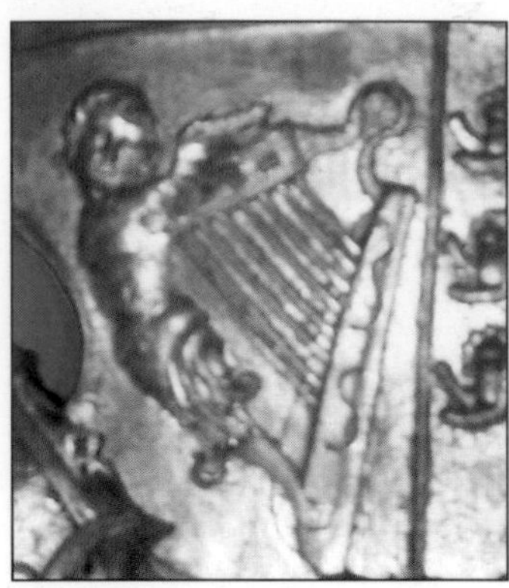

IN SIMPLE terms gilding is the art or craft of spreading gold over a base surface. Wood, stone, leather, glass and other materials are covered with a coating of gold leaf for both protection and ornamentation. Gilding is so ancient that the Greeks, Romans, Egyptians, Chinese and Japanese all have a history of working with sheet gold. The craft is not restricted to gold, for many alternatives and substitutes can be used. Gold powders, bronze powders, platinum leaf, copper and silver have all been used and worked as a decorative finish. There are numerous techniques for working gold leaf. It can be stuck onto a lacquered finish or sandwiched between lacquers, as in oriental work; gold powders can be floated in resins, as in Victorian furniture decoration; or, as with this project, the gold leaf can be floated on a water and size base. Water gilding is straightforward. The base material — in this case carved wood — is first covered with a glue size and plaster mixture called gesso followed by clay and size; this is dampened and then, by means of a knife, brush and burnisher, covered in fine gold leaf.

TOOLS & EQUIPMENT

- Workbench
- Double saucepan or glue boiler
- Small lawn sieve
- Selection of jars, throwaway containers and vessels
- Spatula
- Various brushes and modelling tools
- Flour papers and glasspapers
- Cotton or linen cloth
- Gilder's cushion
- Gilder's knife
- Burnishers
- Gilder's brush or mop
- Delicate liner
- Gilder's tip

MATERIALS

- Article to be gilded
- Parchment or rabbit-skin size (in a raw state or prepared)
- Gilder's whiting
- Bole
- Gold leaf (size and quality to suit)

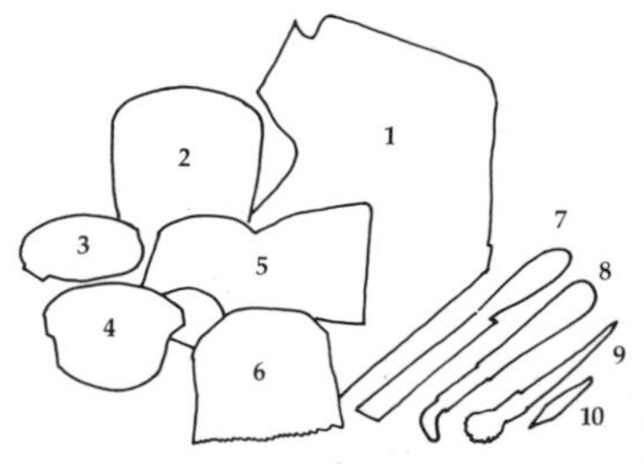

A selection of tools and materials for gilding. **1** *gilder's pad,* **2** *pipkin,* **3** *whiting,* **4** *rabbit-skin glue,* **5** *book of gold leaf,* **6** *squirrel-haired brush,* **7** *gilder's knife,* **8** *agate burnisher,* **9** *gilder's mop,* **10** *modelling tool.*

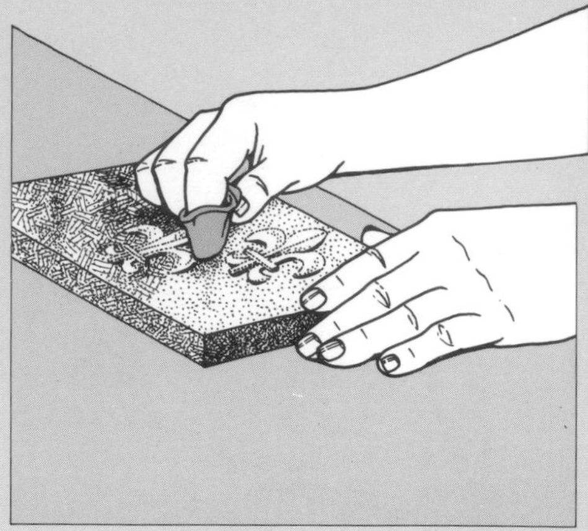

Considering the technique and preparing the size

For water gilding, it is advisable to choose an item that is small and not too deeply carved. You might choose to gild a badge, a name-board, or a small carved item such as a bracket. Notice how this project concentrates not on the coat-of-arms but on the small *fleur-de-lis* detail. It is also important at this point to consider the wood to be gilded. If you can, go for a close, smooth-grained wood such as lime or pine. You could, of course, gild a carving made in another project.

When you have decided what you want to gild, mix a quantity of size stock just before gilding. Take your chosen size material, leave it to soak for the recommended time and then cover it with water, rather like porridge, and heat it slowly. Do not let the water in the outer boiler run dry or the size will over-heat and spoil.

When the base has melted down, strain the resultant soup through a fine lawn sieve and leave it to cool and set. When it has set it should have the consistency of brown jelly. It must not be so hard and firm that it bounces around the workshop, and yet not so soft that it collapses. If necessary, add water and reheat. Size can also be purchased as a ready-made gel to which water is added.

Mixing and applying the gesso

When the size has been reheated arrange on the work surface a heat-resistant jar or throwaway container, a spatula, a quantity of gilder's whiting and the item to be gilded. Start by pouring some of the stock size into the jar, remove the inner pan from the double saucepan and put the jar in the hot water.

Now, bearing in mind that the wood to be gilded needs between five and nine coats of gesso, add the whiting to the size until you have a mixture that looks rather like a thickish cream. When the gesso is well-mixed, free from hard lumps and powder balls and of the correct consistency, you are ready to lay on the first coat. Use a flat long-haired brush to lay the gesso on with a slight stippling action. It should not be heaped on, but the first coat can be given a keyed texture for subsequent coats.

Wait for the gesso to dry and then lay on the second coat. Work the brush with a nice even action — avoid letting the gesso collect in pools and do not let it fill up the fine details of the carving. And so you continue, laying on a coat of gesso, letting it dry, laying on the next coat, and so on, until the whole work looks well-covered.

Finally, take a small soft brush, dampen the gesso slightly and work all the little corners and crannies until they are all nicely contoured.

Rubbing down, applying the bole and burnishing

Once the gesso is dry, take the very finest of flour papers and rub the work over with a light feather touch. Be very gentle and cut back only the imperfections — the little burrs and flecks. This done, take the ready-prepared bole, add a little thinned-down size, then stir until the mixture is of the consistency of thin cream.

When you consider the bole mixture well stirred and ready, take the long-haired brush and lay on a thin, even coat. Let it dry and then lay on three or four more coats until the white gesso has been completely covered. As with gesso the bole must be allowed to dry between coats.

When the whole work has been evenly covered with bole and the final coat is dry take a sheet of flour paper and cut back all the little lumps and gritty imperfections. Now, with a piece of firm cotton or linen cloth, rub and polish the dry bole until the whole surface begins to resemble leather or burnished clay. Do not press too hard or break the surface, just rhythmically rub away until the whole surface shines.

It is most important that the surface to be burnished and the working area are free from dust and fragments of hard bole. To this end, clean up after you have rubbed down, brush the surface of the carving and generally bring the working area to good order.

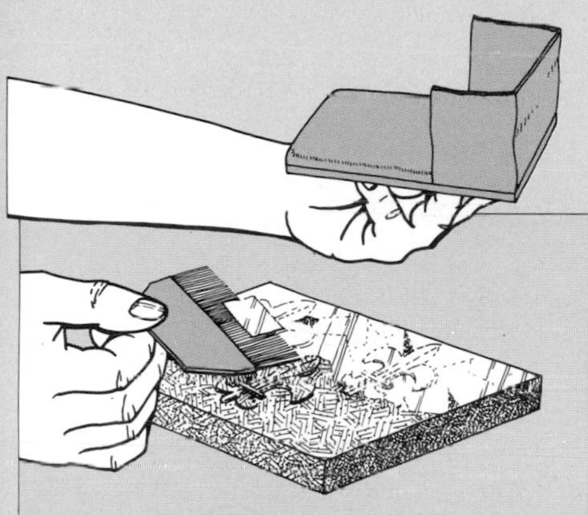

Applying the gold leaf

Set out the gilder's cushion, the knife, a couple of burnishers, a mop and liner, a tub of clean water, a little size, a gilder's tip of suitable size and the gold leaf. Before you start, examine your chosen subject closely and consider how best the dips, undercuts and the high relief areas might be covered. You might also at this stage have a trial run with a scrap of gold leaf; note how the knife cuts, and see that the gilder's tip is brushed against your hair or the back of your hand just before you pick up the gold leaf. When you are ready to start work, hold the cushion in one hand, then with the tip of the knife carefully open the book of gold leaf and manoeuvre a single sheet onto the cushion. Now very gently breathe on the gold leaf and with luck it will flatten out on the cushion. Gold leaf is fragile and likely to blow away at the slightest puff of air, so keep windows shut, fans switched off and do not have children watching.

Cut the gold leaf to shape with a downward press of the whole blade of the knife, then brush the gilder's tip over your arm and pick up the cut piece.

This done, add a little size to the water, dampen the area to be gilded (wet a small area and use the mop), then with great swiftness flip and slip the gold leaf from the tip onto the dampened surface. Finally, use the liner and quickly press the leaf into place.

Working the gold leaf

As with all crafts, there are any number of things that might go wrong. You might forget to add a little size to the water, for example, in which case the leaf might lift; or the work might be too wet, in which case the leaf will stay put but will be stained by the bole. To avoid such problems work with extreme care and caution. Aim to lay the gold little by little; press and cut the leaf into shapes and ribbons, pick it up with the tip, flip it onto the damp bole and push it into place with a liner.

If at first your efforts look wrinkled or horribly overlapped just keep trying and do your best. When you come to a piece of deep carving, such as a hole or an undercut, take care that the leaf does not run straight over the depression and form a bridging skin.

Continue to arrange the jigsaw until the red surface of the bole disappears under the gold. When you have more or less covered the bole, stand back and consider the work as a whole. Finally take scraps of gold leaf, just touch them with water and push them in place over any faults.

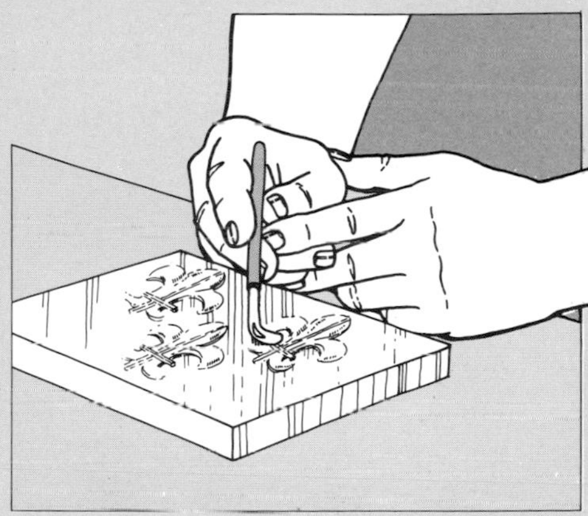

Burnishing

When you have covered the whole carving with gold leaf and you consider it finished, put it aside for at least 24 hours and clear the working area of all tools and waste. Prepare for burnishing by rubbing the tool backwards and forwards on a piece of clean cloth until it is shiny, clean and slightly warm. When this has been done, make sure the piece to be burnished is free from dust, grit and particles of gold leaf — and then to work.

At first, rub the burnisher with a light touch over a small area; after a few minutes, when the gold looks smooth and shiny, increase the pressure. Aim to burnish gradually outwards and across the work. Concentrate on the proud rounded areas and try to make them a feature. When you come to the undercuts and dips, leave them unburnished. Working in this way, it should be possible to vary the textures so that the gilding grades from matt to high shine.

There are a number of critical factors that might affect the burnishing. For example, if you leave the work for longer than 48 hours or if the atmosphere is too dry the gold leaf might not burnish. If this is the case let the work stand in a damp room or cabinet and then try again.

RIGHT PROJECT PHOTOGRAPH *Queen Anne's coat of arms dated 1710. This piece has been covered with fine gold leaf, an addition that not only gives the piece a grander appearance but also brings out sculptural qualities.*

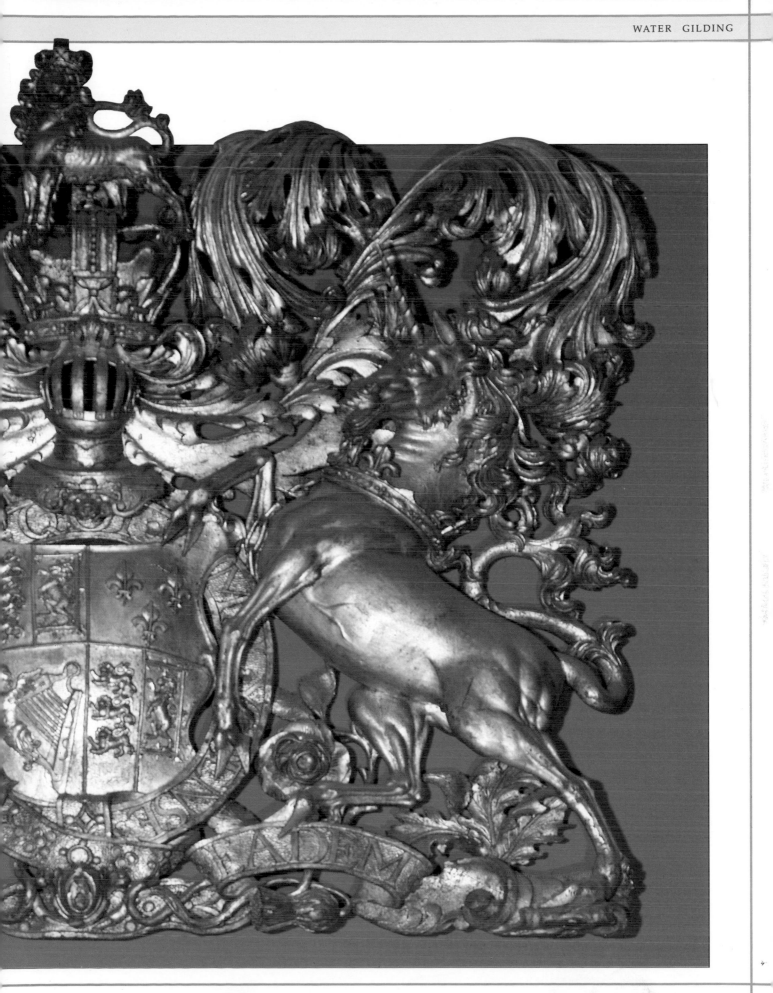

STENCILLING IN THE AMERICAN HITCHCOCK TRADITION

IN THE first quarter of the nineteenth century, an established Connecticut chairmaker called Lambert Hitchcock decided that not only was he going to make quality chairs but also the best and the most beautiful chairs in America, if not in the whole world. He was inspired by traditional American folk stencilling techniques, and eighteenth-century German, Norwegian and English hand-painted furniture such as chairs and dower chests. He set up a factory in Riverton, Connecticut and within a few years Hitchcock chairs had become so popular, that their name had become synonymous with just about any chair that was decorated with stencilling. However, Hitchcock chairs are completely different from most of the other chairs of that period. The actual stencil technique was recorded at the time as follows: 'the piece to be decorated is lacquered, then when the lacquer is almost dry, precious metallic bronze powders are dribbled and brushed through the stencil onto the sticky lacquer. Finally the piece is rubbed down and re-lacquered'.

Hitchcock chairs can be recognized by their characteristic hard-edged, gold designs that blur and tone from side-to-centre. Worked in many lacquer and gold-powder layers, the overall decorative effect is startling. It resembles lacquer-covered inlay or Japanese lacquer. It is interesting to note that Hitchcock chairs are still being made today.

TOOLS & EQUIPMENT

- Plate-glass cutting board
- Sketch pad
- Pencils
- Fine-point scalpel
- Spare blades or an oilstone and strop
- Fine grade glasspaper
- Felt-tip pens
- Painting brushes

MATERIALS

- Piece of furniture to be decorated
- Clear oil-based lacquer
- Fine gilder's gold powders (bronze powders) in different colours
- Cartridge paper
- Tracing paper
- Stencil card
- Rough paper
- Oil-based paint

Adjust the scale to suit the project that you have in mind. Note the use of the small registration points on the stencil plates. In this instance, the registration points are aligned and printed twice.

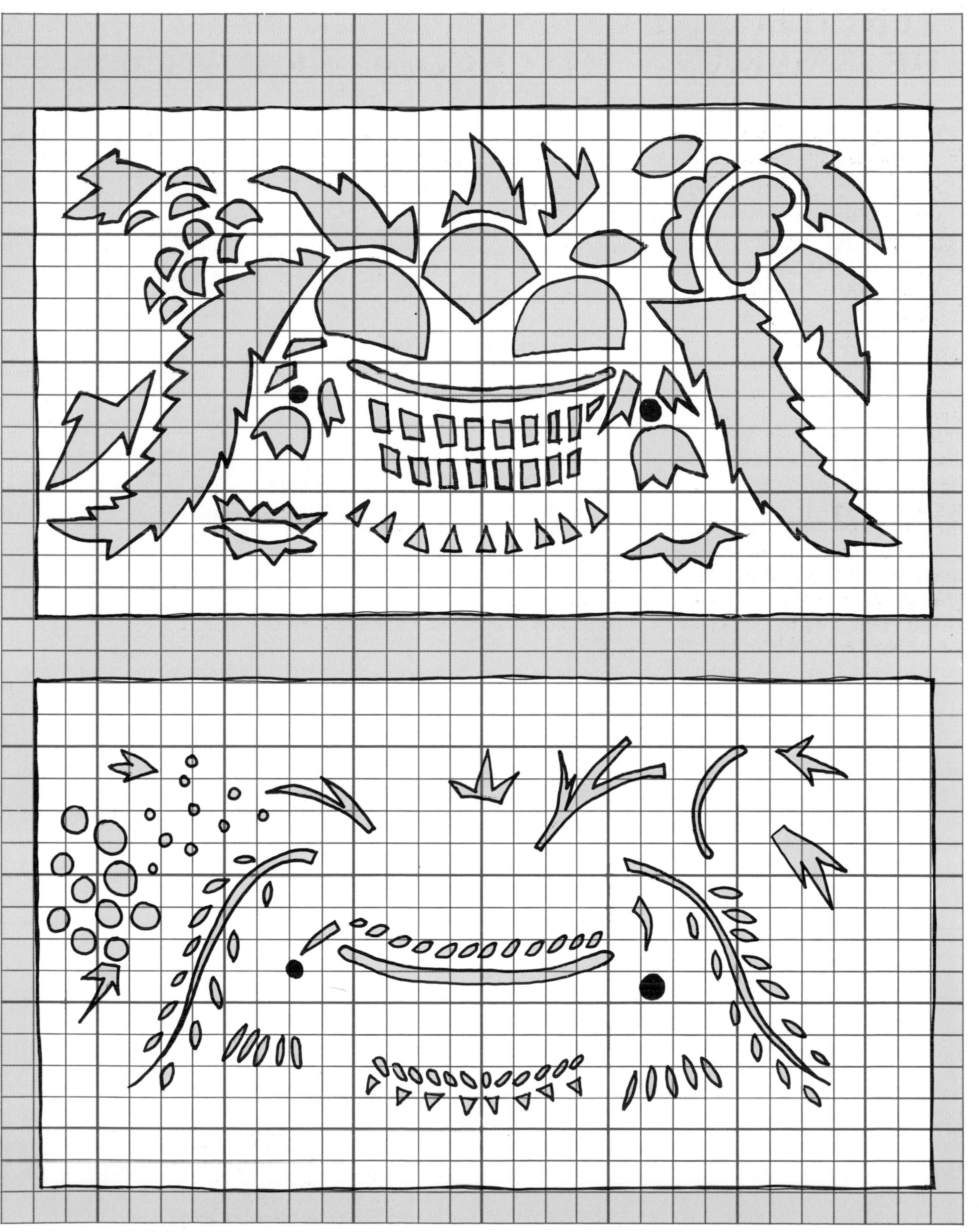

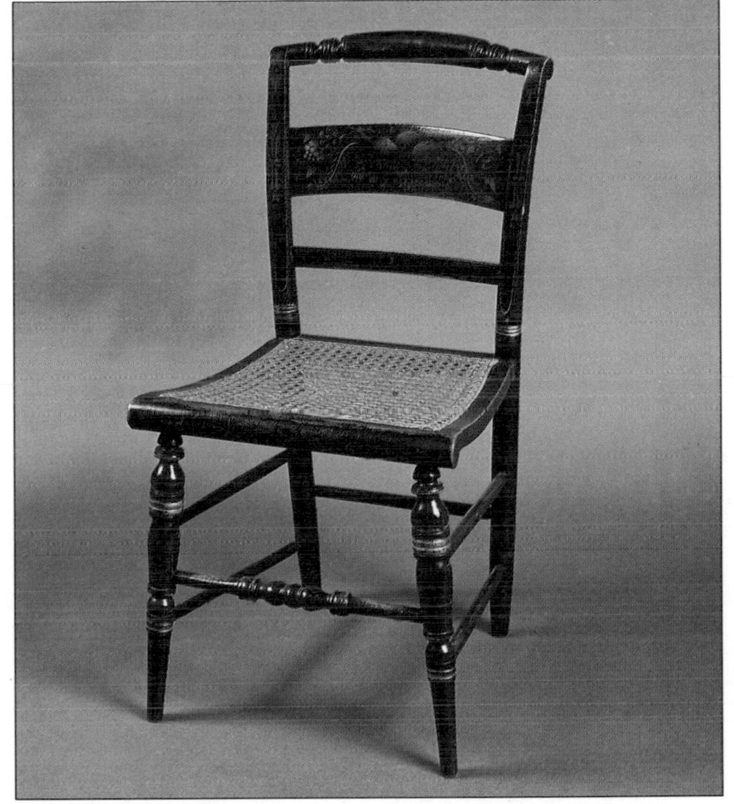

LEFT PROJECT PHOTOGRAPH *Chair-back decorated with Hitchcock stencilling. Complete with the characteristic bowl of fruit and supporting swags, note how the leaf form of the design is built up from two separate stencil printings.*

ABOVE PROJECT PHOTOGRAPH *A classic Hitchcock-stencilled chair. This piece has been worked with bronze powders on a black and lacquer base. See how the various panels and forms have been worked with delicate gold lining, and note how the leg turnings have also been picked out in gold.*

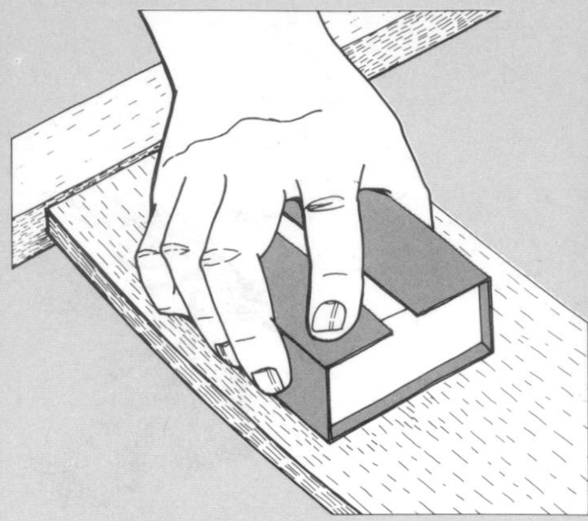

Considering the Hitchcock technique and drawing out the master design

Study the project photographs (see page 173) with a magnifying glass, and see how the stencil design is made up of a number of slightly different gold colours. Focus on the motifs details, such as the two sweeping leaf fronds that spring out either side of the basket of fruit, and note how the design has been worked in two parts. There is a hard edge that sets out the main form and an area of veining that is set against a darker central ground.

Unlike the more ordinary folk stencils, the Hitchcock stencils concentrate on precious powder 'edge-work'. The technique is simple enough: a base lacquer is laid onto a painted ground and, when the lacquer is almost dry, fine powders are trickled and brushed through the windows of the stencils. Finally, the piece is re-lacquered. Working in stages, it is possible to build a very rich deep 'inlay' effect.

When you feel that you understand just how the technique works, take a sheet of cartridge paper, a sketch pad, tracing paper and pencils, and work out a series of design studies. Note how the technique requires a minimum of two stencil plates, and consider how this method of stencilling differs in that the edges of the design are dusted.

Transferring the design and cutting the stencil plates

When you have studied the Hitchcock technique in some detail and you appreciate the design implications, divide the master design so that the various elements are clearly set out. If you decide to work a basic 'two-print' design, you need a main outline stencil plate that establishes the overall motif and a second stencil that picks out some of the finer details such as the veins on the leaves and the various dots and dashes on the fruit.

Take tracings from your master design and transfer the traced lines to the working face of the stencil card. Now, pin the inspirational material up around the working area, and set out the plate-glass cutting surface, the stencil card, the fine-point scalpel and either a pack of spare blades or an oilstone and strop. Cut the stencil card with a clean, crisp line, drawing the knife towards you with one hand, and guiding and manoeuvring the card with the other.

It is important for the second stencil plate to be perfectly aligned with the first so it is necessary to make reference or registration points. The simplest registration method is to have a small window in the second plate that can be matched-up with a detail on the first plate. Alternatively, the second plate might also be pierced with a section of 'edge-print' (see the working drawing and details). When the plates have been cut, take some rough paper and a couple of felt-tip pens, and carry out a trial stencil. If necessary, adjust the plates for a better fit or modify the design.

Surface preparation and laying the ground

Start by rubbing down the surface to be printed. Use a fine-grade glasspaper and work the wood until it is completely smooth and free from dust or old paint. Take your chosen base paint and a soft flat brush, and lay on a thin coat. Wait for the paint to dry thoroughly and then take the fine glasspaper and rub it down – a swift, gentle rubbing is all that is needed, just enough to cut back the surface of the paint.

Set out the lacquer, a soft brush and the first stencil plate. Arrange your chosen fine ground bronze powders and make sure the dusting brush is clean. Shut the windows and generally organize your whole working environment so that you can proceed without interruption. Making sure that the lacquer is well stirred and free from lumps, lay on a thin coat. Do not hurry this stage or over-work the lacquer. Put the piece to one side out of harm's way.

Now, have a trial dusting with the bronze powder. Put the powder in a fold of paper and, with a little finger-tapping action, dribble and control the flow. Try to achieve a coverage that grades from a dense gold cover to a complete fade-out of colour.

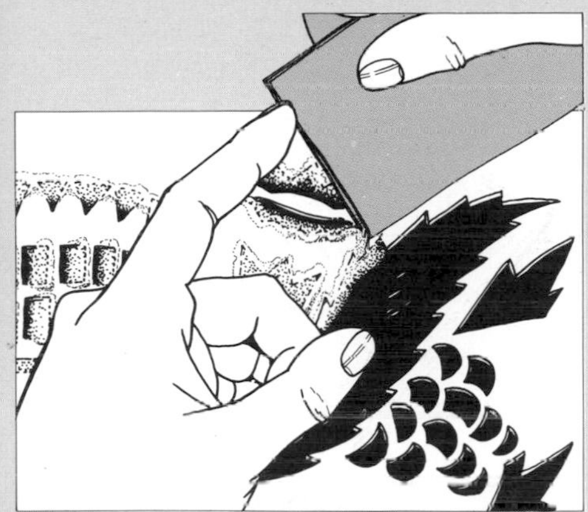

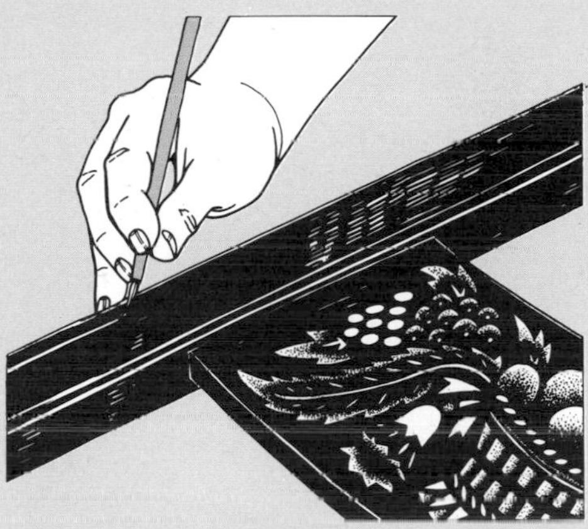

Working the first stencil

Take your prepared piece of furniture and delicately touch the lacquer with a fingertip – it needs to be slightly sticky. Arrange the piece of furniture at a good height so that the surface to be decorated is level and face-up. Now, take the stencil plate, check with your design layout as to the precise placing and carefully position it on the lacquered surface. Note: this next stage is tricky and you have to get it right the first time so work with care and caution.

Hold the stencil plate with one hand, hold a little paper trough of metallic powder with the other, and dribble the powder around the edge of the stencil window with a gentle tapping movement. Aim to leave a trail around the edge of the design.

Remembering that the lacquer is sticky, take a dry soft brush and dab the powder from the edge of the stencil plate and onto the sticky surface. Do not be tempted to heap the powder on or work with a heavy hand, but dust and brush so that the concentration fades from the dense stencil edge towards the motif centre. If you look at the project photographs (see page 173), you will see that the leaves tend to be worked from edge-to-centre, whereas all the round forms, such as the grapes and apples, are worked from side-to-side in order to give a feeling of roundness and shadow.

Working the second stencil

Carefully peel up and remove the stencil plate. Wait for the lacquer to dry and then take the fine glasspaper and rub it down. This should be swift and just enough to cut back the surface. Having done this, re-lacquer the surface with another thin coat.

While you are waiting for the lacquer to almost dry, set out all the tools and materials for the second stencil printing. This should include the stencil plate, the second shade of bronze powder, the paper trough and the dusting brush. Once the lacquer is almost dry, position the second stencil plate.

How you work this stencilling will depend on the motif but the method will be more or less as already described. Make sure the plate is the correct way up, check that the registration window is aligned, and then apply the powder with the brush. Use as little powder as possible, and work it well into the lacquered surface. Be careful to avoid forcing the powder under the edge of the stencil card and this can be achieved by working the brush with a gentle dabbing action.

Remove the plate and let the lacquer dry. Continue working the remaining stencil plates that go to make up your chosen design in the same way.

Finally, when the last stencil plate has been worked and the lacquer is dry, lightly rub down the surface with glasspaper and lay on the last coat of lacquer. Note: by repeatedly rubbing down and re-lacquering, it is possible to achieve a decorative effect similar to Japanese lacquer work.

Striping and finishing

Have a last look at the photographs and note how all the motif clusters have been framed and set within gold-striped panels. Study your stencilled piece and consider how best the striping ought to be set out. For example, you might run a line around the very edge of the piece of furniture and emphasize the form. Alternatively, you might decide to introduce another shape and have the stencilled motif set within a double-line oval frame. There are any number of exciting design possibilities. Some of the earlier Hitchcock chairs made between 1825 and 1832 were a mass of gold stripes along panel edges, stripes around ring-turned legs, stripes on the stretchers, and so on. Note: traditionally Hitchcock chairs were gold-striped with a goose quill pen or trailer.

Set out your finest brushes and a well-stirred pot of gold paint. Arrange the piece to be worked so that it is at a comfortable height. Have a trial run with a piece of scrap wood. Finally, using your fingertips as a gauge, run the gold lines around the stencil as illustrated. When the gold paint is dry, give the piece a final rubbing down and then lay on the last thin coat of lacquer. Note: when you are buying your materials – the various lacquers, paints and bronze powders – it is most important that you spend time matching the products – so tell the supplier what it is you are trying to achieve.

CHAPTER 6

PATTERNS AND MOTIFS

WOODWORKERS in need of additional inspirational patterns and motifs will find them in this section. The idea behind this chapter is beautifully simple: once you have worked through the projects and have achieved a fair degree of expertise and know-how, you will sooner or later want to modify the projects and use them in a way that is unique to your own craft and design requirements. The patterns and designs shown here have been carefully chosen so that they relate to various projects in the book but cover slightly different periods, sources and techniques.

Many designs, patterns and motifs are too large to print full-size, for example, those found on dower chests. So, with this problem in mind, we have selected a number of significant designs, reduced them in size and then printed them on special grids. You can work them to whatever size you require. The designs can be enlarged by using a larger grid and then carefully transferring and reworking the lines of the design one square at a time. If, for example, you take it that the directory is scaled at one square to ¼in (four squares to 1in) you have only to relate the material to a pre-set larger grid in order to increase the overall size and proportion of the design. To work a design that is four times larger, all you need to do is draw up a grid that has one square to 1in, and then transfer the lines of the design accordingly. Using this technique it is possible to select one of these designs, and then to enlarge, modify and personalize it to suit whatever project you have in mind.

BIBLIOGRAPHY

Alexander, J. D. *Making a Chair From a Tree: An Introduction to Working Green Wood* (London, Bell & Hyman, 1978)
Anderson, M. D. *Misericords* (London, Penguin, 1956)
Arnold, J. *The Shell Book Of Country Crafts* (London, John Baker, 1968)
Aronson, J. *The Encyclopedia of Furniture* (London, Batsford, 1965)
Ayres, J. *British Folk Art* (London, Barrie and Jenkins, 1977)
Barber, J. *Wild Fowl Decoys* (New York, Dover, 1954)
Bridgewater, A. & G. *The Craft of Woodcarving* (Newton Abbot, David and Charles, 1981)
Bridgewater, A. & G. *Printing With Woodblocks, Stencils and Engravings* (Newton Abbot, David and Charles)
Bridgewater, A. & G. *A Treasury of Woodcarved Design* (New York, Van Nostrand Reinhold, 1981)
Brough, J. C. S. *Timber For Woodwork* (London, Evans, 1947)
Campkin, M. *The Technique Of Marquetry* (London, Batsford, 1969)
Chinn, G. and Sainsbury, J. *The Carpenter's Companion* (London, Marshall Cavendish)
Gill, M. A. V. *Tunbridge Ware* (Aylesbury, Shire, 1985)
Gordon, H. *Old English Furniture* (London, John Murray, 1948)
Kassay, J. *Book of Shaker Furniture* (Boston, University of Massachusetts Press, 1980)
Lipman, J. and Winchester, A. *The Flowering of American Folk Art 1776–1876* New York, Viking Press, 1974)
Maccarthy, F. *British Design Since 1880* (London, Lund Humphries, 1982)

Opresch, G. *Peasant Art In Romania* (London, Studio, 1929)
Shea, J. G. *Antique Country Furniture of North America* (New York, Van Nostrand Reinhold)
Smith, D. *Old Furniture and Woodwork* (London, Batsford, 1949)
Sparkes, I. G. *English Windsor Chairs* (Aylesbury, Shire, 1981)
Tangerman, E. J. *Whittling and Woodcarving* (New York, Dover, 1962)
Toller, J. *Treen and Other Turned Woodware* (Newton Abbot, David and Charles, 1975)
Vanderwalker, F. N. *Wood Finishing* (Sterling, 1980)
Victoria & Albert Museum, Department of Woodwork *Catalogue Of English Furniture and Woodwork*, 1929, Vols 1, 2, 3 and 4
Wheeler, W. and Hayward, C. H. *Practical Woodcarving and Gilding* (London, Bell & Hyman, 1983)
Wymer, N. *English Country Crafts* (London, Batsford, 1946)

◆

GLOSSARY

ADZE *An axe-like tool with a curved blade set at right-angles to the handle. It is swung like a pendulum and the cutting edge removes scoops of wood.*

BALK *Roughly squared piece of timber.*

BAND CLAMP *Versatile clamp consisting of a tough strip of webbing that is wrapped around the workpiece and tightened by means of a screw mechanism.*

BAND SAW *Mechanically powered saw with an 'endless' blade that runs over wheels.*

BATTEN *Strip of wood.*

BEETLE *Hammer-like tool with a long handle and a heavy head.*

BENCHHOOK *A board that hooks over the bench top, presenting a raised block against which timber is placed for sawing.*

BEVEL *A tool used for setting off angles consisting of a flat rule with a movable arm stiffly jointed at one end; also a flat-sloping moulding.*

BIT *Boring-piece of a drill.*

BOLE *Fine, compact and oily clay, usually yellow, red or brown due to the presence of iron oxide.*

BOW SAW *A thin-bladed saw, set in a wooden frame, for cutting curves.*

BRACE *Tool for boring in which a bit is made to revolve by turning the brace.*

BURNISHER *A rod with a flat surface at one end, used to polish.*

CABINET SCRAPER *A flat piece of steel used to remove thin shavings by means of a 'burr' or hook to its edge.*

CALLIPERS *Compasses with bowed legs for measuring width of a body or cavity and for transferring the measurement.*

CHISEL *A flat-bladed, hand tool for cutting and levering out chips of wood, either pushed by hand or struck on the handle with a mallet.*

CLAMP *Screw device for securing wood to the workbench or for holding tightly together two pieces of wood that have been jointed and glued.*

COMPASS *Two-legged instrument used to draw circles and strike arcs.*

COPING SAW *Narrow-bladed saw tensioned in a U-shaped frame, used for cutting curves in small-section wood. The blade can be swivelled.*

CROSS-CUT SAW *A saw with angled teeth suitable for cutting across the grain.*

DOVETAIL *A joint in which a fan-shaped projection of one piece of timber fits precisely into a similarly shaped recess in another.*

DOVETAIL SAW *A fine-toothed back saw, suitable for very precise work.*

DOWEL *Round peg or pin used in jointing.*

DRAWKNIFE *A two-handled knife that is drawn along the wood towards the body, used for cutting free shapes and curves.*

END-GRAIN *The timber grain seen end-on when a piece is cut traversely.*

FLOURPAPER *The finest grade of glasspaper. Suitable for finishing wood.*

FORSTNER DRILL BIT *A bit which runs on its periphery, used for boring shallow flat-bottomed holes.*

FRAME SAW *Narrow-bladed saw tensioned and supported in a wooden frame.*

FRET SAW *Thin saw stretched on a frame, used for cutting wood in ornamental patterns.*

G-CLAMP *A simple clamp that exerts pressure directly on the work by tightening a screw towards an opposing 'jaw'. It is used for small work.*

GARNET PAPER *An abrasive paper coated with grit from the garnet stone. It keeps its sharpness through prolonged usage.*

GAUGE *A marking tool with a sliding stock that can be screwed tight onto its shaft. It can be pressed against an edge or surface to enable a sharp point to 'scribe' a line on the material.*

GENT'S SAW *A small saw with a thin blade and a round handle, used for cutting dovetails and other precise work.*

GESSO PLASTER *Plaster of Paris prepared for use in modelling or as a ground for painting and gilding.*

GLASSPAPER *Abrasive paper with coating of crushed glass.*

GOUGE *Carving tool which cuts through wood either under hand-pressure or by being struck on the handle with a mallet. The blade section is curved or V-shaped.*

HACKSAW *Saw with narrow blade tensioned in a steel frame, for cutting metal.*

HAND SAW *Saw with a deep, flexible blade, to which the handle is attached directly.*

HOLDFAST *A clamping device which is dropped through a hole in the benchtop and used to secure timber for carving or other work.*

JIG *A device for holding timbers in appropriate positions for drilling, routing and sawing.*

LACQUER *Natural tree sap or synthetic imitation used as a protective and decorative varnish.*

LATHE *Machine on which wood is rotated against a fixed cutting tool.*

LINSEED OIL *Oil from flax which, when applied to wood, preserves it and gives it a soft, natural finish.*

MACARONI CHISEL *Wide U-shaped gouge with square corners, useful for finishing the sides of shallow recesses.*

MALLET *A percussion tool consisting of shaft and head made of beech, the latter having large, flat, rectangular faces. It is used for tapping chisels and gouges.*

MARQUETRY *Decoration of a flat surface by gluing together shaped pieces of wood.*

MORTISE CHISEL *A square-edged chisel, the blade of which tapers in its thickness making it suitable for chopping deeply and for levering out waste wood.*

MORTISE GAUGE *Similar to the marking gauge but with two adjustable points, used for scribing parallel lines on timber to be worked into mortise-and-tenon joints.*

MORTISE-AND-TENON *A joint consisting of a projecting tongue (tenon) on one member which slots into a recess (mortise) in another member.*

OILSTONE SLIP *A shaped oilstone on which gouges are sharpened.*

PARQUETRY *Wood inlays or blocks arranged in a geometric pattern.*

PARTING TOOL *A V-section gouge used to carve V-section cuts for outlining reliefs. Also, a tool for parting off work on the wood lathe.*

PEEN HAMMER *Hammer with a transverse spatulate head on its 'top' side for lightly tapping in pins and nails.*

PLANE *A flat-bottomed wooden or steel tool in which is set an angled blade (the 'iron'). Its function is to shave the surface of the timber along which it is pushed.*

PRIMER *Seal (glue, gesso, oil etc) that prevents wood from absorbing paint.*

PROTRACTOR *Semicircular instrument for measuring and setting off angles.*

PUNCH *Steel shaft hollowed out at its 'point' to fit over a nail or pin in order to drive it below the surface.*

PVA GLUE *A white woodworking adhesive that is ready prepared, easy to apply and quick-drying.*

QUARTER-SAWN *Timber that has been cut radially from the log, with annual rings at right-angles.*

RASP *File used for shaping wood.*

SANDPAPER *The generic term for abrasive papers, although sand is no longer used to provide the gritty surface.*

SANDING BLOCK *Rubber, cork or felt-faced block around which sandpaper is wrapped for hand-sandings.*

SASH CLAMP *A clamp with jaws that travel along a bar, one adjusted by screw thread, the other positioned against a peg which fits into a series of holes.*

SCALPEL *Knife with removable, and therefore replaceable, sharp blade.*

SET-SQUARE *Draughtsman's appliance for drawing angles, consisting of wooden handle with a metal plate set at right-angles to it.*

SIZE *A thin glue applied as a sealant.*

SKEW CHISEL *A flat chisel with an angled cutting edge, useful for working in tight corners.*

SLIPSTONE *See* OILSTONE SLIP.

SPOKESHAVE *Plane-like tool for working small curves. The blade is flanked by a pair of handles.*

TALLOW *Animal fat used in making candles and soap.*

TEMPLATE *A pattern, usually in the form of a metal plate, used as a guide for cutting or drilling.*

TENON SAW *A back saw suitable for cutting tenons and other precise work.*

VEINER *A V section gouge used for carving fine V-section cuts.*

VENEER *Figured slice of timber applied to a basewood, usually for decorative purposes.*

VICE *A large bench-mounted clamping device.*

WHITTLING KNIFE *Available in a variety of shapes, with a high-quality steel blade.*

CONVERSION TABLE

IMPERIAL IN	METRIC MM	IMPERIAL IN	METRIC MM
1/16	1·6	1	25·4
1/8	3·2	2	50.8
3/16	4·8	3	76·2
1/4	6·4	4	101·4
5/16	7·9	5	127·0
3/8	9·5	6	152·4
7/16	11·1	7	177·5
1/2	12·7	8	203·2
9/16	14·3	9	228·6
5/8	15·9	10	254·0
11/16	17·5	11	279·5
3/4	19·1	12	304·8
13/16	20·6	18	457·2
7/8	22·2	24	609·6
15/16	23·8	30	762.0

INDEX

A

adze, 188
  using, 46
American style:
  decoy ducks, 132–7
  dower chest tradition, 146–51, *148*
  Hitchcock stencilling, 170–5
  painted furniture, 145
  stencilling, 158–63, 170–5
Anderson, A. E., *124*
appliqué relief, 106–11
Art Nouveau, *52*
  appliqué relief, 106–11, *108*
Arts and Crafts Movement, 18, *20, 21*, 22
  writing desks, *64*
ash, description, *14*

B

balk, 188
ball-in-a-cage, 88–93
band clamp, 188
band saw, 188
Barnsley brothers, 22
batten, 188
beech, description, *14*
beetle, 188
benchhook, 188
bending wood, 27, 47
bevel, 188
birch, description, *14*
bird's eye maple, description, *15*
bit, 188
bole, 188
  applying, 166
bonheur-du-jour, *108*
Boulle, Charles André, 56, *61*
boulle marquetry, 56–61
bow saw, 188
bowls, quaich, 16, 30–5
boxes, *28*
  marquetry, *52*
  Shaker, 16, 24–29
  Tunbridge ware, *76, 77*
boxwood, description, *14*
brace, 188
burnisher, 188

C

cabinet scraper, 188
cabinets, *20, 21*
  veneered, *20, 61*
callipers, 188
Canadian birch, description, *14*
carving:
  appliqué relief, 106–11
  built up, 126, 128
  decoy ducks, 132–7
  fairground horse head, 120–5
  Grinling Gibbons posies, 126–31
  interlaced chair-backs, 138–43
  love spoons, 100–5
  medieval roundels, 82–7
  misericord, 114–19
  relief, 80–111
  in the round, 112–43
  sunflower panels, 94–9
  treen, 88–93
  whittling, 88–93, 100–5
cedar, description, *14*
chairs:
  Chippendale, *140, 141*
  dining, *140*
  George II, *140*
  Hitchcock-stencilled, 170–5, *173*
  interlaced backs, 138–43
  Majorelle, *108*
  sculptured, *44*
  smoker's, *40*
  Windsor, 16–17, 42–7
cherry wood, *14*
Chessum, Thierry, *44*
chestnut, description, *15*
chests, *7, 8*
  Nonesuch inlay, 68–73, *72*
  painted American dower, 146–51, *148*
  roll-top, *20*
  sunflower, *96*
  thirteenth-century, *85*
chip carving, *7*
  knitting-stick holder, *92*
  medieval roundels, 82–7
  nutcrackers, *92*
  whittling, 91
Chippendale, Thomas, 138
  chairs, *140, 141*
  chair-backs in style of, 138–43
  secretaire, *52*
chisels, 188
clamps, 188
coats of arms, *168*
coloured wood, 144
  see also painting
commodes, Boulle, *61*
compass, 188
containers, *28*
coping saws, 188
Crane, Walter, 18
cross-cut saws, 188

D

decorative construction, 16–47
decorative finish, 144
decoy ducks, 132–7
desks:
  carved, *108*
  secretaire, *52*
  writing, *64*
dining chairs, 140
dovetail joints, 18–23, 188
dowel, 188
dower chests, painted, 146–51, *148*
drawknife, 188
ducks, decoy, 132–7

E

elm, description, *15*
endgrain, 188
Evelyn, John, 126

F

fairground horse's heads, 120–5, *124*
figure heads, ship's, 120, *124*
finishing, 144–75
  French polishing, 152–7
  Hitchcock stencilling, 170–5
  painting, 146–51, 158–63
  stencilling, 158–63
  water gilding, 164–9
flourpaper, 188
Forstner drill bits, 188
frame saws, 188
French polishing, 152–7

G

G-clamps, 188
Gallé, Emile, 106, *52, 108*
games board, parquetry, 62–7
garnet paper, 188
gauges, 188
gent's saw, 188
geometric motifs, *7*
gesso, 188
  applying, 166
Gibbons, Grinling, 126, *128*
  carved posies in the style of, 126–9
gilding, water, 164–9
Gimson, Ernest, *21*, 22
glasspaper, 188
glues, 189
Gothic style, stools, *41*
gouges, 188

H

hacksaws, 188
hand saws, 188
Hitchcock, Lambert, 170
  stencilling in the style of, 170–5
holdfasts, 188
holly, description, *14*
horse's heads, 120–5, *124*

I

inlay work, 48–79
interlaced chair-backs, 138–43

J

jigs, 188
joints:
  dovetail, 18–23, 188
  mortise-and-tenon, 189
  wedged mortise-and-tenon, 36–41

K

knitting-stick holder, *92*

L

lacquer, 188
lathes, 188
  preparing work for, 35
  turning bowls, 35
  turning legs, 46
legs, turning, 46
Lethaby, William Richard, 18, 22
lime, description, *15*
linseed oil, 188
London College of Furniture, *20, 28, 52, 64, 73, 77*
love spoons, 100–5, *105*
love tokens, *92*, 100

M

Macaroni chisels, 188
mahogany, description, *15*
Majorelle, Louis, *108*
mallets, 188
maple, description, *15*
marquetry, 188
  abstract, *52*
  Art Nouveau, *52*
  Boulle tradition, 56–61
  design, 50–5
  Nonesuch inlay, 68–73
  parquetry, 62–7
  Tunbridge ware, *65*, 74–9
mirror frames, *77*
misericords, *2, 117*
  carving, 114–19
Morris, William, 18
mortise-and-tenon joints, 189
  wedged, 36–41
mortise chisel, 188
mortise gauge, 188
mortises, cutting, 39
motifs, 176–85

N

Nonesuch inlay, 68–73
nutcrackers, *92*

O

oak:
  description, *15*
  misericords, 114–19
  panels, 94–9
oilstone slip, 189

P

painting:
  American dower chests, 146–51
  American style, 153–63
  see also stencilling
panels, carving, 94–9
parquetry, 62–7, 189
parting tools, 189
patterns, 176–85
pear, description, *14*
peen hammers, 189
Pembroke tables, *156*
pine, description, *14*
plane, description, *15*
planes, 189
polishing, French, 152–7
posies, carved, 126–9
Post-Modernist style, *20, 28*
primers, 189
protractors, 189
punch, 189
PVA glue, 189

Q

quaich bowls, 16, 30–5
quarter sawn, 189

R

rasps, 189
relief woodcarving, 80–111
  appliqué relief, 106–11
  love spoons, 100–5
  medieval chip-carved roundel, 82–7
  sunflower panels, 94–9
  treen, 88–93
  whittling, 88–93, 100–5
rivet-nailing, 27
roll-top chests, *20*
roundels, chip-carved, 82–7

S

sanding blocks, 189
sandpaper, 189
sash clamps, 189
scalpels, 189
Scottish quaich bowls, 16, 30–5
screens, Art Nouveau, *108*
secretaire, Chippendale, *52*
set-squares, 189
Shaker boxes, 16, 24–9
Shakers, 24
ship's figure heads, 120, *124*
size, 189
skew chisels, 189
smoker's chair, *40*
sofas, George II, *128*
spokeshaves, 189
steaming wood, 27
stencilling, 142
  American style, 158–63
  Hitchcock tradition, 170–5
stools:
  eighteenth century, *41*
  Gothic, *41*
sunflower motif, *8*, 94–9
sunflower panels, 94–9
sycamore, description, 15

T

tables:
  Boulle, *61*
  French polishing, *156*
  marquetry, *52, 61*
  Pembroke, *156*
tallow, 189
templates, 189
tenon saws, 189
tenons, cutting, 38
treen, 88–93
Tunbridge ware, *65*, 74–9, *76, 77*
turning:
  bowls, 35
  legs, 46

V

veiner, 189
veneers, 48–79, 189
  Boulle tradition, 56–61
  marquetry designs, 50–5
  parquetry, 62–7
  Tunbridge ware, *65*, 74–9
vices, 189

W

walnut, description, *15*
water gilding, 164–9
wedged mortise-and-tenon, 36–41
whittling:
  love spoons, 100–5
  treen, 88–93
whittling knife, 189
Windsor chairs, 16–17, 42–7
wood:
  for carving, 81
  types of, 14–15
woodcarving:
  appliqué relief, 106–11
  built up, 126, 128
  decoy ducks, 132–7
  fairground horse head, 120–5
  Grinling Gibbons posies, 126–31
  interlaced chair-backs, 138–43
  love spoons, 100–5
  medieval roundels, 82–7
  misericord, 114–19
  relief, 80–111
  in the round, 112–43
  sunflower panels, 94–9
  treen, 88–93
  whittling, 88–93, 100–5
writing desks, 64
  carved, *108*
  secretaires, *52*

Y

yew, description, *15*

ACKNOWLEDGEMENTS

2 Victoria and Albert Museum; **7** Victoria and Albert Museum; **8** Victoria and Albert Museum; **11** Angelo Hornak (National Trust/Dyrham Park); **20** London College of Furniture (Jonathan Rubinstein), London College of Furniture (Nick Clayton), London College of Furniture (Louise Biggs); **21** Victoria and Albert Museum; **28–29** London College of Furniture, American Museum in Britain, Bath; **32–33** Birmingham Museum and Art Gallery/Dennis Assinder, Bridgeman Art Library; **40–41** Angelo Hornak, Victoria and Albert Museum, Christie's Colour Library; **44–45** London College of Furniture, Bridgeman Art Library; **52** London College of Furniture (P. Vallance), London College of Furniture, Bridgeman Art Library (Victoria and Albert Museum), Bridgeman Art Library (Harewood House); **53** Bridgeman Art Library; **60–61** Christie's Colour Library, Bridgeman Art Library (Victoria and Albert Museum); **64–65** London College of Furniture, P. Niczewski, Tunbridge Wells Museum/Michael Wheeler; **72–73** Bridgeman Art Library, London College of Furniture, Victoria and Albert Museum; **76–77** Christie's Colour Library, Tunbridge Wells Museum/Michael Wheeler, Carole Hogg; **84–85** J. C. D. Smith, Victoria and Albert Museum; **92–93** York Castle Museum; **96–97** Victoria and Albert Museum; **104–105** Welsh Folk Museum, Birmingham Museum and Art Gallery/ Dennis Assinder; **108–109** Victoria and Albert Museum, Christie's Colour Library, Angelo Hornak (Bethnal Green Museum); **116–117** Victoria and Albert Museum; **124–125** Fairground by Night Exhibition, Wookey Hole Caves/Derek Bayes, Fairground Exhibition, Wookey Hole Caves; **128–129** Christie's Colour Library, National Trust, Petworth/Jeremy Whitaker; **136–137** Michael Edwards, American Museum in Britain, Bath; **140–141** Christie's Colour Library, Bridgeman Art Library (Victoria and Albert Museum); **148–149** American Museum in Britain, Bath, Bridgeman Art Library (Henry Francis du Pont Winterthur Museum), Metropolitan Museum of Art, Rogers Fund; **156–157** Angelo Hornak (National Trust/Ickworth), Bridgeman Art Library (Victoria and Albert Museum); **160** Fiona Skrine, American Museum in Britain, Bath; **165** (Inset) Angelo Hornak (John Makepeace Workshop); **168–169** Victoria and Albert Museum; **172–173** American Museum in Britain, Bath.

Quarto Publishing Limited would like to take this opportunity to thank **Alec Tiranti Limited** (London) for supplying tools, **Carvers and Gilders** (London) for supplying gilding materials, **Ardenbrite Products Limited** (London) for supplying a range of French polishing materials, and **Peter Niczewski** for his marquetry and inlay work featured throughout the book.

Pageant and Panorama

Many artists, poets, writers and painters have been attracted by the pageants and panoramas of the city of Venice. Most have been inspired by an awareness that such a magnificently decaying vision could not last and have tried to capture the essence of the city before its eventual and long promised demise. But Venice has been declining for centuries and, one suspects, will go on doing so for many centuries more. It is this sense of brave defiance which accounts for much of the poignant beauty of the city and much of the poetry in the art she has inspired.

Canaletto's response seems more honestly matter-of-fact than that of many other artists. That is not to deny he had genius—for that he indisputably had—but he seems not to have been beguiled by the city into painting other than what he saw. In his time the physical appearance of Venice cannot have been all that different from what it is today, although the period of the city's greatest prosperity was some two centuries nearer and Venice was still the 'Most Serene Republic'. Then, as now, she was much visited, and then as now most visitors liked her and a few loathed her. Liking or loathing Venice, few have denied the magic of the place—a shimmering wonderland rising in a lagoon.

Although, as in *The Stonemason's Yard* (Plate 6), it is only very rarely that Canaletto painted anything other than the 'pageant and panorama', we can see in his paintings, perhaps more than in the work of any other artist, the real Venice. And the fascination of so much of his work lies in the fact that it shows us Venice as we can still see her. Particular favourite spots are easily recognizable; bell-towers and chimney-stacks protrude above roof-tops in exactly the same places as they do today. Church doors and palace windows have awnings in exactly the same shape and colour as they still do, and, most fascinating of all, in their daily life Canaletto's people seem hardly to have changed in the two centuries that have since passed. The one great difference between Canaletto's Venice and the city of today is that nowhere in his pictures can one find a single ancestor of the hordes of pigeons that are now so much part of the Venetian scene.

This fascination with how like Canaletto's paintings are to reality inevitably leads one to wonder how he painted them, for whom, and why so many. And of the painter himself, who was he? How did he train? And where did he live and die?

Canaletto was born in Venice on 28 October 1697. His family, though not patrician, had a certain social status in the city and republic, where social status mattered much. This is best described by the words '*origine Civis Venetus*' used by Visentini under the engraved portrait of the artist published in 1735 (Plate 2). The family were armigerous and used the arms of the da Canal family,